# BEYOND NORTH KOREA: FUTURE CHALLENGES TO SOUTH KOREA'S SECURITY

**Edited by
Byung Kwan Kim, Gi-Wook Shin and
David Straub**

I0125391

SHORENSTEIN
**APARC**
STANFORD

THE WALTER H. SHORENSTEIN
ASIA-PACIFIC RESEARCH CENTER

THE WALTER H. SHORENSTEIN ASIA-PACIFIC RESEARCH CENTER (Shorenstein APARC) is a unique Stanford University institution focused on the interdisciplinary study of contemporary Asia. Shorenstein APARC's mission is to produce and publish outstanding interdisciplinary, Asia-Pacific–focused research; educate students, scholars, and corporate and governmental affiliates; promote constructive interaction to influence U.S. policy toward the Asia-Pacific; and guide Asian nations on key issues of societal transition, development, U.S.-Asia relations, and regional cooperation.

The Walter H. Shorenstein Asia-Pacific Research Center
Freeman Spogli Institute for International Studies
Stanford University
Encina Hall
Stanford, CA 94305-6055
tel. 650-723-9741
fax 650-723-6530
http://APARC.stanford.edu

*Beyond North Korea: Future Challenges to South Korea's Security*
may be ordered from:
The Brookings Institution
c/o DFS, P.O. Box 50370, Baltimore, MD, USA
tel. 1-800-537-5487 or 410-516-6956
fax 410-516-6998
http://www.brookings.edu/press

Walter H. Shorenstein Asia-Pacific Research Center Books, 2011.
Copyright © 2011 by the Board of Trustees of the
Leland Stanford Junior University.

First printing, 2011.
13-digit ISBN 978-1-931368-19-3

# BEYOND NORTH KOREA: FUTURE CHALLENGES TO SOUTH KOREA'S SECURITY

SHORENSTEIN
APARC
STANFORD

THE WALTER H. SHORENSTEIN
ASIA-PACIFIC RESEARCH CENTER

# CONTENTS

# TABLES AND FIGURES

## Tables

## Figures

# ACKNOWLEDGEMENTS

The papers in this volume were initially prepared for presentation at a conference held at Stanford University in March 2009. The inaugural Koret Fellow, South Korean General (Retired) Byung Kwan Kim, played a vital role in planning and organizing the conference, as well as writing one of the keynote chapters in this volume. The editors are grateful to the contributors—Donald W. Keyser, Jongseok Lee, Jae Ho Chung, Benjamin Self, Alexandre Y. Mansourov, Kyung-Tae Lee, Ji-Chul Ryu, Seongho Sheen, and Thomas Fingar. We express our sincere gratitude to the Koret Foundation, especially its chairwoman Susan Koret, whose generous grant made this conference possible.

As always, we are indebted to the late Walter H. Shorenstein for his devotion to strengthening the United States' relations with its friends and allies in East Asia through his years of support for the Center. We also thank all of the Shorenstein APARC staff members who contributed to the conference and this book, especially associate director for research Daniel C. Sneider for his creative input into the conference planning; Heather Ahn, the Korean Studies Program coordinator, who handled all the logistics for a major conference; and former and current publications managers Victoria Tomkinson and George Krompacky, who edited and designed this volume.

The editors believe that South Korea is important not only as a major American ally and partner but as a leading global example of how a country can emerge, only two generations after liberation from colonial rule and a devastating internecine war, as one of the world's largest economies and most dynamic societies. We hope that this fresh look at the long-term security challenges facing the country will be useful both to South Koreans and their friends in the United States and throughout the world.

—Byung Kwan Kim, Gi-Wook Shin, and David Straub

# PREFACE:
## ABOUT THE KORET SERIES ON KOREA

This volume is the first in a new series of policy-related studies on contemporary South Korea. The Koret Foundation of San Francisco made the project possible by a generous grant to the Korean Studies Program at Stanford University. The Koret Foundation's gift allowed Stanford's Walter H. Shorenstein Asia-Pacific Research Center, of which the Korean Studies Program is a part, to establish a Koret Fellowship to bring leading Asian and American policymakers to Stanford to study United States-Korean relations. Koret Fellows conduct their own research on South Korea and the bilateral relationship, with the broad aim of fostering greater understanding and closer ties between the two countries.

Gi-Wook Shin
Professor and Director
Shorenstein APARC
Stanford University

# INTRODUCTION: FUTURE CHALLENGES TO SOUTH KOREA'S SECURITY

## Gi-Wook Shin and David Straub

This book, and the conference on which it is based, were intended to take a fresh look at future security challenges to the Republic of Korea (ROK) or, as it is commonly known, South Korea. For most English-speaking international readers, however, the first question is likely to be "why should I care?" Even in the United States, which fought a major war from 1950 to 1953 to defend South Korea and has been its treaty ally ever since, Korea is not well-known to the average American.

The immediate reason we should care about the security of South Korea is North Korea. The North Korean state is an anachronism, a coelacanth of a country that by a tragic accident of history was bequeathed a Stalinist system in 1945 and whose first leader promoted the development of a Maoist-style cult of personality and a dynasty that persists today. The regime controls its people by means of isolation from the outside world, nationalistic propaganda, and pervasive repression. A Soviet-style command economy has produced absolute poverty for most North Koreans, and even brought about famine and starvation in the mid-1990s.

Facing South Korea, which is one of the world's great developmental success stories and whose security is firmly backed by United States, North Korean leaders must fear for their regime's very survival. Indeed, they appear to recognize the profound dilemma they face—to develop their economy, the long-term underpinning of any regime, they must open up to the outside world, but doing so would expose the people to knowledge of their government's failure and South Korea's success. Having apparently decided that a major opening to the world is fraught with risk, North Korean leaders have instead pursued a "military-first policy," which includes the development of nuclear weapons and is accompanied by bombastic rhetoric against perceived enemies, including South Korea and the United States. In a search for hard currency, North Korea has even engaged in nuclear and missile proliferation.

Although the North Korean leadership does not appear to be suicidal and thus is unlikely to launch a war, its behavior and systemic weaknesses could eventually result in accidental war, domestic chaos involving "loose nukes," or the intentional proliferation of nuclear materials and technologies to regimes or parties that might use them to threaten the United States or other countries. Moreover, North Korea is surrounded by three of the world's major powers, China, Japan, and Russia, as well as, in effect, the United States. Instability on the Korean Peninsula could result in a confrontation among those powers and, in the worst case, lead to war. In fact, the peninsula became a battleground among these powers three times during the last century—the Sino-Japanese War of 1894–95, the Russo-Japanese War of 1904–05, and the Korean War of 1950–53. All these events greatly shaped the contours of regional order in Northeast Asia.

In this context, South Korea's security is important not only to itself but also to peace and stability in Northeast Asia and even the world. While much of the international community's focus on the North Korea problem has been on United States policy—the United States does of course have a key role to play—over the long term South Korea's role may well be more important. Even though the United States will likely remain the world's foremost military power and a firm ally of South Korea for the foreseeable future, no country in the world is perforce more committed or more involved in the security of the Korean Peninsula than South Korea.

If South Korea remains successful—politically stable, economically growing, and militarily strong—North Korea will be less tempted to use military or other means against it, actions that could produce instability or war in the region. A secure and confident South Korea will be more inclined to pursue a long-term, principled approach toward North Korea that will reduce the risks of miscalculation and encourage North Korea to move in a positive direction. In the event of chaos in North Korea, South Korea will be a major—perhaps the central—player, as it certainly will be in the case of unification.

## A Regional and Global Perspective

This volume aims to take a fresh approach to analyzing the security challenges facing South Korea. First, we put South Korea's security in a regional and global context. In chapter 1, former senior U.S. State Department official and East Asia expert Donald W. Keyser offers a tour d'horizon of the regional and global factors that impinge on South Korea's security. Keyser's remarks set the stage for the book's subsequent discussions of specific issues— notably South Korea's relationships to its neighbors and the economic, energy and environmental, and demographic shifts that are transforming a globalizing world. Keyser describes, as he puts it, "a region in sweeping change…transitioning to the unknown." He discusses the implications of the global financial crisis of 2008–2009, especially as they relate to South Korea's defense posture. He looks at the debate in South Korea over the role the country should play in world affairs as a newly emerged middle power. Having served as a U.S. diplomat in China, Japan, and the former Soviet Union, and negotiated with North Korea, Keyser analyzes the interests and policies of all of these players as they affect South Korea. He also explores the prospects for greater regional security cooperation. Keyser does not seek to offer conclusive answers to the challenges facing South Korea but he clearly identifies issues that South Korea and its international friends must address to ensure its security.

### A Long-Term Perspective

The second way in which we aim to take a fresh approach to South Korea's security is by looking to the future. This volume is "bookended" by Keyser's regional and global overview at the beginning and by Thomas Fingar's concluding chapter, on long-term global trends and their implications for South Korea and the U.S.-South Korean alliance. Now the Oksenberg/Rohlen Distinguished Fellow at Stanford, Fingar was the United States' first Deputy Director of National Intelligence for Analysis, from 2005 to 2008. Concurrently, he served as chairman of the National Intelligence Council. In those and other top U.S. intelligence positions, he played a leading role in the National Intelligence Council's continuing and much noted "Global Trends" project. The project looks at how emerging global trends may influence world events. For this book, Fingar reviews the global trends identified in the most recent study, *Global Trends 2025: A Transformed World*, and considers how they might affect South Korea. While eschewing predictions, Fingar clearly sees globalization as a continuing phenomenon. He discusses the "rise of the rest"—above all China—and how regionalization and globalization interact. Finally, he looks at economic, energy, environmental, and demographic changes throughout the world and their possible impact on South Korea. Like Keyser, Fingar offers no easy answers, but suggests ways to think productively about the global challenges that will likely affect South Korea in the future.

## *South Korean Leadership Perspectives*

In addition to contributions by leading experts such as Donald Keyser and Thomas Finger, this volume contains important analyses of the North Korea problem written by two former senior South Korean officials, General (Retired) Byung Kwan Kim (in his first major publication in English) and former Unification Minister Jongseok Lee. Both have devoted their careers to studying North Korean issues and, as former top officials, in actively responding to them.

These two South Korean experts approach North Korea from quite different perspectives, reflecting the divergence of views in South Korea about how to deal with its northern neighbor. Kim focuses on the military dimension, and his views broadly represent conservative South Korean opinion about North Korea and South Korea's alliance with the United States. Lee, on the other hand, is a leader of South Korean progressive thinking about North Korea. As such, he discusses the internal situation in North Korea, as well as diplomatic efforts to mitigate the threats it poses to South Korea, the United States, and the international community. Interestingly, despite their different vantage points, both Kim and Lee start from the premise that North Korea is—or soon will be—in crisis, and that South Korea's security depends on making the right policy choices.

In his chapter, "Responding to the Coming North Korean Crisis: Assessing South Korean Military Requirements," General Kim outlines what he believes South Korea must do militarily to prepare for a coming North Korean internal crisis. He asserts that the interests and actions of South Korea's neighbors will be a key factor in such a crisis situation; thus, he first analyzes the regional military situation, and then compares North and South Korean military capabilities. Kim systematically assesses four North Korea crisis scenarios, along with the likely responses from the United States, Korea's neighbors, and the international community. Finally, he makes specific recommendations on how South Korea should prepare militarily, both to address a coming North Korea crisis and for the unified Korean state he believes could follow.

Minister Lee, one of South Korea's top academic experts on North Korea, offers his insights on North Korean internal leadership dynamics, based on a lifetime of study and personal experience in government, including negotiations with North Korea's top leaders. He believes that North Korea is now suffering from two overlapping crises, economic and political, which could result in the regime's collapse and internal chaos, and in turn cause unpredictable and possibly disastrous consequences for South Korea. He interprets North Korea's pursuit of nuclear weapons as a response to its own weakness, but sees its possession of nuclear weapons as a profound challenge to both South Korea and the United States. Rather than focus exclusively or first on denuclearization, Lee argues that the international community, led by the United States and South Korea, must simultaneously seek to prevent instability in North Korea and to secure its denuclearization. Arguing that the George W. Bush administration provides a case study in how not to deal with North Korea, Lee offers specific policy recommendations to the South Korean and U.S. governments.

### Bilateral Perspectives

This book also features chapters on South Korea's relations with its other neighbors. China, Japan, and Russia are, and will remain, key states in terms of South Korea's security. Historically, all three have fought with—or over—Korea.

China is the world's most populous country and its switch to a market-based economy has set it on a trajectory that could also make it the world's largest economy in coming decades. Since China implemented economic reforms and normalized relations with South Korea two decades ago, most South Koreans have regarded its rise as a great opportunity. Indeed, South Korea has become one of the largest investors in, and traders with, China. Traditionally, however, China had an unequal relationship with Korea, and South Koreans today are increasingly concerned that the giant country might someday again seek to exercise overweening influence over the Korean Peninsula. South Koreans worry also about how potential instability in the PRC—with its one-party system, widespread poverty, a rapidly aging population, and serious ethnic divisions—might affect their own country.

In chapter 4, Jae Ho Chung, a professor of international relations and director of the Institute for China Studies at Seoul National University, reviews the history of South Korea's relations with the PRC since diplomatic normalization in 1992. He describes how quickly the honeymoon period after normalization ended due to an "incongruence of expectations and outcomes" on both sides. Chung analyzes the *realpolitik* factors that have resulted in increased tensions and wariness between these two neighbors, as China sought to wean Seoul away from Washington and increase its diplomatic influence over both North and South Korea. He also explains why South Koreans increasingly are anxious about China posing economic, normative, and security threats to their country. Chung concludes with a discussion of the delicate strategic position in which South Korea finds itself—between the PRC and its American ally.

Both North and South Koreans are wont to describe their relationship with Japan as "close but far." Although near neighbors, Japan's colonization of Korea from 1910 to 1945 meant that both Korean states formed after liberalization would base their identity and legitimacy in significant part on hostility toward Japan. To the surprise and disbelief of most Americans, not only the general public in South Korea but also many intellectuals and officials genuinely fear that Japan may someday experience another bout of militarism and engage again in international aggression. Further, Seoul and Tokyo have much in common—both are democracies and have market economies, and are major trading partners that conduct considerable people-to-people exchange. Both are likewise American allies, and deeply concerned about North Korea and the security potential implications of the rise of China. Despite these similarities, diplomatic relations between Japan and South Korea are regularly roiled by disputes over historical issues, and direct security cooperation between the two has been almost nonexistent. Outside experts have long predicted that the bilateral diplomatic and security relationship would necessarily improve eventually—and in some important respects it has—but national identity factors have proven to be surprisingly durable.

In chapter 5, Benjamin Self, the Takahashi Fellow in Japanese Studies at Stanford's Shorenstein Asia-Pacific Research Center, takes a fresh look at the South Korean-Japanese relationship. Self focuses on the history of direct and indirect security cooperation between Seoul and Tokyo, and trilaterally with the United States. He argues that, contrary to widespread perception, there is a longstanding de facto security partnership between Seoul and Tokyo that has "endured and even blossomed." Like Jae Ho Chung, Self is concerned with how South Korea will deal with the rise of China. He concludes that the optimal long-term course for South Korea, despite the lingering historical tensions, is to cooperate in security affairs with Japan to retain its independence from Beijing.

Russia has played a lesser but still major role on the Korean Peninsula. At the end of the nineteenth century, it competed with other great powers for influence on the peninsula, and its loss in the Russo-Japanese War of 1904–1905 set the stage for Japan's colonization of Korea. As the Soviet Union, it supported Koreans' struggle against Japan. It occupied the northern half of the peninsula after Japan's defeat in World War II and set up a Stalinist-style government there that continues to this day. It approved North Korean leader Kim Il-sung's failed invasion of the South in 1950, which cost millions of Korean lives and, ironically, resulted in the United States permanently committing itself to the security of the Republic of Korea. After the collapse of the Soviet Union, Moscow gradually re-engaged in Korean affairs, albeit in a more limited and pragmatic way.

In chapter 6, Russian-born scholar Alexandre Y. Mansourov offers an informative and insightful overview of current South Korean-Russian relations. Noting that the North Korea problem dominates news of Russia's engagement with the Korean Peninsula, Mansourov describes a South Korean-Russian relationship that is much broader and more significant than is generally known. For example, he details political relations that involve the exchange of many high-level visits, and the rapid increase of bilateral trade, with a potential for much more. Further, he notes that Russia is becoming a key supplier of advanced technology to South Korea, including in the areas of space and military arms; cultural and other exchanges are also burgeoning. Mansourov concludes that, after a hiatus following the collapse of the Soviet Union, Moscow is now "back" on the Korean Peninsula—by dint of its proximity, size, and history—and intends to stay.

In this volume, we intentionally do not focus on the U.S.-South Korea relationship. The United States has been the main foreign player on the Korean Peninsula since 1945, and will remain a key factor there for the foreseeable future. As a result, there is a tendency, among not only Koreans and Americans but also the international community, to have an exaggerated view of the United States' influence. As we argue in these pages, many other countries and factors impinge on South Korea's long-term security, above all of course South Korea itself, and these entities may ultimately play more important roles than will the United States. In any event, many useful studies on U.S.-South Korean relations are readily available and most of the authors in this volume include discussion of the U.S. factor in their chapters.[1]

## Nontraditional Challenges to South Korea's Security

The final part of this volume, and another of its distinguishing features, is its emphasis on nontraditional, or functional, challenges to South Korea's long-term security. Security is all too often regarded largely as a matter of interstate relations, but the long-term basis of a state's security rests, more often than not, on its own domestic policy choices. A country that lacks a stable and flexible political system, a thriving economy, and, most crucially, human resources is unlikely to maintain its security for long. We thus include chapters on South Korea's economy, energy and environmental resources, and demographic problems. Compared to most countries, South Korea is in an enviable position. In the one hand, it is a vibrant democracy, the world's fifteenth-largest economy, and is the sixth-largest exporter. With nearly 50 million people, it is by no means a small country. On the other hand, it is sandwiched between the low-cost economy of China and the high-tech economy of Japan. It imports virtually all its oil, and its birth rate is among the very lowest in the world, just over one child per woman.

In chapter 7, Kyung-Tae Lee, current president of the Korea International Trade Association's Institute for International Trade, assesses economic challenges to South Korea's security. Lee examines the relationship between economic strength and national security, including how economic deterioration in either South or North Korea might threaten South Korea's security. He argues also that increased economic power allows a country to respond more effectively to nonmilitary security threats, such as natural disasters, pandemics, and terrorism. He explores the effects of inter-Korean economic ties and East Asian regional economic cooperation on South Korea's security. As an economist, Lee concludes by acknowledging the importance of a strong economy, but cautions that while it may be a necessary condition it is not sufficient to guarantee a nation's national security.

In chapter 8, Ji-Chul Ryu, a senior fellow at the Korea Energy Economics Institute, provides an overview of the energy and environmental challenges facing South Korea. With few indigenous energy resources, industrialized South Korea is largely dependent on foreign sources of energy, a serious problem for the world's 10th-largest energy consumer. Ryu reviews the history of Seoul's efforts to cope with this challenge, including by diversifying its types and sources of energy, conservation, and investments in renewable energy. As for the future, he discusses how Seoul may be able to secure a stable supply of energy from overseas, increase low-carbon energy use, and cooperate in the energy sectors with North Korea and the United States.

In chapter 9, Seongho Sheen, a professor at Seoul National University's Graduate School of International Studies, discusses South Korea's aging and decreasing population and what that could mean for national security. As he notes, South Korea's birthrate is the second-lowest in the world, which will mean that in coming decades the country will also have one of the world's oldest populations. With fewer than 30,000 American military personnel now remaining in the South, after decades of gradual reduction, Sheen says that South Korea will increasingly have to "Koreanize" its military defense. As he explains, however, South Korea's demographics will not only reduce the manpower pool from which Seoul can recruit its servicemen and women, it will also slow economic growth. Rising demands from an aged population for more social welfare benefits will be an additional drag on the economy and thus on the defense budget. Sheen concludes with an analysis of South Korean policy options to address these very serious—but, in South Korea, not often seriously regarded—challenges to the country's security.

## Looking to the Future

As we hope this book persuasively shows, South Korea's security is critically important to regional and global security in an increasingly globalized world. South Korea is a tremendous success story, and there is every reason to believe that its leaders and people will continue to make wise decisions that will maintain the current trajectory of progress and increased security. But, as we also hope this book demonstrates, national security involves many factors, including the careful management of interstate relations and domestic policy choices. South Koreans and their friends have every reason for confidence about the country's future—but no room at all for complacency about it.

## Notes

1 The Walter H. Shorenstein Asia-Pacific Research Center (Shorenstein APARC) has produced two books on U.S.-ROK relations in recent years. See Gi-Wook Shin, *One Alliance, Two Lenses: U.S.-Korea Relations in a New Era* (Stanford, CA: Stanford University Press, 2010), and Donald A. L. McIyntyre, Daniel C. Sneider, and Gi-Wook Shin, eds., *First Drafts of Korea: The U.S. Media and Perceptions of the Last Cold War Frontier* (Stanford, CA: The Walter H. Shorenstein Asia-Pacific Research Center, 2009). The center sponsors New Beginnings, a study group of distinguished American experts on Korea and Northeast Asia, which has published reports annually since 2008. The most recent New Beginnings report can be found at http://aparc.stanford.edu/events/report_release_new_beginnings_2010. Shorenstein APARC also co-hosts the Korea-U.S. West Coast Strategic Forum in collaboration with Korean colleagues; see http://ksp.stanford.edu/events/series/koreaus_west_coast_strategic_forum/.

# OVERVIEW

# REGIONAL AND GLOBAL CHALLENGES
# TO SOUTH KOREA'S SECURITY

## Donald W. Keyser

Lee Myung-bak's (Yi Myŏng-bak) crushing electoral victory in December 2007 was widely interpreted in South Korea (or Republic of
Korea, ROK) and abroad—despite relatively low voter turnout and
with less than 50 percent of the popular vote—as a stark repudiation of ten
years of progressive policies under Presidents Kim Dae-jung (Kim Tae-jung)
and Roh Moo-hyun (No Mu-hyŏn). Living up to the sobriquet "Bulldozer"
he earned as the aggressive, no-nonsense CEO and chairman of Hyundai
(Hyŏndae) Engineering and Construction and subsequently as mayor of
Seoul, Lee betrayed no dearth of confidence that he had indeed won a man-
date for sweeping change in South Korea's domestic and foreign policies.
During the presidential transition and the public events surrounding his February 2008 inauguration, Lee and his team laid out a detailed policy agenda
notable for its clarity of vision, apparent coherence and unabashed return
to traditional conservative verities. This spawned a cornucopia of expert
analyses by domestic and foreign observers projecting evolution of a new
South Korean strategic posture that envisaged, inter alia, renewed energy in
the ROK-U.S. alliance, a skeptical, hard-nosed attitude toward Pyongyang,
a more reserved though cordial policy approach toward Beijing, an active
effort to mend fences with Tokyo and a determined pursuit of oil, gas and
other commercial interests with Moscow.

And then, figuratively speaking, the roof caved in. President Lee's early
Washington summit with President Bush in April 2008 produced the images
he coveted of alliance harmony smilingly restored, but swiftly exposed the
deep political fissures undiminished in South Korean society. Lee's domestic opposition seized upon his agreement to resume U.S. beef imports to
mobilize massive street demonstrations, challenge his competence, send his
approval ratings plummeting into the low 30 percent range, and knock him

off his political stride.

Pyongyang countered Lee's new policy line with cold disdain, bellicose rhetoric and a studied retreat from cooperative endeavors including those within the Kaesong special industrial region. Pyongyang's accusatory tone and hostile gestures accelerated following Kim Jong Il's (Kim Chŏng-il) August health episode and amidst speculation about a looming succession scenario. Beijing signaled a certain wariness regarding the substance and intent of Lee's foreign policy adjustments. The early promise of more constructive Seoul-Tokyo relations soon foundered over familiar issues of history and contested maritime claims. The vision of broad Russian-South Korean cooperation centering around energy and infrastructure projects in eastern Siberia failed to yield an early harvest of shared goals, let alone concrete, profitable contracts.

Finally, the sudden onset of the global financial and economic crisis required in Seoul, as in other Asian capitals and around the world, a shift in leadership attention, a reordering of priorities and a recalibration—at minimum—of national strategy. Slightly over one year into his five-year term in office, President Lee faced a global and regional canvas that had altered significantly, even fundamentally, from the one he saw and anticipated a year ago. It may then be both worthwhile and timely to examine the topography of this altered Asian landscape in terms of its impact on Seoul's strategic calculus and future policy options.

Broad questions that Seoul's policymakers should be—and likely are—pondering would include:

How is the global economic crisis most likely to shift Northeast Asian power relationships? Will these changes be principally of a subtle, longer-term nature, or will they fundamentally alter the current paradigm? How might Seoul reorient its external political relationships and economic strategies, especially within Northeast Asia, in seeking to ameliorate the fallout from the economic crisis?

How should Seoul's defense posture and projected defense spending be assessed—or altered—in light of the new economic realities?

What are Seoul's comparative advantages in the region, and how can these be best brought into play in the service of Seoul's national interests?

Does Lee's early commitment to a revitalized U.S. relationship still make sense? Should it be best understood as a bow to domestic political requirements? An anachronism? A least-bad strategy to hedge against the unknown and the unknowable? Or a still viable organizing approach to meet Seoul's domestic needs and advance its broad spectrum of external relationships and requirements?

What unilateral, bilateral and multilateral initiatives and arrangements are most likely to help Seoul successfully address the challenges posed by North Korean nuclear and missile programs and the range of conceivable North Korean leadership succession scenarios?

If China's continued rise is a given, what are its trajectory, the implications for China's weight in the region and Seoul's options for accommodating it?

Assuming that Japan recovers early from political confusion and economic stresses, what course will Tokyo pursue with respect to constitutional reform, military modernization and assumption of new international roles and responsibilities? How should Seoul seek to shape the outcome, to the extent possible, in its own choice of policies?

What opportunities and risks exist in Moscow's renewed assertion of great power status including explicit use of energy resources as a political chip to enhance national influence?

What are the prospects for building—or building toward—a Northeast Asian regional security architecture, a mid- or long-term policy goal long ascribed to Seoul's policymakers by many outside analysts? Is such an aspiration a viable strategy? If so, what shape might it have and what implications would it hold for Seoul's foreign policies more generally?

For South Korean policymakers, then, the tasks are as difficult as it is imperative to get them right: to assess what the shifting tectonic plates have fundamentally altered, and what they have not; to work out the intricate pattern of emerging new interrelationships and influences as it bears upon Seoul's national security calculus; and to identify and implement those options that best meet Seoul's current and longer-term national interests. This chapter will seek to explore some of these considerations that emerge from the changing Northeast Asian regional landscape.

## A Region in Sweeping Change, Transitioning to the Unknown

One unaltered reality since President Lee's inauguration is Asia's global importance and the broad contours of intra-regional relationships; the implications are well appreciated throughout Asia, but perhaps less fully understood and assimilated elsewhere.

On the one hand, artifacts of the Cold War (and before) remain: a divided Korean Peninsula, Taiwan as a potential flash point, and U.S. alliances and security relationships forged to counter the threat posed by "international communism" and left in place, essentially unchanged, to meet ill-defined new challenges to "peace and stability" in the region. Three of the world's nuclear powers—the United States, China and Russia—assert strategic interests and maintain forces in the region. North Korea has tested a nuclear device, while Japan, South Korea and Taiwan are widely assumed technically capable of initiating a successful nuclear weapons program in short order. China, Russia, South Korea and North Korea maintain four of the world's largest standing armies; the United States enjoys unrivalled power projection capabilities, while China, Japan and South Korea are investing substantial sums to modernize their armed forces and develop their own power projection assets. Under a tacit "Pax Americana," however, intra-regional relationships remained remarkably conflict-free, if not precisely harmonious, following the withdrawal of U.S. troops from Vietnam in 1975 and what was, in a sense, that conflict's final gasp, the brief Sino-Vietnamese War in early 1979.

On the other hand, precisely because the region's nations managed to avoid debilitating internecine struggles, and virtually without exception assigned top priority to economic development, the face of Asia—and the shape of global commerce—were transformed in the span of a generation. First came the rapid advances of the so-called four Asian tigers: the highly industrialized economies of Singapore, Taiwan, Hong Kong and the Republic of Korea. South Korea's "Miracle on the Han River" and "The Taiwan Miracle" inspired similar policies and nearly as striking successes in Thailand, Malaysia and Indonesia. And then China emerged in 1979 from Mao's radical socialist autarky to embrace, under Deng Xiaoping, an export-driven market economy that has registered nearly three decades of annual double-digit GDP growth, produced by 2009 the world's third-largest GDP, and served as the primary engine for regional economic development and increased global prosperity. China's massive size, political stability, low wages, government encouragement for foreign investors and rapidly improving infrastructure made it an irresistible magnet for relocation by East Asia's richest, most technologically advanced economies—Japan, South Korea, Taiwan—of substantial percentages of their industrial production. Those nations reaped tangible benefits in profits and reduced consumer prices even as concerns began to be voiced about the hollowing out of domestic industry, exponential growth in China's military capabilities and international clout, and the concomitant longer-term implications for power relationships among East Asia's major nations.

India's more recent economic takeoff strengthened the gathering sense of Asia's rise even as it added new permutations and combinations of factors into the emerging security calculus to be considered by other Asian nations. Today, the three major Asian powers—China, India and Japan—together with the Republic of Korea and Association of Southeast Asian Nations (ASEAN) member nations account for over 40 percent of the world's GDP, roughly double the comparable figure in 1981. East Asia's absolute poverty rate stands at only 16 percent in 2009, compared with 78 percent in 1981.[1] Asian quality in education, innovation, entrepreneurship and scientific R&D is well reflected in U.S. patent filings: Asian businesses and research institutes now account for double the annual applications of their European counterparts, and for over a quarter of all filings in the United States. Meanwhile, despite the ongoing crisis in the global financial system, China and India continue to be looked at as the most promising potential "saviors" of other economies, and hence to attract foreign direct investment and buyers.

All of that is well understood in the region and around the world. What is perhaps less well grasped, especially outside Asia, are the subtle changes occurring in Asian psychology and strategic thinking: a propensity to set the regional agenda without according outside (read: U.S.) views primacy, let alone veto power; an emphasis on intra-regional commercial and economic relationships; an embrace of explicitly "Asian" norms and principles—in parallel, to be sure, with acceptance of international rules and practices as in the World Trade Organization—to govern intra-regional dialogue and transactions; and a nascent move toward formation of something akin to an East Asian community.

In short, while the trappings of the U.S.-centric order in East Asia persist, especially in robust American alliance ties to Japan and to the Republic of Korea, it is not difficult to discern a drift, by no means glacial, away from the old logic and verities. Both South Korea and, less overtly, Japan have questioned the meaning and implications of the U.S. concept of "strategic flexibility" enunciated as the centerpiece of President Bush's force reposturing in Asia and the Pacific. Northeast Asian states have displayed growing enthusiasm for an array of regional multilateral institutions and regimes where the United States has but one voice, or none at all: the ASEAN Regional Forum, ASEAN Plus Three, the East Asian Summit (EAS) and the recent inauguration of annual tripartite China-Japan-ROK leadership meetings. China and Russia have taken the lead in the newly formed and still deliberately opaque Shanghai Cooperation Organization—a mechanism ostensibly created to address Central Asian energy and counter-terrorist cooperation but which has invited Iran's participation as an observer, conducted joint training exercises in waters off northeast China whose scenario reportedly simulated an amphibious assault on Taiwan's beaches, and called for the prompt withdrawal of those U.S. bases and forces in Central Asia supporting the U.S. war in Afghanistan. On March 9, the Institute for International

Policy Studies, a Japanese think tank, released a report asserting the lack of American wherewithal to single-handedly resolve the global economic crisis and calling for creation of an Asian currency unit to be coequal with the U.S. dollar and the euro.

Yet these illustrate but one dimension of the complex crosscurrents that are reshaping the Northeast Asian economic and security landscape. Government officials and academic observers commonly point with justification to "fluidity" as the hallmark of the region. There are strong centripetal forces at play in the region—but no real center as yet. To the contrary, it remains an open question whether current vectors point toward an East Asian community or rather toward a classical struggle for power and influence among the major nations of the region. The old order is fast eroding and disintegrating, but nothing has yet crystallized to take its place that promises a commensurate degree of peace, stability, predictability and security. At present, the common aspirations witnessed in the web of regional economic relationships and movement toward regional institutions coexist with enduring mutual suspicion, jockeying for national influence and advantage, and preoccupation with potential existential security threats and the means of countering them. Northeast Asians increasingly share a common identity with respect to economics and, to some extent, cultural and societal features that they judge have underpinned the regional economic "miracle." All are in accord that they must work to preserve the open global trading system. All see a surpassing requirement to act singly or in concert to ensure a stable regional balance. All seek to prevent or neutralize incipient security challenges. All simultaneously compete for increasingly scarce energy resources and assert a need to rationalize and contain such competitive impulses. All suffer, to a greater or lesser degree, from environmental degradation resulting from their own and their neighbors' rapid economic development and wish to ameliorate it.

But how to do all this? That remains far from clear to any of the regional actors, and for the simplest of reasons: the multiplicity of forces and interests, their interplay and evolution, cannot possibly be charted with confidence. So the visible pattern is one in which nations simultaneously cling to old security arrangements still deemed useful, explore the possibility of new structures to supplement or supplant the existing ones as circumstances mature, and adopt multiple hedging strategies to prepare for an unknown and still largely unknowable future.

## Seoul's Economic Standing and Outlook on the Eve of the Financial Crisis

When Lee Myung-bak campaigned for the presidency and assumed power a year ago, there were only faint intimations of troubles in the U.S. economy, while South Korea's fundamentals seemed strong. As recently as last September, Prime Minister Han Seung-soo (Han Sŭng-su), addressing a Seoul conference, foresaw no dark clouds on the horizon and pointed proudly to a litany of South Korean achievements: the world's 13th largest economy; the world's 3rd largest producer of intellectual patents; a global provider of cutting-edge IT products and services; an annual per capita income surpassing $20,000; a world leader in shipbuilding, automobiles, steel products, petrochemical products and electronics; and a recently upgraded rating as an "advanced economy" by the FTSE global equity index.[2]

At the same September conference in Seoul, Defense Minister Lee Sang-hee (Yi Sang-hŭi) added that of the more than 140 nations founded in the world since the conclusion of the Second World War, only seven, the ROK among them, had achieved a per capita annual income over $10,000—a figure that the ROK had already doubled. Comparing the ROK's economic performance to that of North Korea, the Bank of Korea reported a South Korean gross national income (GNI) in 2007 of $902.5 billion—36.4 times greater than the estimated figure for the North.[3] The British scholar Aidan Foster-Carter underlined what this meant in terms of "competition" on the Korean Peninsula: a modest South Korean annual growth rate of 3 percent—the average for the years since the Asian financial crisis had been 5-6 percent—would add the equivalent of the entire North Korean economy.[4] The World Bank in 2008 assigned to the ROK the ranking of 30th place in its assessment of national competitiveness globally.[5]

Based on these rosy statistics, projections and assessments President Lee had formulated his ambitious economic agenda and premised South Korea's plan—"Defense Reform 2020"—for future improvements in its defense capabilities. As campaigner and newly inaugurated president, Lee offered his "National Vision"—South Korea as "a country that stands tall in the world through advancement." He aimed to lay the foundation for South Korea to become within a decade the 7th largest world economy, with a per capita income of $40,000 and standing in 15th place in World Bank national competitiveness ratings. He proposed to achieve this through a program of "small government, big markets," entailing substantial reduction in taxes, elimination of burdensome government regulations on private enterprise and relaxation of restrictions on foreign investment. His presidential transition committee had issued a blizzard of unusually specific "national tasks"—192 of them.[6]

### The Global Economic Crisis: Accelerating Strategic Readjustments (But Still to an Unknown Destination)

It has become a cliché that the financial crisis originating in the United States, and initially thought by many containable there, now threatens the entire global economy. Asian economies, initially considered secure for structural reasons, including high national savings rates and astronomical holdings of foreign exchange reserves, are uniformly suffering from the ripple effects. The World Bank predicted in January 2009 that overall world trade would decline in 2009 by 2.9 percent—the first decline after 27 consecutive years of growth.[7] China, held out in late 2008 to be the potential "savior" of the U.S. and other advanced economies, was hard hit by the sharp falloff in export markets and announced the layoff of 20 million industrial "migrant workers" from interior rural areas. Export-dependent southern Chinese cities became boarded-up ghost towns. As the magnitude of the shock waves became apparent, Beijing launched a $586 billion stimulus package in November 2008 targeted at supporting domestic job creation and boosting domestic consumption, followed that with $124 billion appropriated to revamp China's health care system, and recently announced, without details, at the annual March meeting of China's legislative body, another stimulus package. Meanwhile, China's national leaders and central bankers had consulted closely both with American and regional counterparts, creating a Northeast Asian currency swap arrangement in mid-December and pledging to consider financial support for a regional economic recovery package. Chinese Premier Wen Jiabao, expressing measured optimism at the health of the nation's economy, projected overall Chinese GDP growth of 8 percent in 2009—considerably below the double-digit annual growth figures sustained for 30 years, but sufficient to maintain social stability at home and support economic recovery programs elsewhere.

Counterpoised against this image of Chinese leadership—and ample financial resources to back it up—were grim statistics and projections virtually everywhere else in the region and throughout the world. In January 2009, Taiwan's exports fell 44 percent compared with the previous year. Japan announced that it expected negative growth for the year.

### South Korea's Economic Crisis: Grimmer than Most

For its part, South Korea confronted a situation all too reminiscent of the 1997–98 Asian financial crisis; indeed, it showed a sharper decline in exports and higher rate of capital flight than it had a decade earlier. The Korean won was by far the region's worst performing currency in 2008, falling by 26 percent against the dollar. (It fell another 20 percent against the dollar during the first two months of 2009.) GDP growth in 2008 was only 2.5 percent, the lowest annual figure since the Asian financial crisis year 1998. Industrial production was hit hard by a double-digit decline in exports during the fourth quarter of 2008. In response, Hyundai and Kia slashed working hours in their factories; GM Daewoo (Taeu) and Renault Samsung (Samsŏng) idled plants in December; and Samsung Electronics, Asia's largest manufacturer of chips, announced its largest restructuring in a decade that entailed consolidation of four major subsidiaries into two and reduced the number of corporate executives. Meanwhile, fourth quarter figures showed a 16 percent decline in South Korean facility investment.[8]

In January, President Lee declared that his nation was "facing a state of economic emergency" and announced a $100 billion stimulus package (including tax cuts). After Lee sacked Finance Minister Kang Man-soo (Kang Man-su) late in the year, responding to popular impressions and accusations that he was not up to his job, the new finance minister Yoon Jeung-hyun (Yun Chŭng-hyŏn) offered in early March a set of "unpleasant" but "honest" forecasts: the South Korean economy would contract more quickly than earlier anticipated, by 2 percent in 2009, and it would lose some 200,000 jobs.[9] Even Yoon's "unpleasant news" fell well short of outside forecasts: the Economist Intelligence Unit (EIU) saw South Korea's GDP shrinking by 5.9 percent in 2009[10]; Standard & Poor in mid-February amended its January prediction of zero growth in 2009 to a forecasted contraction of 3.5 percent; and the International Monetary Fund (IMF) envisaged a 4 percent contraction for the year. The historical and psychological reference point for all these prognostications must be 1998—a year when South Korea's economy contracted by 6.9 percent and the nation barely averted financial collapse by means of a $60 billion international bailout.[11]

On March 4 the conservative Seoul daily *Chosun Ilbo (Chosŏn Ilbo)* observed editorially, not without sarcasm, that it was "easy to get the impression that Korea's economy is the most endangered in Asia...the Government is ... missing the point (and) needs to state the actual facts in order to inspire public trust..." The piece drew attention to South Korea's dubious status as the only country in Asia whose banks have loan-deposit ratios surpassing 100 percent, and to the nation's extremely poor comparative standing with other Asian countries in its ratio of short-term debt to foreign exchange reserves: 77 percent for South Korea versus 7 percent for China, 9 percent for India, and 26 percent for Taiwan.[12]

## *Implications of the Financial Crisis*

This chapter cannot explore the detailed economic ramifications of the financial crisis but will simply pose the question: How has the ongoing crisis impacted on regional, especially South Korean, evaluation of current policy requirements and future strategic choices? More confident answers will need to await developments over the coming months and year, but one can now sense in elite commentary and analyses a number of themes holding distinct implications for relative power and influence in the Northeast Asian region.

For starters, faith in the magic of self-regulating market mechanisms and minimal governmental intervention in national economic life has been profoundly shaken around the globe and in Northeast Asia. Toyoo Gyohten, a former Japanese vice minister of finance and chairman of the Bank of Tokyo, wrote on March 12 that "economic and geopolitical factors have been undermining the unipolar world order centered on the United States.... The global center of gravity is shifting away from the G7 framework ... the G5 and G7 that once led the global economy are no longer groups exercising leadership with adequate capabilities and authority."[13] Ambassador Shyam Saran, until a year ago the Indian foreign secretary and still today a special envoy in the Indian prime minister's office, suggested in late February to an Indian gathering that "it is possible that New York and London cannot regain undisputed status as central financial markets of the world."[14] Premier Wen Jiabao has publicly chastised the U.S. government for profligate spending, insufficient saving and mismanagement of the institutions that underpin the American economy; on March 12 he "confessed" publicly that he was indeed worried whether China's substantial investment in U.S. Treasury bills was secure.[15] And these are the public, muted and more diplomatic expressions of what is plainly being discussed in more colorful, starker terms behind the scenes in each of the major Asian and world capitals and financial centers.

In short, each nation in Asia as elsewhere is preoccupied with management of its own situation amidst the global financial turmoil. Korea, Japan and China must all adjust to the reduction of overseas export markets. They must all be alert to the rise of protectionist sentiments, both within and outside the region, that could further adversely affect the outlook for recovery. Each must carefully assess the probable impact on key national export industries, e.g., automobiles, the IT sector, heavy machinery, as well as the domestic economic fallout of reduced foreign direct investment from the United States and Western Europe.

While designing a program to address those immediate worries, each of the Northeast Asian countries will simultaneously be making its own calculus regarding an optimal economic, political and strategic course in the future. Barring an unexpectedly rapid U.S. economic recovery and/or major industrialized nation unanimity at the April G20 meeting in London, continuing erosion of U.S./Western European prestige and leadership ability seems a given. In the eyes of Asian decision makers, the center of gravity— with respect to financial affairs and geopolitics—is discernibly shifting toward Asia, China in particular. Put more concretely, political power and influence are being redistributed globally commensurate with the demonstrated economic strength and weakness of nations in the face of the global crisis.

What might this imply strategically for Asia, and for Seoul? While it is too early to predict outcomes with confidence, particularly given that economic factors are only one part of the strategic equation, the economic crisis has arguably provoked the following shifts:

China emerges a regional and global winner, despite its own serious structural imbalances and domestic political challenges, because its financial reserves, continuing projected annual growth of around 8 percent, and image of solid, sober economic management have presented to the world a "Beijing model" that challenges the "Washington consensus" even as Beijing's leaders show a disposition to do what Washington plainly cannot— help other nations in Asia to ameliorate the worst effects of the crisis.

Northeast Asian nations will have greater strategic space in which to explore options both for effecting some distancing from Washington and for testing new, more multipolar models encompassing stronger regional partnerships and mechanisms. While the December 13 Japan-China-South Korea governmental leaders meeting in Fukuoka represented no explicit challenge to U.S. interests or alliance relationships, for example, the subtle message conveyed by the visual imagery and the announced agreements was unmistakable: the three major Northeast Asian nations were ready to work more closely together to address their common economic agenda. The final communiqué from that one-day gathering announced that joint statements had been signed on "trilateral partnership"; "international financial and economic issues"; "trilateral disaster management"; and an "action plan" relating to future cooperation. China's official news agency Xinhua reported two days later that Premier Wen had introduced six "initiatives" at the gathering, including broader financial cooperation to include "expansion" of the just-agreed-on Northeast Asia currency swap arrangement. Wen also proposed establishment of a regional foreign exchange reserve; promotion of an Asian bond market; joint feasibility studies on a tripartite free trade zone;

enhanced customs cooperation; and closer cooperation among the respective central banks. For its part, Wen continued, China was prepared to offer a regional economic recovery package. Finally, Wen called for a "cementing" of regional cooperation and coordination on "major international and regional issues" and a "strengthening" of the East Asia Summit as a "strategic platform."[16]

Northeast Asian nations will diversify to a greater degree their international relationships. They will be more inclined—here, the possible shift of Japan's government to Democratic Party of Japan (DPJ) leadership is especially relevant—to seek a tighter web of economic and political ties with the BRIC (Brazil, Russia, India, China) nations and other economically significant partners such as Indonesia and Mexico. While this in no way necessitates a radical alteration in the existing framework of the ROK-U.S. and Japan-U.S. security relationships, it does imply a more diffuse international order and a more "global" perspective on the part of the ROK and Japan.

Where Seoul is concerned, the straws in the wind are already there to be seen. In March 2009, on arrival in Jakarta, President Lee hinted strongly at an ongoing diplomatic repositioning to take into account the new circumstances and challenges. According to one press account of his private meeting in Jakarta with South Korean diplomats, Lee proclaimed a new Asia focus: "Korea needs to consolidate relationships with our Asian neighbors to brace for the era of Asia.... I believe Korea is capable enough to become a leader in Asia and represent the continent on the global stage."[17] Elaborating subsequently in a not-for-attribution press backgrounder, an official ROK government spokesman told journalists "Korea will strengthen relations with countries in the Asia Pacific region in various areas, including economy, security and culture.... Under the new diplomatic doctrine, Korea will seek a leading role in resolving regional issues, including the Asian monetary fund."[18]

## The Economic Crisis, Shifting Geopolitical Realities and Seoul's Defense Posture

When Lee took office, he inherited from the outgoing Roh administration a 2006 program outline for defense modernization called "Defense Reform 2020." The conceptual underpinnings of that program reflected both the Roh administration's policy/ideological prism and the best judgment of South Korea's senior professional military officers regarding the nation's future strategic environment, defense requirements, acquisition priorities, funding needs and demographic factors. The explicitly "political" drivers of the program seemed to include (1) Roh's wish, in embracing the essence of Kim Dae-jung's "Sunshine Policy," to reduce tensions with a nonthreatening North while promoting increased engagement; (2) Roh's push for both the appearance and reality of greater "equality" in ROK-U.S. relations, symbolized and given substance by the U.S. agreement to transfer wartime operational control to the ROK armed forces by 2012; and (3) steady progress toward accomplishment of greater autonomy in defense and military affairs. Unarticulated, but no doubt factored into formulation of the program, was a sense that the ROK-U.S. alliance might be entering a sunset phase and that the U.S. security commitment, for whatever reason, was waning. Equally unarticulated, and no less present in the calculations of the planners, was the need to prepare, or hedge, against various "new" (i.e., not emanating from North Korea, but perhaps from China or Japan) threats in the region. The program assumed continuing annual GDP growth rates in the 7 percent range, programmed annual defense spending increases of almost 10 percent through 2020, anticipated pressures on manpower availability from sharply declining birth rates, and counted on ability to harness technological advances and integrate new systems coming on stream—a South Korean version of the U.S. "revolution in military affairs"—to field a significantly smaller but substantially more capable modern force.

Key targets embraced by "Defense Reform 2020" included: reduction of ROK ground forces manpower by 2020 from 680,000 to 500,000, of army corps from ten to six, and of ground divisions from 47 to 20; commensurate upgrading of the air force and navy to ensure a rapid-response capability; and greater localization of arms production so as to promote an arms export industry and take advantage of technological innovations occurring in South Korean's industrial and R&D enterprises. The initial (2006) version of the plan foresaw that the ROK armed forces would be able, by 2011, to conduct surveillance over the entire Korean Peninsula and adjacent area; to upgrade long-range strike and counter-fire attack capabilities; to carry out air combat operations over the entire Korean Peninsula; and to have in operation a command-communication system supporting real-time integrated combat power. To that end, priority was accorded to purchase of such big-ticket equipment as high-tech reconnaissance and surveillance systems (four Global Hawk drone aircraft, multipurpose satellites, four E-737 AWACs) and long-range strike forces (three AEGIS-class destroyers, six Type-214 submarines, 48 Patriot missiles, and 20 additional F-15K fighters).[19]

Succinctly stated, Lee was bequeathed a defense spending program whose underlying premises did not correspond to his policy vision and priorities, that lacked analytical rigor, that rested upon faulty assumptions about future economic growth rates, that presumed an unsustainable level of military spending increases, and that was already yielding a yawning gap between targets and realities. For example, while Roh had won U.S. agreement to turn over wartime operational control by 2012, the resulting budget requirements were not adequately factored into the defense program . Furthermore, the plan assumed that new systems and capabilities coming on stream would compensate for the reduction in manpower, while the declining number of troops would produce cost savings that could be channeled into procurement, technical training and other costs associated with the programmed upgrades. However, as budget shortfalls threatened funding of the planned procurement, questions were raised about the logic of a steadily diminishing force size.

Lee's incoming team initially elected, however, to make adjustments rather than to perform radical surgery on the plan handed over to them. Roh himself had been forced to retreat on some of his initial goals in response to budgetary pressures: to an 8 percent increase in defense spending in 2006, and then 8.8 percent in 2007 and 2008. Lee's first 2009 budget further scaled back the annual defense spending increase to 7.5 percent as it also slowed the Roh administration's shift of emphasis from army to air force and navy. In so doing, Lee sent an early, clear signal that North Korea continued to pose a threat. His administration would therefore need to carefully evaluate the validity and implications of that threat assessment, the military priorities flowing from the administration's intent to restore ROK-U.S. alliance relations as the centerpiece of South Korea's strategic posture, and what the domestic budget would permit. Furthermore, some senior ROK military leaders publicly hinted following Lee's election that they were studying afresh the possibility of joining the U.S.-sponsored theater ballistic missile defense architecture. Roh's decision to the contrary was ascribed to three principal considerations: it would send the wrong message vis-à-vis North Korea; substantial sums of money were required for an initial buy-in; and joining would likely provoke a strong Chinese reaction deleterious to South Korea's larger security equities. If the Lee administration were to opt to join those arrangements, the decision would carry significant implications for the magnitude of the defense budget, the priorities within it, and South Korea's strategic posture.

The global financial tsunami has sharpened debate within South Korea's already polarized society on all these matters even as it has further circumscribed the Lee administration's ability to entertain costly policy departures. The logic of the current situation—South Korea's anticipated sharply negative growth in 2009, emerging Northeast Asian trilateralism to forge a common approach toward the economic crisis, absence of any obvious security threat on the immediate time horizon demanding a response, an unaltered U.S. security commitment despite the Bush era global force reposturing—argues powerfully for a prudent scaling back of ambitions as Seoul reassesses its evolving strategic requirements. In short, the ROK for now has little choice but to slow the pace of its military modernization drive for a restructured, technologically capable armed force that can self-sufficiently shoulder the burden of providing for the nation's defense. And this, in fact, is the essence of what Lee has recently outlined. He has extended the defense plan's completion date to 2025, deferred certain big-ticket procurements, pared away some spending deemed nonessential, sought to fill certain pressing capability gaps through procurement of used hardware rather than the most modern replacement system, and allocated stimulus package funds to subsidize defense industries in order to support both domestic employment and revenue-earning arms exports. Otherwise, review of the conceptual and concrete content of the defense plan has in effect been kicked down the road until the overall economic and political situation has clarified.

## Global Korea: Rebranding South Korea's Image and Leveraging its Comparative Advantages

South Korea's post-Cold War leaders, whatever their backgrounds and ideological leanings, have all grappled with the same dilemma: how to leverage the nation's comparative advantages, regionally and globally, to ensure its security, develop its economy, and maximize its influence. One aspect of this, quite apart from grand strategy, formal alliances and military planning, involves how the nation should present, or "brand," itself in its external relationships. This is not a trivial dilemma, nor one whose solution is evident or simple. The starting point (and usually the ending point) for ROK leaders has become a cliché: the nation is akin to a shrimp (or a minnow) among whales, and may have few realistic choices in a brutal environment beyond a minimalist posture of remaining invisible and inoffensive. Recent South Korean leaders have seen the country as a classical "middle power," whether aspirational or actual. But while those judgments, not inaccurate on the face of it, serve to set the parameters for thinking about the world beyond the Korean Peninsula, they do not lead inexorably to an approach whose success is assured.

Early in his 2003–2008 tenure in office, Roh advanced a vision of the ROK as a regional "hub" for economic activity. Later, without rejecting that notion, and presumably intending to offer a gloss on it, Roh suggested that

South Korea could play the role of "balancer." Neither concept was ever provided much flesh for the bones. As a matter of national branding, the two concepts proved problematic with South Korea's treaty ally, the United States, and perplexing to nations in Northeast Asia. South Korea's diplomats, presenting the ideas under instruction from their capital, seemed as unable to explain the underlying thinking as they were nervous about hearing and having to report home the formal and informal reactions. To the extent that the hub concept was fleshed out in official or quasi-official statements from Seoul, it seemed to mean simply that South Korea would economically engage with all comers, to the mutual advantage of each partner. In so doing South Korea, aiming to bolster its exporting prowess, would take full advantage of cheap Chinese and North Korean labor, emphasize development of its national high technology sector, and support so-called champion companies that were, or promised to be, highly competitive in the global marketplace. The ROK-U.S. alliance would continue to provide the necessary security umbrella. All this seemed, in the Washington optic, to be inchoate but inoffensive.

The balancer idea, however, rang alarm bells in Washington and puzzled other nations in Northeast Asia. Balance what? Balance whom? The question was the same no matter where it was asked: How exactly does a nation formally aligned in a half-century-old mutual defense alliance propose to balance between its treaty partner and other nations, including potential adversaries, in the region? No definitive answer emerged from Seoul, though some sought to allay concerns by explaining that the concept was never intended to connote "negotiate" or "mediate," nor to call into question the strength and viability of the ROK-U.S. alliance. It was, they suggested, more a matter of serving as bridge than as balancer—of clarifying and interpreting such misunderstandings as might arise between stakeholders in the region, given South Korea's excellent relations with all concerned. In Washington, and very likely elsewhere, the balancer idea solidified an impression that Roh was determined to hold the United States at arm's length, to distance the ROK very gradually from the security alliance, while pursuing engagement with North Korea and forging ever-closer ties with China.

On assuming office, Lee Myung-bak swiftly discarded that failed effort at re-branding South Korea and proposed another: "Global Korea." The concept aimed to raise South Korea's international profile and expand its influence by leveraging its principal assets: economic strength, high-tech capabilities, an educated population and experience in building the institutions of civil society.

Prime Minister Han Seung-soo explained the vision of "Global Korea" concisely: it meant simply that the ROK should "assume its fair share" in the global community of nations. Speaking in late 2008, Han sketched some of the goals: (1) joining the OECD Development Assistance Committee (DAC) in 2010 to better coordinate South Korea's assistance policy with the international community; (2) tripling South Korea's overseas development assistance (ODA) to reach over $3 billion by 2015; (3) offering in 2009-11 over $100 million in assistance, exclusive of aid to North Korea, for emergency food aid and strengthening of agricultural capacities of developing countries; (4) dispatching of Korean technical experts to assist developing countries in farming infrastructure, technology and relevant policy making; (5) launching of an "East Asian Climate Partnership," funded at $200 million over the next five years, to support countries in the region in seeking patterns of economic growth consistent with reducing global warming; (6) making available, on request, election monitoring and related advice to those wishing to study Korea's experience in "accelerated democratization"; and (7) challenging substantial appropriations at home into pilot "New Engine of Growth Industries" focusing on environmentally-friendly technologies that could support green policies in Korea and in neighboring countries.[20]

Other ROK governmental officials have flagged elements of the "Global Korea" vision that bear more directly on traditional security concerns. South Korea intended, for example to "review" and "strengthen" efforts to combat proliferation of weapons and technologies of mass destruction. In keeping with tribute paid South Korea by the United Nations as an "Exemplary Nation in Peacekeeping Activities," the nation would continue and expand PKO participation that has already involved over 30,000 South Korean service members in operations conducted in 17 countries.

Speaking directly to the issue of South Korea's international image, President Lee warned in his August 15, 2008 National Liberation and Founding Day speech that the "very first images that come [into] foreigners' minds are labor-management disputes and street rallies...if the nation wants to be labeled an advanced country, it will be necessary to improve its image and reputation significantly."[21] Taking up this theme in a speech to a Seoul gathering later in the year, U.S. Heritage Foundation President Ed Feulner, long associated with staunch support for the U.S.-ROK alliance, ripped into the policies of the ROK government under its recent progressive presidents and wondered aloud whether Seoul's image—and policies—could again inspire confidence in its bilateral partners and among prospective foreign (i.e., western) business investors. Feulner identified Seoul's major difficulties—to some extent continuing under the new Lee administration—as: (1) President Roh's "anti-foreign sentiment" coupled with "vacillating but generally antibusiness economic policies"; (2) the massive anti-beef street demonstrations that "affirmed investor perceptions" that Korea remains a problematic investment environment; and (3) the "fierce public nationalism" aroused over the Dokdo (Tokto, J. Takeshima) island dispute, which the ROK government basically endorsed, thus strengthening a foreign (i.e., American and Japanese) perception of South Korea as "an immature democracy."[22]

In general, Lee seems to have identified a winner in terms of re-branding South Korea's international image and utilizing its assets to advantage. Moreover, this approach holds only positive connotations—if able to be implemented conscientiously—for South Korea's relations with regional stakeholders. That said, questions about pace and impact of the "Global Korea" concept arise in the context of the economic and financial crisis. It remains to be seen whether Seoul will be able to follow through on its announced spending goals and commitments.

### Defining a Revitalized U.S. Relationship

ROK-U.S. relations inarguably suffered serious strains during the years when Presidents Bush and Roh Moo-hyun led their respective nations. Several Washington think tanks, including conservative ones traditionally strongly supportive of the U.S.-ROK alliance, hosted public symposia at which participants conjured up vivid images of a near-term "sunset of the alliance," "end of the marriage," and need for the United States to "cut bait." In Seoul, public and private discussions were no less pointed and heated. The reasons were complex: rooted in history, emotions, diverging perspectives on the evolving post-Cold War threat environment and what to do about it, and the personalities and political personas of the two leaders. Volumes of analysis have already been written, but nothing approaching a consensus—let alone what to do about it—has surfaced in either nation.

U.S. government officials breathed an almost audible sigh of relief when Lee Myung-bak won his election and put an end to the decade of progressive rule in Seoul. Perhaps an equivalent sigh of relief went up from many Seoul offices as the era of George W. Bush drew to a close—no matter whether candidates McCain or Obama succeeded him. As he took office in February 2008, well in advance of the lame-duck phase of Bush's presidency, Lee tacitly acknowledged the fissures, strains and mutual mistrust that had developed during the immediately preceding years by assigning revitalization of the ROK-U.S. alliance pride of place in his initial policy statement.

Speaking before the Korea Society in New York at the outset of his five-day trip to the U.S. in April 2008, Lee declared that "Korea and the United

States should work out a common strategy for peace and prosperity not only for the Korean Peninsula, but also for Asia and the rest of the world....That strategic vision should be called the 'Korea-U.S. Strategic Alliance' [having the three core principles of] common values, trust and peace."[23] Lee struck the same note during his subsequent meeting with a smiling President Bush; following their meeting, the two announced agreement that they intended to begin work immediately on drafting of a joint strategic vision to be unveiled at their follow-on July summit in Seoul. That summit was postponed, however, in the wake of Seoul's massive street demonstrations against Lee's agreement in Washington to permit resumption of U.S. beef imports at the alleged risk of exposing Korean citizens to illness or death from mad cow disease. Bureaucratic interest in formulating a joint strategic vision swiftly waned in both countries.

Were the "revitalized alliance" theme and the beef import agreement merely intended to inspire greater U.S. sympathy and momentum in support of congressional ratification of the Korea-U.S. Free Trade Agreement (KORUS)? Had President Lee calculated that setting a new tone in bilateral dialogue would win Seoul a greater assurance that U.S. policymakers would hear its voice? Were his statements in the nature of political theater, or did he in fact mean to ground the ROK's evolving security posture firmly in the established alliance? Whatever the case, neither side thus far has been able to work through the complexities and articulate a new vision. Journalist-scholar Mike Chinoy quoted one unidentified Pentagon official as asking querulously in spring 2008: "Why do we have an alliance...If it isn't about stopping the North Koreans at the border, what is it? If we don't get out there and articulate it, there will be a greater erosion of public support in both countries."[24] In similar vein, U.S. Forces Korea (USFK) Commanding General Burwell B. Bell commented on the eve of Lee's U.S. trip that the two countries needed to "recast the alliance as something beyond simply a confrontational alliance to prevent aggression against South Korea by North Korea and recognize that the treaty we signed in 1953 doesn't even mention North Korea. It talks about mutual defense against any aggression in the Pacific region on either partner."[25]

The basic question posed here is whether, given the shifting geopolitical landscape, a revitalized alliance with the United States will best serve the majority of Seoul's core national interests. The follow-up question is whether the ongoing economic crisis alters that calculus to any significant degree.

From Seoul's perspective, ending the alliance outright has never seemed a plausible option. Indeed, even during the Roh years, South Korean attitudes seemed to fluctuate wildly between resentment of perceived alliance inequality and fear of U.S. abandonment. Both threatened exposure of South Korea to unacceptable risks, the former to being dragged into an unwanted regional conflict precipitated or joined by the United States, and the latter to being vulnerable to the ambitions of potentially voracious neighbors. More concretely, ROK think tank studies have consistently shown that termination of the alliance or unilateral withdrawal by USFK would impose heavy costs on Seoul. A Korea Institute for Defense Analysis (KIDA) study calculated that Seoul's defense burden would immediately double, other factors remaining constant, from 2.7 percent of GDP to 5-6 percent.[26] Beyond that, the removal of U.S. security guarantees would very likely result in additional costs: decline in foreign investments owing to an increased risk perception, and imposition by the United States of domestic controls on future transfer of certain advanced technologies to the ROK.

Other predictably negative consequences of a significant scaling back or termination of alliance ties would include exposure of ROK imports of oil, now under protection of unmatched U.S. naval superiority, to greater potential risks; and weakened ROK direct and indirect security links to Japan, resulting in diminished expectations of future Japanese investment, technological cooperation and good will.

But does it then make sense for Seoul, under current circumstances, to consider seriously revitalizing the alliance or even maintaining the status quo? No immediate answer suggests itself. Lee must first look to his own domestic situation; the South Korean people remain polarized around generational, ideological and political fault lines. While South Korean citizens seem today to be more attuned to potential threats from North Korea and a rising China, and to the utility of the U.S. alliance in dissuading and deterring any adversaries, they remain hesitant to endorse a more far-reaching alliance system whose purpose, costs, risks and potential benefits they cannot adequately assess.

They understand—or at least speculate—that a more robust alliance would anticipate ROK assumption of higher burden-sharing costs and shouldering of increased responsibilities for specified roles and missions. If the U.S. concept of "strategic flexibility" implies that bases in the ROK, and even ROK troops, might be brought to bear in a future conflict involving China, for example one arising from a situation in the Taiwan Strait, many Koreans are not persuaded that this is consistent with Korean national interests. This conviction, however, exists in parallel with a contradictory anxiety that China might after all harbor future ambitions toward Korea that could be successfully countered only through maintenance of strong alliance ties to the distant power, the United States. Apart from the China factor in the equation, perceived U.S. aggressiveness during the Bush administration—the doctrine of preemptive military strikes, a "global war" on terrorism, declaring North Korea a member of the "axis of evil," interdiction of suspected shipments of weapons of mass destruction under the proliferation security initiative apparently targeting North Korea—brought to the fore in South Korean society profound reservations about the merits of an overly close association with American strategic designs. It is not yet clear to South Koreans whether and how the Obama administration's strategic intentions and tactical approach might differ.

If Lee elects to make good on his stated vision of a revitalized U.S. alliance, he faces an early need to explain and sell the expected mid- and long-term benefits to a larger majority of his people. It will not be enough to stick with homilies, as he did in New York when declaring the need to (re)join hands to "proactively engage countries plagued by terrorism, environmental degradation, disease and poverty with the goal of improving human security on the basis of humanitarian ideals."[27] By the same token, it will not be enough for Americans to focus narrowly on bilateral alliance matters as they have typically done in the past. If there is to be meaningful movement toward Lee's notion of a revitalized alliance, this will also require an American effort to articulate more specific expectations of the alliance, and the South Korean side, in the larger global arena.

The overall picture that emerges with respect to ROK-U.S. alliance ties, then, is one of contradictory impulses, conflicting pressures, a fluid strategic landscape and still unanswerable questions. The inherent difficulty of cutting through the policy thicket to produce a new strategic concept for ROK-U.S. ties has been exacerbated by the global economic crisis. For the present, Seoul is constrained from pursuing more autonomous capabilities, assuming additional alliance burdens and risking antagonism with China, whose cooperative posture is seen to be indispensable in addressing the economic crisis.

## North Korean Challenges and What to do About Them

Lee Myung-bak also signaled a sharp break with his two predecessors in tone and substance of national policy toward North Korea. Lee's remarks at his February 2008 inaugural and in the days following left no doubt that Kim Dae-jung's "Sunshine" policy and Roh Moo-hyun's "Peace and Prosperity" policy had been evaluated and found wanting. Lee indicated that his administration's new strategy would place emphasis on transparency, mutual benefits and pragmatism. He and his principal advisers made plain that the previous approach, which they characterized as "one side giving and the other side receiving," would be discarded. In effect, they had taken on board the criticism, advanced by conservatives in South Korea and synthesized acidly by U.S. Heritage Foundation President Edwin Feulner who asserted that "by providing billions of dollars in unconditional aid and promises of yet more largesse, Seoul minimized its influence over Pyongyang and marginalized its effectiveness in the Six-Party Talks."[28]

Tougher tone and newly hard-nosed negotiating strategy aside, South Korea's core policy interests and assumptions probably had not altered. South Korea sought to forestall any North Korean regime collapse/chaos scenario; to preclude any actions by the United States or others likely to prompt the same, or outright military conflict; and to monitor and dissuade any Chinese exercise of greater influence over Pyongyang that might culminate in the incorporation of North Korea into Beijing's implicit sphere of influence.

President Lee very likely was in sync with majority public sentiment in his country. A Chicago Council on World Affairs poll in 2006, for example, revealed that 65 percent of South Korean respondents—as compared with only 41 percent only two years earlier—saw North Korea as posing a "security threat" to the South.[29] What had happened? Most importantly, and obviously, North Korea had moved ahead on its nuclear program, taking advantage of the twists and turns in the frequently stalled Six-Party Talks to test a nuclear device on October 9, 2006. While foreign scientific analysis of the test prompted questions regarding the nature of the device and success of the detonation, the test underscored Pyongyang's determination to ignore appeals from six-party talks participants and to scorn the prospect and effectiveness of any UN-imposed sanctions regime. That in turn suggested the bankruptcy of the international approach, including Chinese blandishments, U.S. veiled threats ("all options are on the table"), on-again, off-again six-party talks, and Roh Moo-hyun's studied refusal to acknowledge any potential threat from the north. North Korea's survival tactics had evolved; one element in its strategy was the single-minded pursuit of nuclear capability as a legitimate and necessary deterrent against possible foreign attack.

ROK Defense Minister Lee Sanghee acknowledged publicly in autumn 2008 that efforts to build trust and reduce military tensions with the North had stalled. There had been zero progress in South-North exchanges and cooperation. He offered a stark appraisal of the ROK's threat environment: North Korea possessed a "vast military force" with over 75 percent of its million ground forces forward-deployed; it retained the capability to launch a surprise attack on the South "at any time"; and it continued vigorously to pursue weapons of mass destruction programs including nuclear weapons, biochemical weapons and missile delivery systems.[30]

Today, relations on the Korean Peninsula seem frozen. North Korea, facing the prospect of a difficult leadership succession in the wake of Kim Jong-il's health episode last August, is focused inward while projecting outward a belligerent determination to defend itself against all comers, to maintain its "deterrent" until (wildly unrealistic) asserted conditions are met, and to regard South Korea's conservative leadership with contemptuous animosity. Pyongyang reacted with customary ferocity and bombast to President Lee's enunciation of a new approach featuring reciprocity and linkages. The official daily *Rodong Sinmun* almost immediately denounced Lee as a "traitor" and scornfully rejected as "reactionary pragmatism" his proffer of assistance in raising North Korean per capita GDP to $3,000 in return for its abandonment of the nuclear program and openness to exchanges with the outside world.

Such rhetoric has not subsided, but has rather intensified and been coupled with concrete manifestations of anger such as imposition of new constraints on South Korean activities within the Kaesong industrial project zone and North Korea's March 2009 warning that the safety of South Korean civil aircraft flying customary routes near its air space could not be guaranteed. Stressing that they did not fly routes through North Korea's asserted airspace, South Korean flag carrier Korean Air and Asian Airlines nevertheless announced that they would re-route—at the cost of several thousand dollars per flight.

Preparations for an early April "satellite launch"—widely suspected to be a Taepodong (Taep'odong) missile test—proceed apace. Pyongyang reportedly rebuffed the U.S. proposal of an early visit by newly named special envoy Ambassador Stephen Bosworth on condition that it forgo the planned launch. The new U.S. administration has not yet put its senior Asia policy team in place, Bosworth excepted, and is evidently still conducting a policy review as a prelude to discussions and coordination with partners in the Six-Party Talks process. China, Japan and Russia seem to be marking time, awaiting developments from Pyongyang and Washington and, in Tokyo, also anticipating the probable early advent of a new, opposition-led government and possible policy adjustments toward North Korea and regional issues generally.

What does all this dictate as a near-term strategy for the Lee Myung-bak administration? Once again, watchful waiting would seem to be the order of the day. For at least two decades Pyongyang's strategy has been remarkably consistent in one respect: seek a direct negotiating channel with

Washington that serves to marginalize Seoul; deflect quiet pressures from Beijing or Moscow; cast Tokyo as the outlier; and thus drive wedges between the United States, U.S. allies (ROK, Japan) and partners (China, Russia). Whatever the logic and merits of the Roh Moo-hyun approach, it played into the hands of this strategy; the South wielded the very hammer that drove the wedge between itself and the United States. That is an outcome that the Lee administration plainly intends to avoid through his adoption of a revitalized alliance approach vis-à-vis Washington and a new policy toward Pyongyang featuring quid-pro-quo linkages. But this is only a starting point and the easiest part, assuming reciprocal intentions on the part of Washington. President Lee will still need to weigh the larger, longer-term issues: Is there sufficient strategic congruity between the United States and the ROK? Will the evolving U.S. approach buttress the ROK's stance, or will it implicate the ROK in implementation of policies toward the North it deems risky or counterproductive? What about Kaesong and its assumption that the best hope for peaceful regime transformation in the North lies in subtle, incremental, often frustrating efforts to seduce Pyongyang into the global community? Specifically, can the validity of this assumption be empirically proven or at least persuasively argued and, if so, will the U.S. administration agree and support the approach? Finally, as the Lee administration sorts all this out, it must do so with one eye fixed on Beijing's equities, expectations and actions with respect to North Korea.

## China's Rise: Its Trajectory and Implications for Seoul's Strategic Posture

Book-length dissertations have been written on China's so-called rise and the impact on evolving strategic relationships within the Northeast Asian region and beyond. Whatever else may be said, it is difficult to challenge the view that the trajectory of China's rise has been breathtaking since Deng Xiaoping 30 years ago proclaimed a national development strategy of openness (to the outside world) and reform (of the economy on market capitalist principles). China's rapid development of export industries and domestic infrastructure, stunning accumulation of national wealth, quiet accretion of international power and influence, and striking expansion of military capabilities all bespeak the most significant global development since the implosion of the Soviet Union. That China has achieved all this without provoking extreme nervousness elsewhere testifies to a sophisticated diplomacy that dispelled fears of a looming menace and cast the nation as a benign neighbor and indispensable economic partner.

South Korean administrations extending from Chun Doo-hwan (Chŏn Tu-hwan) to the final year of Roh Moo-hyun bought into this paradigm as a means of expanding South Korea's international strategic space, developing the nation's exporting capacity by taking advantage of China's tax incentives and low labor costs, and, particularly in the 1990s, promoting peaceful reunification with the North. China was seen as prepared, in return for preferred access to South Korean capital, technology and economic partnerships, to distance itself from a North Korean strategic ally once described as "closer than lips and teeth." And so a "China mood" enveloped Seoul in the years following the ROK's strategic departure represented by its 1992 establishment of diplomatic relations with Beijing.

That near-euphoria reached its high tide during the first years of the Roh administration. The watershed year was 2003. Reflecting both a public attitude of profound disquiet toward Bush administration policies and a corresponding enthusiasm for the tone and substance of Chinese policies, a *Dong-A Ilbo (Tonga Ilbo)* poll in that year found that 61 percent of respondents saw China as more important to Seoul's diplomatic strategy than the United States. In the same year, China first surpassed the United States as the number one destination for ROK exports (18.1 percent versus 17.7 percent). When Roh visited Beijing in 2003, against that backdrop of public perceptions and expectations, he proposed that ROK-Chinese relations should be promoted to the status of a "comprehensive cooperative partnership," with one component being explicit cooperation in military affairs and regional security. By March 2005, the ROK Defense Minister called for establishment of cooperation "not below the level of South Korea and Japan." During a meeting with his Chinese counterpart, he discussed establishment of military hot lines and agreed on cooperation between the respective air forces and navies to "secure the security of the West Sea."[31]

Those trends were mirrored in South Korea's larger strategic posture. South Korean military planners showed little disposition in the alliance framework to entertain discussion of China contingencies. Under President Roh, South Korea declined to participate in the U.S.-sponsored scheme of theater missile defense and responded coolly to the American presentation of a new doctrine of "strategic flexibility" with respect to its forces and bases stationed in South Korea. Seoul plainly aimed to avoid arousing concerns in Beijing that it might participate in an incipient architecture aimed at containment of China. Within the Six-Party Talks framework, a de facto China-ROK entente was formed, with the two tacitly coordinating policies in the hope of thwarting U.S. military action against North Korea.

When President Lee assumed office, however, the China mood had receded and been superseded by a more balanced appraisal of China's strategic intentions and the opportunities that could be successfully milked in an expanding ROK-China bilateral relationship. If not quite the proverbial perfect storm, a concatenation of events and impressions occurred from 2004 onward that produced an increasingly ambivalent attitude toward China among South Koreans. Chinese academics conducted a so-called Northeast Project that asserted a historical claim to the Goguryeo (Koguryŏ) Kingdom, provoking a nationalistic counter-reaction in South Korea along with suspicions that Beijing might somehow be laying the foundation to assert its primacy as a North Korean leadership or other transition eventually unfolded. Media images of Chinese mistreatment of North Korean refugees and South Korean missionaries working among them in the China-North Korea border region galvanized emotional reactions in South Korea. Perhaps emboldened by its recent success in branding itself as a "peacefully rising" power lacking any hegemonic designs, Beijing overstepped the mark. By suggesting publicly that ROK-U.S. and ROK-Japan-U.S. security ties were inconsistent with the modern era, Beijing provoked resentment. Yonsei University's Professor Kim Woo Jun (Kim U-jun) commented in August 2004 that "the anti-U.S., pro-China atmosphere has changed.... [W]e saw the hegemonic side of China."

Those incidents festered and others occurred that further burdened the ROK-China relationship. Throughout 2007–08, the Korean business community voiced new worries about the economic impact of China's rise on Korean competitiveness. Fishing rights disputes erupted in the Yellow Sea (West Sea). Chinese product quality and consumer safety issues provoked outrage and fears among South Koreans. There was a spate of cyber attacks, phishing incidents and identity theft cases whose provenance was thought to be Chinese. The Beijing Olympics torch relay that passed through Seoul in April 2008 produced images that highlighted the ugly side of China's pride in its sudden rise: nationalistic Chinese students physically confronting South Koreans peacefully protesting China's Tibetan policies and dissident policies, and in one scene, replayed frequently on South Korean media, beating an elderly Korean man who had apparently been innocently riding a bicycle.

Thus, when Lee early in his tenure met with Chinese president Hu Jintao and proclaimed another incremental promotion in bilateral ties—to a "strategic cooperative partnership"—it did not go unnoted that the concept lacked detail and seemed merely aspirational. South Korea's new image of China seemed back in harmony with Washington's optic and policies. On the one hand, China had become far and away South Korea's number one trading partner. Reservations about competitiveness and specific structure of the relationship aside, the South Korean business community continued to see China as a land of opportunity. On the other hand, Seoul increasingly viewed China as being fundamentally no different than other rising (or risen) powers: a nation prepared to brandish its new influence, potentially backed by military strength, in support of its national objectives.

In that regard, Seoul worried increasingly about China's opaque attitude and strategy toward North Korean developments, in particular the looming leadership succession to Kim Jong Il. Beijing's support for Korean unification—the key factor that had prompted the 1992 ROK opening to China—was in doubt. Beijing's defended its refusal to apply its undoubted leverage over Pyongyang to compel a cessation of its nuclear program and other provocations in terms of the greater need to support stability and predictability, but others perceived a different strategic design. Some saw signs that China's "real" intention toward North Korea amounted to creeping annexation: the Chinese Goguryeo "usurpation" represented the ideological underpinning for the policy, while China's massive assistance and related relationships ensured that Pyongyang, whatever its public face, would be economically subservient and politically docile before Beijing. China's studied refusal—going beyond polite indifference—to entertain U.S. and South Korean suggestions that the three might productively share views and synchronize policies relating to North Korean contingencies has further deepened suspicions about Beijing's private calculations.

On the eve of the global economic crisis, then, the Lee administration apparently saw no inherent contradictions between revitalizing alliance ties with the United States, pursuing mutually advantageous economic ties with China, and promoting an "Asia diplomacy" featuring South Korea's active involvement in regional and supra-regional mechanisms. At the same time, Lee seemed ready to embrace an unspoken hedging strategy toward China not dissimilar from those adopted by the United States, Japan and others. While none of that must necessarily change as a consequence of the economic crisis, it is also true that, as noted above, China's economic clout (and America's relative lack of it) has been brought to bear in a way that will probably prompt further refinements in the emerging ROK strategy. Hedging against China's rise, yes; but increased deference to China's views, probably.

## Is Japan Becoming a "Normal" Country, and Does it Matter to Seoul?

The essential ROK-Japan story has been one of economic interdependence, shared values, similar security outlooks and enduring frictions rooted in historical memory. Despite the pull of the first three factors, the last has tended to trump all else and to abort periodic efforts by leaders of both countries to achieve closer policy coordination. In that respect, from the ROK side, despite the sharply differing strategic outlooks of the Roh and Lee administrations, there has been a continuity of philosophy, effort and exceedingly imperfect results.

Regional suspicions—and worse—about Japan's future strategic intentions arose more from symbols and rhetoric than concrete deeds. This was especially true in South Korea, where memories of Japanese colonial rule left festering wounds in the national psyche. South Koreans, North Koreans and Chinese were all put on edge by Prime Minister Koizumi's official visits to the Yasukuni shrine; Chief Cabinet Secretary (later Prime Minister) Abe's hawkish rhetoric on North Korea; Japanese politicians' and opinion leaders' periodic rationalization or denial of Japan's militarist, colonial past; and the Japanese right wing's clarion calls for Japan to be a more "normal" country in military defense. All this seemed to represent not simply an attitude to project Japan's status internationally and mobilize domestic electoral support, but the visible aspect of qualitative changes underway in Japan's security posture. Japan—already packing a conventional military punch in the Asia-Pacific region second only to that of the United States—was building a more capable force, extending its reach and deepening its defense cooperation with the United States. China expressed its dissatisfaction with the U.S.-Japan agreement in 2006 to include the Taiwan Strait in their "area of common strategic interest." Under the charismatic Koizumi, Japan was seen in the region to be pursuing a more aggressive diplomatic strategy while charting a new course to a worrisome and unknown destination.

There was much less to all this than met the eye. The U.S.-Japan security relationship witnessed no major changes: Japan's Self-Defense Forces assumed no significant new roles and missions, while the United States and Japan hammered out only tentative accords even on long-festering issues involving relocation of U.S. bases, facilities and troop units on Japanese soil. Koizumi's public embrace of President Bush and the Bush administration's Iraq invasion and global war on terrorism aside, which produced enduring images in Washington and many other capitals, Japan made a relatively small commitment of military forces to the Iraq "coalition"—exclusively for "peaceful reconstruction" activities—and indeed much smaller than the openly skeptical South Korean government's contribution. Japan dispatched civilian construction crews to Afghanistan for road building and, significantly in terms of the precedent, a tanker to the Indian Ocean to help refuel U.S. and other forces engaged in the Afghanistan conflict. Despite appeals by Japanese conservatives, Koizumi included, to do more in the interest of supporting the U.S. ally and putting Japan firmly on the path to becoming a "normal" country unimpeded by constitutionally imposed constraints on collective self-defense activities, the Japanese political consensus budged only a degree or two from the postwar approach. Japanese boots were on the ground in Iraq, but without authorization to fire a shot in anger. In fact, the Japanese contingent at Samawah had to be protected by other coalition forces. The tanker was dispatched under the standard one-time Diet authorization having a sunset provision; renewals were required, provoking spirited controversy and explicit opposition from the DPJ that seems poised to assume power in 2009.

Japan's actual external policies over the past decade—as distinct from the *sturm und drang* attending rhetoric and symbolic actions by Liberal Democratic Party (LDP) Prime Ministers Koizumi, Abe and Aso (Fukuda having been a brief exception, much welcomed by Japan's neighbors)—have generally won the Asian region's positive appraisal on their merits. While more or less explicitly seeking to balance Chinese influence, Japan proceeded with customary caution in emphasizing multilateralism and regionalism even as it behaved somewhat more assertively on matters (like North Korea) touching directly upon its core security interests. In early 2002, Koizumi undertook a major tour of Southeast Asia and called upon his regional counterparts to join with Japan in developing a "community that acts together [and] advances together." Japan subsequently signed ASEAN's Treaty of Amity and Cooperation, expressing welcome for the concept of an East Asian Summit and readiness to participate in it. In response to the December 2004 tsunami that devastated Indonesia and Thailand, Japan quickly assumed a leadership role in humanitarian relief and recovery efforts. Tokyo actively pursued new free trade agreements (FTAs) with other nations in the region, South Korea included among them. It has participated enthusiastically in burgeoning Northeast Asian trilateral cooperation: first, in the context of ASEAN+3, and then in the process culminating in the Japan-ROK-China governmental meeting in Fukuoka in December 2008.

President Lee entered office determined—as his two immediate predecessors also had been—to put aside historical memories and relatively inconsequential territorial conflicts in the interest of forging stronger bilateral ties with Japan and trilateral ties with Japan and the United States. Following his election, Lee outlined his outlook and aspirations in a phone conversation with Japanese prime minister Fukuda. The short summary: South Korea and Japan "share basic values" (democratic political systems, market economic systems) that argue for another effort to build stronger links and closer policy coordination on regional concerns, especially North Korea.

Responding to that message, Fukuda attended Lee's inaugural ceremony in February and remained to hold a bilateral dialogue. The two agreed in principle to resume the one-time pattern of regular "shuttle summits" between Tokyo and Seoul; to avoid historical on issues, with Lee pledging that he would eschew requests for Japanese apologies; to resume talks on a bilateral FTA stalled for three years over the issue of opening agricultural markets; and to enhance their consultations and coordination within the Six-Party Talks framework.

President Lee's April 2008 "shuttle summit" visit to Tokyo—the first by a South Korean president since Roh Moo-hyun had traveled there in December 2004—formalized the February understandings on FTA negotiations and seemingly accelerated the process of policy coordination on North Korea and otherwise. Lee reiterated to Fukuda that he would make no demands of Japan for apology or soul-searching regarding the past, adding that he would not respond personally "in knee-jerk fashion" to any provocative remarks by Japanese politicians. The take-away sound bite from the April meeting was "a more mature partnership"—a concept to which the two leaders both pledged their best efforts.

Mutual good intentions notwithstanding, bilateral progress on the political/security track halted not long after the conclusion of President Lee's meetings in Tokyo after the Dokdo/Takeshima islet dispute erupted yet again, inflaming opinion in South Korea and spurring another round of street demonstrations. Strongly adverse reaction in Seoul and elsewhere greeted news reports in late October that Japanese Air Self-Defense Forces Chief of Staff General Tamogami had won a prize for an essay contending that Japan had been lured into Manchuria, had never imposed Japanese names or onerous conditions on Koreans, had been trapped into attacking Pearl Harbor and had committed no wartime atrocities whatsoever. All this served to underscore yet again that historical issues resonated emotionally in South Korean politics and society, and would impose a relatively low ceiling on any efforts by a South Korean leader to advance political and security ties with Japan—whatever the abstract "logic" of promoting such ties otherwise. For his part, President Lee held firm to his pledge to Fukuda, and reacted publicly to the controversies in understated fashion rather than adding fuel to the fire. Development of relations on the economic and commercial track continued apace, highlighted by the Sino-Japanese-Korean trilateral accord in Fukuoka to expand mutual currency swap arrangements to $30 billion each and to launch common efforts immediately toward future conclusion of a trilateral free trade agreement.

From the standpoint of South Korea's evolving security posture, the Japan factor thus is essentially unchanged. Japan's military posture neither threatens South Korea's interests nor offers compelling arguments to explore a new strategic paradigm entailing enhanced ROK-Japan coordination. Otherwise, Seoul remains determined to strengthen economic links with Japan, to enhance regional cooperation with Japan's involvement, to coordinate more closely on North Korean matters and to move tentatively with Japan, China and others toward creation of an informal security structure to address future regional challenges.

## How Much of a Strategic Factor is Moscow?

Russia is indisputably "back" on the world stage, albeit in a far different role than during the Cold War contest with the United States, and often as a mere afterthought in the strategic calculations of major nations in Northeast Asia. Its new influence derives not from its nuclear arsenal and the potency of its armed forces, but from its accumulation of wealth earned from its abundant mineral, oil and natural gas resources. President and now Prime Minister Putin proved himself both ruthlessly adroit and nationalistically tough-minded in achieving unchallenged state domination over the relevant industries, negotiating (and enforcing) the terms of specific contractual arrangements and parleying pipeline routing decisions and contracts into explicit economic leverage and political influence over foreign nations.

Under Putin, Russia has also managed to gradually rebuild its military assets, including in the Russian Far East; to make arms and defense technology sales a crucial component of its efforts to earn hard currency while consolidating existing security relationships or building new ones; and to strengthen security and strategic links with China, Central Asian republics and South Asian nations through the vehicle of the Shanghai Cooperation Organization. The turnaround in these areas has been striking if little remarked upon publicly. In the mid-1990s, following the collapse of the Soviet Union and Warsaw Pact, Russia was reeling economically and psychologically. By the end of 1992, Mongolia was independent in fact as well as name, and Russia had withdrawn 100,000 ground forces from that nation. The once-formidable Russian Pacific Fleet submarine force fell by over 75 percent, while the overall number of surface combatants dropped by nearly 50 percent; maintenance issues and lack of fuel further degraded the fleet, as did low morale among the sailors resulting from unpaid salaries, decaying living conditions and an overall sense of Moscow's neglect and inability to reverse the deterioration. By the early 2000s, however, Moscow had accumulated enough wealth to begin a continuing program of steady upgrading in the quantity and quality of Russian assets in the Far East. It announced plans for modernization of defenses in the southern Kuriles—the area the Japanese call the Northern Territories. It invested substantial funds in an upgrading of a strategic submarine base at Rybachiy on the Kamchatka Peninsula; it scheduled deployment to the field by 2010 of the first of a new generation Borey-class SSBM; and it accelerated plans to introduce new high-performance fighter aircraft and missile systems into the theater.[32]

Despite Russia's progress—preceding eruption of the global economic crisis, in any case—in the military and strategic arena, South Korea has looked at Russia principally through the prism of its energy/mineral resource assets and its residual notional influence over North Korea. For those reasons President Lee also scheduled a visit to Moscow during his first year in office. The September 2008 visit broadly supported Lee's vision of improving relations with all nations in the region so as to expand South Korea's strategic possibilities and break through the stalemate in North Korea discussions by harnessing all potential diplomatic and economic assets. Lee, received warmly in Moscow by President Medvedev, announced with his host an expansive bilateral agenda that envisaged broad across-the-board cooperation in areas of mutual interest. In comments to journalists in Moscow and St. Petersburg, and on return to Seoul, Lee and his senior aides spoke enthusiastically about future ROK-Russian cooperation in developing projects under the rubrics of an "iron silk road," an "energy silk road," and a "green silk road." They outlined plans, or more precisely ambitions, to construct a "win-win" railway that might help integrate North Korea into the economic life of the region; to sign contracts for Siberian infrastructure and development projects; and to cooperate on new energy and natural resources projects. Revealing one principal focus of his opening toward Russia, Lee told journalists: "If a Russian natural gas pipeline goes through North Korea, it will be very beneficial to the North Korean economy."[33]

No results and no apparent forward movement have been witnessed in these areas. In the first place, the euphoria of the moment certainly exceeded the concrete preparations. Second, Moscow has seen diplomatic and strategic merit in highlighting its resource assets and dangling them before all comers. A variant of the pipeline game pitting Japan against China for Moscow's favor has spawned countless conflicting hints over recent years, all without any firm Moscow decision thus far. The game, from Moscow's standpoint, involves not only bottom-line economic computations but also expectations of a concomitant political payoff. It is very doubtful that Russian leaders foresee any meaningful prospect of such where South Korea is concerned. South Korea is tied firmly into the U.S. alliance system, preoccupied with North Korean challenges and scenarios, focused otherwise on complex political and economic relations with China and Japan, and unlikely to risk or detract from those priority relationships by any cross-cutting opening toward Russia. Third, Moscow has been exceptionally hard hit economically by the twin impact of plummeting oil prices and the global financial crisis, and like other nations has turned its attention inward over recent months.

With respect to North Korea, and utilization of the Six-Party Talks mechanism, Moscow's involvement has been relatively insubstantial to date. While it has shown no disposition to block consensus, support North Korea's position against others or introduce mischievous distractions into the process, neither has it displayed any particular policy creativity or demonstrated an ability to utilize persuasion and pressures to modify North Korean behavior. For Moscow, the Six-Party Talks process offers a chance to monitor developments and stay usefully engaged with other parties; to maintain some influence in North Korea by presenting itself as an "objective" friend willing to contribute economic assistance and dissuade others from adopting aggressive measures; and to remain in policy lockstep with Beijing, visible in the U.N. Security Council, the Shanghai Cooperation Organization and elsewhere, in the tacit common objective of countering troublesome U.S. initiatives. In all of this, there seems nothing for South Korea to harness to its own strategic advantage.

Some analysts have conjectured that South Korea might look in the future to Russia as a classic "outside balancer" should China or Japan threaten its interests and the United States no longer be willing or able to respond effectively. That would presuppose a virtually unimaginable constellation of low-probability events and surrounding circumstances, and probably figures not at all in any contingency planning under consideration in Seoul. Should such possibilities loom even remotely on the horizon, South Korea's far likelier strategic options would include an unquestionably autonomous defense capability including nuclear weapons and/or a regional security structure sufficiently potent to mitigate threats against any member state.

## Northeast Asia Regional Security Architecture: Does Anyone Outside South Korea Share the Dream?

Of all the regional stakeholders in Northeast Asia, South Korea has consistently been the one most attracted to multilateralism and most supportive of a formal regional security. The seductiveness of the concept flows naturally from South Korea's geopolitical status. A "shrimp among whales" that also happens to be one of the world's leading economies is understandably prone to be wary of the appetites of neighbors and attentive always to any intimations of "strategic abandonment" by one's principal ally.

ROK interest in the possibilities of regional security systems began in the early 1990s, spurred by the end of the Cold War, the impressive early success of ASEAN, the concurrent example of European integration, and doubts in the efficacy of the GATT/World Trade Organization regime to protect its own economic interests. Seoul proposed various initiatives for nascent Northeast Asia security dialogues that were essentially stillborn. Support for regional mechanisms and institutions picked up steam in Seoul, and elsewhere, in the wake of the 1997-98 Asian financial crisis that highlighted both the unexpected fragility of the international system and, most pertinently, the initial U.S. impotence or disinclination to do much to ameliorate the economic fallout for its allies. Meanwhile, ASEAN's expansion of membership, broadening of its scope to include "dialogue partners" in the ASEAN Regional Forum, and presentation of initiatives for stronger regional cooperation served as a spur to the three Northeast Asian countries to develop their own regional agendas, including cooperation on energy, environmental protection, development of transportation networks and conclusion of FTAs. ASEAN's later inauguration of ASEAN+3 annual meetings to include China, Japan and Korea further advanced Northeast Asian regional cooperation and inspired a more serious look at ways and means of emulating the Southeast Asian experience.

While ASEAN's core mission and raison d'etre had been almost exclusively economic, the three Northeast Asian countries from the outset looked equally to economic and political/strategic objectives. For its part, the ROK saw a principal function of a Northeast Asian regional "dialogue"—leading toward a formal structure—as relating explicitly to security issues on the Korean Peninsula. In 1994 it officially proposed a mechanism to that end; it saw the Korean Peninsula Energy Development Organization (KEDO), formed to implement the 1994 U.S.-North Korea "Agreed Framework," as holding potential to be a nascent security organization; and it later launched a "Northeast Asian Cooperation Initiative" that would be similarly focused on ways to promote regional cooperation to maintain peace on the Korean Peninsula. The Tumen River Area Development Program (TRADP), inaugurated by both Koreas, China, Russia and Mongolia to develop jointly the Tumen River area bordering North Korea, Russia and China, ran afoul of North Korean political concerns, insufficient start-up money and conflicting goals and interests of the various participants.

Hence, while looking primarily to U.S. security ties for defense, and pursuing a network of reinforcing bilateral relationships, South Korea has been the strongest proponent of transforming the Six-Party Talks process into a permanent regional security mechanism, possibly modeled initially on Europe's Helsinki process and the resultant Organization for Security and Cooperation in Europe (OSCE). Seoul's logic is probably unassailable: with the longer-term prospects for ROK-U.S. alliance relations clouded, a structural mechanism is needed to constrain the power and ambitions of a rising China and a militarily potent Japan. Furthermore, given the unfortunate truth that Seoul enjoys (and can expect) relatively small leverage over the United States, China, Japan or, for that matter, Russia and even North Korea, nurturing stronger relations with each of these regional actors can only partially satisfy South Korea's abiding security concerns.

President Roh's approach was seemingly animated less by a desire to win buy-in by all relevant parties than to erect ultimately a kind of pan-Asian regional counterweight to U.S. influence. If so, the concept was deeply flawed and doomed from the outset. That notwithstanding, all participants in the Six-Party process, North Korea as usual excepted, paid formal support to the hope that this mechanism could eventually be transformed into a regional security architecture. To that end, the September 19, 2005 Joint Statement by Six-Party Talks participants made reference to "new ways and means for promoting security cooperation in Northeast Asia." The February 13, 2007 Joint Statement formally created working groups on a "Northeast Asia Peace and Security Mechanism" (NEAPSM) and "Economic and Energy Cooperation." Seoul and others explained that the two groups taken together constituted the germ of a future regional organization to address both security and economic matters.

There still remain ample reasons to suspect that the concept has been oversold, that it is more chimera than vision, and that most participants are simply paying pious lip service to a concept that is worthy but impossible to implement. One fails to see a logical progression from NEAPSM to permanent security structure. If the Six-Party Talks flounder and fail, the NEAPSM holds little appeal as a rudimentary mediating mechanism for the future. If the talks succeed, or if the North Korean nuclear issue is resolved in some other fashion, it is difficult to imagine the issue or basket of issues that would capture the imagination of regional leaders sufficiently to invest time and resources in constructing something entirely new.

When all is said and done, the psychological and security terrain in Northeast Asia bears scant resemblance to the more fertile soil in Southeast Asia that inspired creation of ASEAN. Most importantly, ASEAN was launched to promote intraregional cooperation for sure, but its larger purpose was to strengthen member nations' profile and bargaining power within broader Asia and the international community. While some charter members were inevitably more powerful than others, and while cultures, religions and political systems differed, no state posed any genuine security threat to any other and all agreed that the organization's mantra should be peace, cooperation and consensus. There was no single colossus looming over the region or the organization. Such was not and is not the case in Northeast Asia. History still weighs heavily on each of the nations; nationalisms flourish and vie with each other. Disparities in history, culture, area, political system, income, and economic strength are far more sharply defined—even without inclusion of North Korea and Mongolia—than was the case for the newborn ASEAN. A regional "outsider," the United States, enjoys half-century-old security alliances with two nations in the region, and these alliances are increasingly seen by the rising regional powerhouse, China, as a direct or implicit threat to its own future ambitions. Even without the U.S. aspect, China and Japan have historically regarded each other as rivals, and this has not diminished—quite the contrary—despite economic cooperation and recent improvement in the tone of their relations.

President Lee, evidently grasping all this quite well, has taken a more muted approach to advancing regional schemes that go beyond strengthening the two Northeast Asia "triangles"—the ROK-U.S.-Japan relationship to support Seoul's security requirements, and the ROK-China-Japan relationship to foster economic cooperation that is not without a security dimension as well.

## Charting South Korea's Strategic Course

What, then, is Seoul left with in devising an "optimal" national security strategy under current circumstances? Put simply: there probably is no such animal! Each conceivable security posture involves costs, risks and tradeoffs. Given the murkiness and dynamic complexity of the contemporary scene, and the incalculable number of permutations and combinations of outcomes that might plausibly be projected, no single course of action could suggest itself definitively to a prudent national leader. In the final analysis, the ROK is what it is: a middle power in a tough neighborhood, with potential and aspirations to enhance its stature and influence internationally, but obliged to adhere to the core principles and policies that have taken it to this stage of national power. Pragmatism, tough-mindedness and flexibility must continue to be prominent attributes of South Korean diplomatic behavior. Its principal national security goals must be to minimize external threats, increase its space for autonomous decision-making, expand its international profile and bargaining power, and reduce the costs to the nation of contingencies both foreseeable (e.g., North Korean transition, implosion and unification scenarios) and only remotely imaginable.

It is easier to identify what South Korea ought *not* do than to suggest what course it should adopt. Surely the riskiest conceivable strategic course would be for Seoul to pursue some variant of nonalignment—whether aloof neutrality or neutrality within the context of a regional security system yet to emerge—that is predicated upon an autonomous defense capability including a nuclear deterrent. Simply getting to that point of recognized autonomous capabilities would entail financial costs and security risks of unacceptable magnitude.

The most obvious, and arguably logical course for the ROK to pursue is adaptation of the existing U.S. alliance to meet emerging security requirements for the future. There are two major dilemmas here. The first is that it takes two to tango—and the two have been out of the dancing-in-step habit for the better part of a decade. Both partners need to establish that there remains sufficient mutual trust and strategic congruity to undergird a revitalized alliance, as President Lee has proposed, that takes on expanded joint endeavors in the region and internationally. This demands clarity of thinking and candor of articulation that have thus far not been in evidence. It also presupposes an ability to sell the new concept to each nation's people, an ability perhaps warranting greater skepticism within South Korea given the degree of political polarization, concerns about U.S. policies and reluctance to assume new costs and burdens.

The second dilemma involves China. South Korea's leaders need to ask if an alliance-plus approach with the United States would best serve its strategic interests within Northeast Asia, specifically vis-à-vis China's influence, perceptions and ambitions. Can South Korea in fact afford to arouse Chinese suspicions—already voiced publicly from time to time in the recent past—regarding the thrust of an alliance system seen as a Cold War anachronism unless implicitly intended to contain China and thwart its legitimate national aspirations? And if China were to draw such an inference, would China's response involve a potentially devastating retreat from indispensable economic understandings and arrangements? How would all this, moreover, impinge upon China's stance toward North Korean nuclear and leadership succession matters?

Given such considerations, South Korea seems more likely for the present to stick with the approximate status quo—President Lee's public statements to the contrary notwithstanding—and to opt for an alliance-minus approach with the U.S. (i.e., a somewhat more limited relationship, without "revitalization" and broadening) coupled with stronger emphasis on exclusively Northeast Asian arrangements and expansion of South Korea's international footprint per Lee's "Global Korea" vision.

None of this can operate in a vacuum. Seoul's strategic calculus would obviously need to adjust in the face of unanticipated external events, including paradigm-altering actions by one or more of the relevant nations.

## Notes

1 Edward Gresser & Daniel Twining, "Shock of the New: Congress and Asia in 2009," *NBR Analysis*, The National Bureau of Asian Research, February 2009.

2 Han Seung-soo, "Charting a New Frontier: Global," Special address, IISS Korea Forum Conference, Seoul, Korea, September 26, 2008.

3 Lee Sanghee, "Korea's Role in Global Security," Keynote address, IISS Korea Forum Conference, Seoul, Korea, September 26, 2008.

4 Aidan Foster-Carter, "Lee Outflanked," *NAPSNet Policy Forum* 08-059A, July 31, 2008.

5 "Half-Finished: What Lee Myung-bak Still Needs To Do," *Economist*, September 25, 2008.

6 Nishino Junya, "A New Era in South Korean Foreign Policy?" The Tokyo Foundation, February 2008.

7 Quoted in Terry Cooke, Foreign Policy Research Institute, February 27, 2009.

8 "Rumors of a Korean Economic Crisis Should Be Properly Addressed," *Chosun Ilbo*, March 4, 2009.

9 Kurt Achin, "South Korea Reverses Economic Growth Prediction," *VOA News*, February 10, 2009.

10 "Forecast," Economic Intelligence Unit, *The Economist*, February 17, 2009.

11 Reuters, untitled news report, February 3, 2009.

12 "Rumors of a Korean Economic Crisis Should Be Properly Addressed," *Chosun Ilbo*, March 4, 2009.

13 Toyoo Gyohten, "The Financial Crisis: Address Structural Problems Immediately," *AJISS-Commentary*, March, 12 2009, accessed at http://www.jiia.or.jp/en_commentary/200903/12-1.html.

14 Shyam Saran, unpublished speech before Indian Foreign Ministry audience, February 28, 2009.

15 See, for example, "China's Premier Worries about US Treasury Holdings, AFP, March 12th, 2009.

16 "Wen Jiabao Attends Meeting of Leaders of China, Japan and South Korea," Xinhua News Service, December 15, 2008.

17 Cheong Wa Dae, "President Announces 'New Asia Initiative,'" March 8, 2009, accessed at http://www.korea.net/news/issues/issueDetailView.asp?board_no=20334.

18 "Lee Promises New Cooperative Diplomacy for Asia," *Chosun Ilbo*, March 9, 2009, accessed at http://english.chosun.com/site/data/html_dir/2009/03/09/2009030961029.html.

19 See, inter alia, John Feffer, "China and the Uses of Uncertainty," *Foreign Policy*

*in Focus*, December 12, 2006, and Bruce Klingner, "Evolving Military Responsibilities in the U.S.-ROK Alliance," *International Journal of Korean Studies* XII, no. 1, (Fall/Winter 2008): 25–42.

20 Han Seung-soo, "Charting a New Frontier."

21 *Chosun Ilbo* (English-language edition), Seoul, August 16, 2008.

22 Edwin J. Feulner, "The ROK-US Relationship: A View from Washington," lunch address at IISS Korea Forum Conference, Seoul, Korea, September 26, 2008.

23 "President Lee Myung-bak Addresses The Korea Society," April 15, 2008, podcast accessed at http://www.podanza.com/podcast/the-korea-society/afedfdbc3da03c007fcb56cba50c6857/.

24 "S. Korea's Lee Calls for Strategic Alliance with U.S.," *Asian Political News*, April 21, 2008.

25 Klingner, "Evolving Military Responsibilities."

26 Kim Taeho, "Balancing U.S. Alliance and Chinese Cooperation: Korea's Emerging Security Challenge," in *Asian Perspectives on the Challenges of China* (Washington, DC: Institute for National Strategic Studies (INSS), 2000): 29–38.

27 "President Lee Myung-bak Addresses The Korea Society."

28 Feulner, "The ROK-US Relationship."

29 Cited in Kim Choong Nam, "Redefining ROK's Strategic Posture in the Twenty-First Century," *International Journal of Korean Studies* XI, no. 2 (Fall 2007): 28–66.

30 Lee Sanghee, "Korea's Role in Global Security."

31 Jae Ho Chung, "South Korea's Strategic Thinking toward China: From Park Chung Hee to Roh Moo Hyun," Brookings Institution, October 18, 2006, transcript accessed at http://www.brookings.edu/events/2006/1018china.aspx.

32 Alexey D. Muraviev, "The Red Star of the Pacific: The Forgotten Player is Back," *Independent Analysis/Policy Advice*, Australian Strategic Policy Institute (ASPI), August 28, 2007.

33 See Cheong Wa Dae, "Korea-Russia Joint Statement," September 30, 2008, accessed at http://www.korea.net/news/Issues/issueDetailView.asp?board_no=19659; "Russian, S. Korean Presidents Discuss Trade Ties, Nuclear Issue," *People's Daily Online*, September 30, 2008, accessed at http://english.peopledaily.com.cn/90001/90777/90853/6508707.html; and "Lee, Medvedev to Discuss Energy Cooperation, *Korea Times*, September 29, 2008, accessed at http://www.koreatimes.co.kr/www/news/include/print.asp?newsIdx=31808.

## Select Bibliography

Achin, Kurt. "South Korea Reverses Economic Growth Prediction." *VOA News*, February 10, 2009.

*The Age* (Australia). "South Korean Economy Shrinks 5.6 percent." January 22, 2009.

Ahn, Byung-joon. "Directing a Diplomatic Concert toward Pyongyang." *The National Interest*, April 2, 2003.

Ahn, Se Hyun. "Energy Security in Northeast Asia: Putin, Progress and Problems." Asia Research Centre Working Paper 20, London School of Economics & Political Science, 2007.

Arvizu, Alexander A. Statement before the House Foreign Affairs Committee Subcommittee on Asia, the Pacific and the Global Environment. "A New Beginning for the U.S.-South Korea Strategic Alliance," April 23, 2008.

*Asian Political News*. "S. Korea's Lee Calls for Strategic Alliance with U.S.." April 21, 2008.

Auslin, Michael R. "Japan and South Korea: The New East Asian Core." *Orbis* 49, no. 3 (Summer 2005): 459–473.

Auslin, Michael and Christopher Griffin. "Time for Trilateralism?" *Asian Outlook*, AEI Online, March 6, 2008.

Babson, Bradley O. "Toward a Northeast Asian Security Community: Implications for the North Korean Economy." Korean Economic Institute (KEI) paper prepared for conference "Towards a Northeast Asian Security Community: Implications for Korea's Growth and Economic Development," held in Washington, D.C. October 15, 2008.

Bandow, Doug. "Seoul Searching." *The National Interest Online*, November 11, 2008.

Bell, Gen Burwell B., testimony in hearing, Fiscal Year 2009 National Defense Authorization Budget Request for U.S. Pacific Command and U.S. Forces Korea, Committee on Armed Services, U.S. House of Representatives, March 12, 2008.

Bertelsmann Stiftung. Bertelsmann Transformation Index (BTI). "BTI 2008: South Korea Country Report."

Brooke, James. "Seeking Peace in a Once and Future Kingdom." *New York Times*, August 25, 2004.

Cha, Victor. "U.S.-Korea Relations: A New Day." *Comparative Connections* 10, no. 1 (April 2008), 37–45.

Chan, John. "South Korean Economy Heading toward Negative Growth in 2009." *World Socialist Web Site*, December 12, 2008.

Cheon, Jong-woo and Yoo Choonski, "South Korean Economy Shrinks Most in 11 Years," *Reuters*, January 21, 2009.

Chinoy, Mike. "South Korea Straddles the Politics of Change." *CNN.com*, December 21, 2007.

Choi, Young Jong. "South Korea's Middle Power: Diplomacy and Regional Security Cooperation." *AsiaViews*, edition 43/v/Nov/2008.

*Chosun Ilbo*. "Korea, Russia Agree to Forge Closer Energy Ties." September 30, 2008.

*Chosun Ilbo*. "Lee Arrives for State Visit to Moscow." September 29, 2008.

*Chosun Ilbo*. "Lee Hails Benefits of Russia Deals for Korean Integration." October 1, 2008.

*Chosun Ilbo*. "Lee, Hu Hammer Out Strategic Partnership." August 26, 2008.

*Chosun Ilbo*. "Rumors of a Korean Economic Crisis Should Be Properly Addressed." March 4, 2009.

*Chosun Ilbo*. "Russian Deputy Prime Minister Sechin to Visit Seoul." October 30, 2008.

*Chosun Ilbo*. "The US Should Not Go Overboard." April 15, 2008.

Chu, Shulong. "The Security Challenges in Northeast Asia: A Chinese View" in *East Asian Security: Two Views*. Strategic Studies Institute monograph, November 23, 2007, http://www.StrategicStudiesInstitute.army.mil/.

Chung, Jae Ho. "South Korea's Strategic Thinking toward China: From Park Chung Hee to Roh Moo Hyun." Presentation at Brookings CNAPS, October 18, 2006, http://www.brookings.edu/events/2006/1018china.aspx.

Chung, Mong-Joon. "Opening Remarks—Korea in the Emerging Asian Power Balance." IISS Korea Forum Conference, Seoul, Korea, September 26, 2008.

Cossa, Ralph. "ROK-US Relations: Revitalizing the Alliance." *PacNet* #12, February 15, 2008.

Cronin, Patrick and Audrey Cronin. "Challenging Deterrence: Strategic Stability in the 21st Century." Special Joint Report of the IISS and the Oxford University Changing Character of War Programme, February 2007.

Easley, Leif-Eric. "Defense Ownership or Nationalist Security: Autonomy and Reputation in South Korean and Japanese Security Policies." *SAIS Review*, XXVII no. 2 (Summer-Fall 2007).

*Economist*. "Half-Finished: What Lee Myung-bak Still Needs To Do." September 25, 2008.

*Economist Intelligence Unit*. "Country Briefings: South Korea: Economic Data." January 6, 2009.

*Economist Intelligence Unit*. "Country Briefings: South Korea: Forecast." February 17, 2009.

Feffer, John. "China and the Uses of Uncertainty." *Foreign Policy in Focus*, December 12, 2006.

———. "Ploughshares into Swords: Economic Implications of South Korean Military Spending." *KEI Academic Paper Series* 4, no. 2, Korea Economic Institute, February 2009.

———. "South Korea: Still Dreaming of Regionalism." *Foreign Policy in Focus*, October 3, 2008.

Feulner, Edwin J. "Lunch Address—The ROK-US Relationship: A View from Washington." IISS Korea Forum Conference, Seoul, Korea, September 26, 2008.

Finnegan, Michael J. "What Now? The Case for US-ROK-PRC Coordination on North Korea." *PacNet* #48, September 11, 2008.

Flake, L. Gordon. "The Future of Regional Security Cooperation, and Korea's Role." Paper prepared for presentation at the 18th annual conference of the Council on US-Korean Security Studies, October 9-10, 2003.

Gilson, Julie. "Strategic Regionalism in East Asia." *Review of International Studies* 33, no. 1 (2007): 145-163.

Glaser, Bonnie, Scott Snyder, and John S. Park. "Chinese Debates on North Korea." *PacNet* # 11, February 8, 2008.

Glosserman, Brad and Scott Snyder. "Confidence and Confusion: National Identity and Security Alliances in Northeast Asia." *Issues & Insights* (Pacific Forum CSIS) 8, no. 16, September 2008.

Goodby, James E. "The Emerging Architecture for Security and Cooperation in Northeast Asia." *Brookings CNAPS*, March 2008.

Gresser, Edward & Daniel Twining. "Shock of the New: Congress and Asia in 2009." *NBR Analysis*, February 2009.

Haggard, Stephan and Marcus Noland. "A Security and Peace Mechanism for Northeast Asia: The Economic Dimension." *Peterson Institute for International Economics Policy Brief* 08-4, April 2008.

Hamm, Taik-young. "The Self-Reliant National Defense of South Korea and the Future of the U.S.-ROK Alliance." *Nautilus Institute Policy Forum Online* 06-49A, June 20, 2006.

Han, Seung-soo. "Special Address—Charting a New Frontier: Global," IISS Korea Forum Conference, Seoul, Korea, September 26, 2008.

Han, Sung-Joo. "Opening Remarks—Korea in the Emerging Asian Power Balance," IISS Korea Forum Conference, Seoul, Korea, September 26, 2008.

Han, Sung-Joo. "Strategic Diplomacy in an Age of Globalization." *The Tokyo Foundation Tenth-Anniversary Website*, speech presented at the sixth symposium Diplomatic Strategy in the Age of Globalization, May 9, 2008.

Harrison, Selig. "Gas and Geopolitics in Northeast Asia: Pipelines, Regional Stability and the Korean Nuclear Crisis." *World Policy Journal* (Winter 2002/03).

Heseltine, Colin. "Australia and South Korea: New Governments … New Opportunities?" *Austral Policy Forum* 08-08A, August 14, 2008.

*Chosun Ilbo*. "Hyundai Aims for Slice of Russia's Booming Car Market." June 9, 2008.

Ikenberry, G. John, Chung-in Moon, and Mitchell Reiss, co-directors. "The Search for a Common Strategic Vision: Charting the Future of the US-ROK Security Partnership." A Report of the US-ROK Strategic Forum (February 2008).

Inkster, Nigel. "Assessing Political Risk." Dinner address, IISS Korea Forum Conference, Seoul, Korea, September 26, 2008.

*International Institute for Strategic Studies*. "The Conventional Military Balance on the Korean Peninsula," 2009.

Japan Ministry of Foreign Affairs. "Japan-Republic of Korea Joint Declaration: A New Japan-Republic of Korea Partnership towards the Twenty-first Century." Provisional translations, http://www.mofa.go.jp/region/asia-paci/korea/joint9810.html.

*JoongAng Ilbo*. "A Military Isn't a 'Balancer'." April 9, 2005.

Kang, Choi. "Toward ROK-US Strategic Alliance." *The Korea Herald*, March 27, 2008.

Kang, David. "Forging an Enduring Foundation for U.S.-ROK Relations," circa May 2007.

———. "Getting Asia Wrong: The Need for New Analytical Frameworks." *International Security* 27, no.4 (Spring 2003): 57–85.

Kang, David and Ji-Young Lee. "Japan-Korea Relations: In a Holding Pattern with Hope on the Horizon." *Comparative Connections*, January 2009.

———. "Japan-Korea Relations: Inaction for Inaction." *Comparative Connections*, April 2008.

———. "Japan-Korea Relations: Lost in the Six-Party Talks." *Comparative Connections*, January 2008.

———. "Japan-Korea Relations: Tentative Improvement through Pragmatism." *Comparative Connections*, July 2008.

———. "Japan-Korea Relations: Who's In Charge." *Comparative Connections*, October 2008.

Kihl, Young Whan. "Inter-Korean Strategic Relations and Security Forum in Northeast Asia." *International Journal of Korean Studies* XII, no. 1 (Fall/Winter 2008): 61–81.

Kim, Choong Nam. "Redefining ROK's Strategic Posture in the Twenty-First Century," *International Journal of Korean Studies* XI, no. 2(Fall 2007): 28–66.

Kim, Hyung-a. "South Korea's 'Bulldozer' Seeks a Partner in Rudd." *The Canberra Times*, March 4, 2009.

Kim, Jae-kyoung. "Korea Braces for China Shock." *Korea Times*, January 27, 2009.

Kim, Soung-chul. "Multilateral Security and Economic Cooperation in Northeast Asia." *Sejong Policy Studies* 4, no. 2 (2008): 265–98.

Kim, Soung-chul. "(Outlook): Forge Alliance with U.S., China." *JoongAng Ilbo*, March 18, 2005, accessed April 17, 2006 via OSC Doc # KPP20050317000198.

Kim, Sung Min. "ROK-US Security Relations: 'The China Factor' and a Turning Point." Thesis, Naval Postgraduate School, Monterey, California, December 2002.

Kim, Sunhyuk and Wonhyuk Lim. "How to Deal with South Korea." *The Washington Quarterly*, Spring 2007.

Kim, Tae-ho. "Balancing U.S. Alliance and Chinese Cooperation: Korea's Emerging Security Challenge." *Asian Perspectives on the Challenges of China* (2000): 29–38.

Kim, Tae-ho. "Pragmatism in National Security." *Korea Focus, Hankook Ilbo*, December 29, 2007.

Kim, Tae-Hyo. "Korea's Strategic Thoughts toward Japan: Searching for a Democratic Alliance in the Past-Driven Future." *Korean Journal of Defense Analysis* 20, no. 2 (June 2008): 141–154.

Klingner, Bruce. "Evolving Military Responsibilities in the U.S.-ROK Alliance." *International Journal of Korean Studies* XII, no. 1 (Fall/Winter 2008): 25–42.

———. Prepared Statement before Committee on Foreign Affairs, Subcommittee on Asia, the Pacific and the Global Environment, U.S. House of Representatives, Hearing on "Remaking U.S. Foreign Policy in North Korea," February 12, 2009.

Klingner, Bruce. "Transforming the US-South Korean Alliance." Backgrounder No 2155, Heritage Foundation, June 30, 2008.

Koo, Kab-woo. "The Reality Behind South Korea-US Alliance." *Nautilus Institute Policy Forum Online* 04-09, March 12, 2004.

"Korea, China Upgrade Relations to Strategic Cooperative Partnership." *Korea.net*, May 27, 2008.

*Korea Times*. "Half of Koreans Disapprove of Seoul's Foreign Policy." January 27, 2009.

*Korea Times*. "True Alliance?" April 10, 2008.

Lee, Chang Choon. "Whither South Korea? President-elect Roh's Dubious Foreign Policy Posture." *The National Interest* 2, no. 4, January 29, 2003.

Lee, Chul-kee. "Strategic Flexibility of U.S. Forces in Korea." *Nautilus Institute Policy Forum Online* 06-19A, March 9, 2006.

Lee, Chung. "A View from Asia: The NK Missile Threat and Missile Defense in the Context of South Korea's Changing National Security Debate." *Comparative Strategy* 24, no. 3 (July-September 2005): 253–275.

Lee, Dong-hwi. "Korea-US FTA Negotiations and East Asian Regional Cooperation." *Korea Focus*. Korea Foundation, November 27, 2006.

Lee, Jong-Heon. "South Korea US Alliance at Risk." Seoul (UPI), March 13, 2006.

Lee, Sanghee. "Changes in Perceptions of the ROK-US Alliance: and the way ahead to achieve common interests." The Brookings Institution, July 11, 2007.

Lee, Sanghee. "Korea's Role in Global Security." Keynote address, IISS Korea Forum Conference, Seoul, Korea, September 26, 2008.

Levin, Norman D. "Do the Ties Still Bind? The US-ROK Security Relationship after 9/11." RAND Corporation, Santa Monica, California, 2004.

Loo, Bernard. "How to Avoid a Nuclear Arms Race in Northeast Asia." IDSS Commentaries, September 13, 2004.

Manosevitz, Jason U. "Japan and South Korea: Security Relations Reach Adolescence." Asian Survey XLIII, no. 5 (September/October 2003): 801–825.

Moon, Chung-in. "Theory of Balancing Role in Northeast Asia." Chosun Ilbo, April 12, 2005. Accessed April 20, 2006 through OSC, Doc #KPP 20050412000011.

Muraviev, Alexey D. "The Red Star of the Pacific: The Forgotten Player is Back." Australian Strategic Policy Institute (ASPI) Independent Analysis/Policy Advice, August 28, 2007.

Nanto, Dick K. "East Asian Regional Architecture: New Economic and Security Arrangements and U.S. Policy." CRS Report for Congress RL 33653, January 4, 2008.

Nishino, Junya. "A New Era in South Korean Foreign Policy?" The Tokyo Foundation, February 2008.

Oh, Kongdan. "US-ROK: The Forgotten Alliance." Brookings, October 2008.

Park, Hyeong Jung. "Looking Back and Looking Forward: North Korea, Northeast Asia and the ROK-U.S. Alliance." Brookings, December 2007.

Pollack, Jonathan D. "The Korean Peninsula in U.S. Strategy: Policy Issues for the Next President." in Ashley J. Tellis, Mercy Kuo and Andrew Marble, eds., Strategic Asia 2008-09: Challenges and Choices (Seattle, WA: The National Bureau of Asian Research, 2008) 135–164.

Reuters. "IMF Predicts South Korean Economy to Contract 4 percent in 2009." February 3, 2009.

Romberg, Alan D. "Rethinking Northeast Asia" The Henry L. Stimson Center, November 2008.

Rozman, Gilbert. "Security Challenges to the US in Northeast Asia: Looking Beyond the Transformation of the Six-Party Talks." in East Asian Security: Two Views. Strategic Studies Institute monograph, November 23, 2007, http://www.StrategicStudiesInstitute.army.mil/.

Ruan, Zongze. "China's Role in a Northeast Asian Community." Asian Perspective 30, no. 3 (2006): 149–157.

Savage, Timothy. "Big Brother Is Watching: China's Intentions in the DPRK." China Security 4, no. 4 (Autumn 2008): 53–57.

Secretariat of the National Security Council, Republic of Korea. "Theory on Balancer in Northeast Asia: A Strategy to Become a Respected State in International Cooperation." Accessed April 27, 2005 through Open Source Center, Doc # KPP20050428000225.

Snyder, Scott. "China-Korea Relations: Establishing a "Strategic Cooperative Partnership." Comparative Connections, July 2008.

———. "China-Korea Relations: Establishing a "Sweet and Sour Aftertaste." Comparative Connections, January 2009.

———. "China-Korea Relations: Post-Olympic Hangover: New Backdrop for Relations." *Comparative Connections*, October 2008.

———. "China-Korea Relations: Lee Myung-bak Era: Mixed Picture for China Relations." *Comparative Connections*, April 2008.

———. "China-Korea Relations: Underhanded Tactics and Stolen Secrets." *Comparative Connections*, January 2008.

Snyder, Scott. "Inauguration of Lee Myung-bak: Grappling with Korea's Future Challenges." Brookings Institution, February 2008.

Snyder, Scott. "Smart Power: Remaking U.S. Foreign Policy in North Korea." Testimony before the House Committee on Foreign Affairs, Subcommittee on Asia, the Pacific, and the Global Environment, February 12, 2009.

"South Korea-U.S. Summit Statement." Camp David, Maryland, April 20, 2008.

Suh, Young-Kil. "The Future of the U.S.-South Korea Alliance." *Strategic Insight*. Center for Contemporary Conflict, October 1, 2003.

Tanaka, Hitoshi. "Revisiting the North Korea Issue." *East Asia Insights* 3, no. 5 (October 2008).

Tanaka, Hitoshi with Adam P. Liff. "The Strategic Rationale for East Asia Community Building." In *East Asia at a Crossroads*, edited by Jusuf Wanandi and Tadashi Yamamoto, 90–104. Tokyo: Japan Center for International Exchange, 2008.

Thuy, Do Thi. "China, Japan, South Korea: Time for Trilateralism?" *RSIS Commentaries*. S. Rajaratham School of International Studies, Graduate School of Nanyang Technological University, August 5, 2008.

Toloraya, Georgy. "Russia's East Asian Strategy: The Korean Challenge." *Russia in Global Affairs* no. 1 (January/March 2008).

U.S. Department of Energy, Energy Information Administration. "Country Analysis Briefs: South Korea." Last updated June 2007.

U.S. Department of State. "Secretary Clinton's Remarks with South Korean Foreign Minister Yu." Seoul, Korea, February 20, 2009.

——— "U.S. to Host Inaugural Strategic Consultations with South Korea." January 10, 2006.

World Nuclear Association, "Nuclear Power in Korea," country briefing, accessed March 2009 at http://www.world-nuclear.org.

Xinhua News Service. "Hu Calls on China, S Korea to Strengthen Economic Cooperation." August 26, 2008.

———. "Wen Jiabao Attends Meeting of Leaders of China, Japan and South Korea." December 15, 2008.

Yang, Jung A. "President Lee Meets Hu Jintao." *The Daily NKK*. August 25, 2008.

Yoo, Cheong-mo. "Lee, Hu Set New Milestone in South Korea-China Relations." Yonhap News Agency, August 2008.

Yoo, Choonsik. "S&P Sees South Korean Economy Shrinking 3.5 pct." Thomson Financial News, Reuters, February 16, 2009.

Yoshida, Reiji. "Government downplays jets warned off by Seoul." *The Japan Times*. March 18, 2005.

Zhao, Lin. "Strategic Cooperation Between China and South Korea and Strategic Structure of Northeast Asia." East-West Center Working Paper no. 31. Presented at 5th East-West Center International Graduate Student Conference, February 16–18, 2006 in Honolulu, HI.

# THE NORTH KOREAN CHALLENGE TO SOUTH KOREA'S SECURITY

# RESPONDING TO THE COMING NORTH KOREAN CRISIS: ASSESSING SOUTH KOREAN MILITARY REQUIREMENTS

## Byung Kwan Kim

In the contemporary global security environment, local conflicts and non-military threats have increased, but the risk of large-scale inter-state conventional warfare has declined. Northeast Asia is an exception. Despite deepening economic and cultural interdependence in the region, large-scale conflict remains a significant possibility there. It is home to six of the world's largest militaries: China, Russia, Japan, North Korea, South Korea, and the United States, which has an extensive military presence in the region.

Competing to expand their national influence, regional actors are engaged in an accelerating arms race. Differences of national interests over territorial, historical, and natural resource issues continue to have the potential to lead to conflict among them. With Northeast Asia expected to be responsible for a third of the world's gross domestic product by 2025, major instability in the region—not to mention war—could have a devastating impact globally.

North Korea (Democratic People's Republic of Korea, or DPRK) represents one of the most serious threats to peace and stability in Northeast Asia. The regime's pursuit of nuclear weapons, long on the regional agenda, became an even more acute challenge when it tested its first nuclear device in October 2006. In the wake of North Korean leader Kim Jong Il's (Kim Chŏng-il) apparent stroke in August 2008, another North Korean threat emerged. The succession process there may result in regime instability, which would increase the risk of North-South conflict and of intervention in North Korea by other powers, not to mention risk a loss of control over nuclear devices and materiel and other weapons of mass destruction in the country.

In this chapter, I will assess what South Korea (Republic of Korea, or ROK) must do militarily to respond to the challenges posed by the changing North Korean situation. I will first outline the current security situation in

Northeast Asia in regard to North Korea, then consider scenarios for major change in North Korea and the likely responses of the regional powers. In particular, I will discuss what ROK military capabilities are needed to address successfully the range of possible change in North Korea, with reference to the ROK's "Defense Reform 2020 Plan." Finally, I will look at the security situation in Northeast Asia after Korean unification and assess the ROK's military needs then.

South Korea's military posture is vital to peace and stability in Northeast Asia due to the country's geographically central position in the region and its status as part of the divided Korean Peninsula. Based on my career as a South Korean military officer, I will offer recommendations for ROK military capabilities sufficient to meet the challenges posed by a changing North Korea. It is my sincere hope that wise leadership in the ROK and in the region will bring lasting peace and stability to the Korean Peninsula and Northeast Asia as a whole.

## The Current Security Situation in Northeast Asia

Unlike most other parts of the globe, Northeast Asia continues to witness a struggle for regional hegemony amidst peace and economic prosperity. The United States has led efforts for regional security based on its cooperation with each of the countries of Northeast Asia, but the People's Republic of China's (PRC) political, economic and military influence has dramatically expanded in recent years. Meanwhile, Japan and Russia are also aggressively engaged in a competition for prestige and influence in the region.

Northeast Asia is home to six of the world's largest militaries, densely positioned in or near the Korean Peninsula. In 2006, their military expenditures amounted to nearly 60 percent of the global total and the average annual rate of increase in their military budgets was 8 percent. Given that the global rate of increase was 3.5 percent, these figures indicate that there is an ongoing, intense arms race in the region. Moreover, every country in the region is expected to continue to enhance its military capabilities, especially its high-technology forces, which will further complicate efforts at regional security cooperation.

Unlike Europe, where the devastation and trauma of World War II produced an absolute consensus for peace, pacifist sentiment is not as strong among the countries of Northeast Asia.[1] Also unlike Europe, there is as yet no regional security consultation mechanism in Northeast Asia. The resulting difficulties of conflict management thus make for a high probability that inter-state conflict could escalate into armed conflict.

A number of issues could lead to hostilities in Northeast Asia. In addition to the North Korean situation, PRC-Taiwan relations have the potential to erupt in military conflict. The region is also home to many territorial disputes over islands, competing claims to exclusive economic zones and maritime resources, and strong nationalist sentiment and longstanding historical disputes, especially among Korea, China, and Japan. These factors are unlikely to be resolved soon; regional instability and uncertainty will thus likely persist.

If North Korea experiences abrupt change, countries in the region will likely compete for influence over North Korean territory. Such competition, along with other factors, could result in a regional conflict. The Korean Peninsula is thus expected to play a critical role in influencing change in Northeast Asian power relations.

### The Big Four: United States, Japan, China, and Russia

In Northeast Asia, the PRC has by far the most ground forces, while the United States has the strongest air force and navy. Due to a long "line of contact," its 880-mile land border with North Korea, the PRC has the greatest strategic influence on the Korean Peninsula, followed by Russia and Japan. The PRC has reinforced its ground forces along the border with North Korea and could immediately commit those troops in a North Korean contingency, with the only obstacle being opposition from Russia, Japan, South Korea, and the United States. For the foreseeable future, the long-standing friendly relationships between the PRC and Russia and between the United States and Japan will likely continue. The United States will continue to contribute to Northeast Asian security by serving as a stabilizing force in the region. The forces of these four non-Korean powers are detailed in Table 2.1 and Figure 2.1.

Table 2.1 Military Forces of the Four Non-Korean Regional Powers

|  | Personnel (million) | Tanks | Artillery | Carriers/ Submarines | Aircraft |
|---|---|---|---|---|---|
| United States | 1.47 | 7,620 | 6,530 | 12/72 | 9,074 |
| Japan | 0.24 | 880 | 630 | 0/16 | 636 |
| PRC | 2.21 | 7,660 | 17,000 | 0/62 | 2,883 |
| Russia | 1.13 | 22,150 | 18,545 | 1/112 | 1,954 |

Source: The Military Balance 2008.

**Figure 2.1 Military Forces**

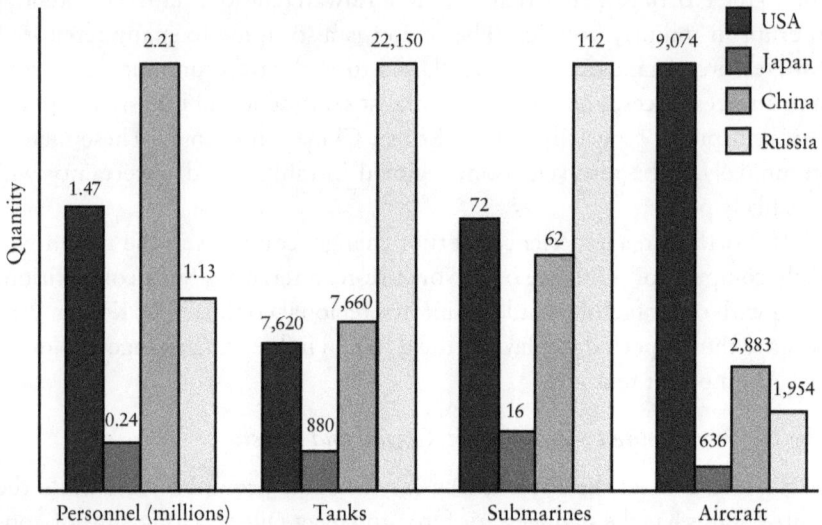

*Source: The Military Balance 2008.*

### United States

The U.S. military has 1.47 million uniformed personnel, including a 522,000-person army, and its weaponry is the world's most capable. The United States has been transferring forces from the Atlantic to the Pacific region, improving its strategic nuclear forces, and deploying missile defense (MD) systems in the continental United States and on the territory of its allies. U.S. forces are detailed in Table 2.2.

### Japan

Japan has 240,000 uniformed military personnel, including 150,000 in its army and small but modern Naval Self-Defense Forces and Air Self-Defense Forces (see details in Table 2.3). Since 1995, Japan has been moving away from its traditional Exclusive Defense-Oriented Policy to a New Basic Policy for National Defense.[2] The new policy calls for Japan's forces to be modernized to enhance their capability to respond to crises in the homeland and in the region. It also provides that Japan will develop its space capabilities.

### PRC

The Chinese military has 2.21 million personnel in uniform, including 1.6 million soldiers and 100,000 in the Second Artillery, the PRC's medium-long range missile corps. The PRC has been improving its intelligence capabilities and expanding its navy, air force, and strategic weapons (see Table 2.4 for details). It is also attempting to close the space technology gap with the United States.

**Russia**

The Russian military has 1.13 million uniformed personnel, including 395,000 Army personnel and separate missile and space forces (see Table 2.5). Since 2003, Russia has increased its defense budget by 20–30 percent per year to modernize its military. Russia is also replacing its traditional system of separate services system with three "Regional Integrated Commands." It is employing triads[3] (ICBMs, SSNs, and strategic nuclear bombers) to deter the strategic forces of the United States and other countries.

### The North-South Korean Military Balance

There is an overall balance in conventional military forces between North and South Korea. Although North Korea has more personnel and equipment than South Korea, its weaponry is superannuated and inadequately maintained. South Korea has far fewer military forces, but its weaponry and repair and maintenance systems are superior.

The situation regarding non-conventional forces is different. With only a very limited budget to import new weapons systems or even to maintain its existing weapons, the North Korean leadership's confidence in its conventional weapons is expected to continue to weaken. It will thus likely rely even more on nuclear devices and medium- and long-range missiles, which provide it with an "asymmetrical" advantage over South Korea. (Under various international agreements, South Korea does not have or seek such weapons.) North Korea's superiority in these areas will allow it to stage limited provocations.

The ROK-U.S. alliance, including the United States' "nuclear umbrella" over South Korea, is a crucial deterrent against North Korea. The ROK-U.S. Combined Forces Command system, with its overwhelming air superiority on the Korean Peninsula, further enhances the alliance's deterrent power. Combined ROK-U.S. forces can operate rapidly and effectively against any North Korean provocation, including the use of weapons of mass destruction.

**Table 2.2 U.S. Military Forces**

| Army | Navy | Air Force | Marines |
|---|---|---|---|
| Marine Expeditionary Forces: 3 | Regional Fleets: 5 <br> Carrier Strike Groups (CSG): 12 | Functional Commands: 6 <br> Pacific & Europe Commands | Marine Expeditionary Forces: 3 <br> Marine Maneuver Brigades: 2 <br> Marine Air Group: 1 |
| Personnel: 522,000 | Personnel: 337,000 | Personnel: 338,000 | Personnel: 186,000 |
| Tanks: 7,620 <br> Armored Vehicles: 14,300 <br> Strykers: 600 | Aircraft Carriers (CV): 12 <br> Submarines: 72 <br> Cruisers: 27 | Reconnaissance Aircraft: 239 <br> Tactical Aircraft: 3,513 <br> Cargo Aircraft: 1,020 | Tanks: 403 <br> Light Armored Vehicles: 252 <br> Amphibious Armored Vehicles: 1,311 |
| Artillery: 6,530 <br> Helicopters: 4,597 | Destroyers: 49 <br> Escort & Patrol Vessels: 51 <br> Landing Ships Tank (LST): 39 <br> Aircraft: 3,230 | Tanker Aircraft: 659 <br> Long-range Bombers: 203 <br> Helicopters: 219 | Fighters: 213 <br> Helicopters: 70 |

*Source: The Military Balance 2008.*

## Table 2.3 Japanese Military Forces

| Ground<br>Self-Defense Force | Maritime<br>Self-Defense Force | Air<br>Self-Defense Force |
|---|---|---|
| Armies (corps equivalent): 5 | Self-Defense Fleet: 1 | Air Defense Forces: 3 |
| Divisions: 9 | District Fleets: 5 | (Air Group: 6) |
| Composite Units: 1 | | (Composite Group: 1) |
| Central Rapid Response Group: 1 | | |
| Personnel: 150,000 | Personnel: 45,000 | Personnel: 45,000 |
| Tanks: 880 | Submarines: 16 | Fighters: 362 |
| Armored Vehicles: 960 | Escort Vessels: 53 | Early Warning Aircraft: 17 |
| Artillery: 630 | Large Transporters: 3 | Tankers: 2 |
| Helicopters: 458 | Minesweepers: 31 | Cargo Aircraft: 42 |
| | Aircraft: 213 | Helicopters: 50 |
| | | Military (Recon) Satellites: 4 |

Source: *The Military Balance 2008.*

## Table 2.4 PRC Military Forces

| Army | Navy | Air Force | Second Artillery |
|---|---|---|---|
| Military Regions: 7 | Fleets: 3 | Military Regions: 7 | Missile Corps: 6 |
| Personnel: 1,600,000 | Personnel: 255,000 | Personnel: 255,000 | Personnel: 100,000 |
| Tanks: 7,660 | Submarines: 62 | Tactical Aircraft: 1,730 | ICBM: 46 |
| Armored Vehicles: 3,500 | Battleships: 318 | Bombers: 82 | IRBM: 35 |
| Artillery: 17,000 | Support Vessels: 204 | Reconnaissance Aircraft: 179 | SRBM: 725 |
| Helicopters: 375 | Aircraft: 870 | Early Warning Aircraft: 4<br>Tankers: 18 | SLBM: 12 |
| | | Military Satellites: 10 | |

Source: *The Military Balance 2008.*

Table 2.5 Russian Military Forces

| Ground Forces | Naval Forces | Air Force | Strategic Forces |
|---|---|---|---|
| Military Districts: 6 | Fleets: 4 | Military Districts: 6 | Strategic Missile Forces |
| | Flotillas: 1 | | Space Forces |
| | | | Airborne Units |
| Personnel: 395,000 | Personnel: 142,000 | Personnel: 160,000 | Personnel: 437,000 |
| Tanks: 22,150 | Aircraft Carriers (CV): 1 | Fighters: 1,525 | ICBMs: 508 |
| Armored Vehicles: 27,040 | Submarines: 112 | Bombers: 214 | ABMs: 100 |
| Artillery: 18,545 | Battleships: 180 | Tankers: 20 | Military Satellites: 90 |
| Helicopters: 1,278 | Fighters: 175 | Early Warning Aircraft: 20 | |

*Source: The Military Balance 2008.*

Although South Korea is modernizing its conventional forces in accordance with its "Defense Reform 2020 Plan," military tension can be expected to persist on the peninsula as long as North Korea maintains its current regime. See Table 2.6 and Figure 2.2 for a comparison of North and South Korean military forces.

### North Korea

Under its "military first" policy,[4] the North Korean government is maintaining large-scale conventional forces, enhancing domestic control, and strengthening its nuclear and missile capabilities. Its nuclear and missile programs bolster regime security and provide leverage in international negotiations. While maintaining friendly relations with both the PRC and Russia, North Korea has also sought to improve relations with the United States and Japan, in part by exploiting nuclear negotiations.

### South Korea

While the ROK has established cooperative relations with its neighbors Japan, the PRC, and Russia, it is transforming—and further strengthening—its alliance with the United States into a forward-looking, strategic partnership. The two governments have agreed to transfer wartime operational control over ROK forces from the United States to the ROK in April 2012. In preparation, they are establishing a joint ROK-U.S. system in which the ROK will play the leading role and the United States a supporting role in the defense of the Republic of Korea.

## Table 2.6 North and South Korean Military Forces

| | | | South Korea | North Korea |
|---|---|---|---|---|
| Total Military Personnel [Army/Navy/Air Force] | | | 674,000 (540,000/68,000/65,000) | 1,170,000 (1,000,000/60,000/110,000) |
| Ground Forces | Units | Corps | 12 | 19 |
| | | Divisions | 50 | 75 |
| | Equipment | Tanks | 2,300 | 3,700 |
| | | Artillery/MRL | 5,100/200 | 8,500/4,800 |
| | | SSM | 20 (launchers) | 80 (launchers) |
| Navy | Surface Battleships | | 120 | 420 |
| | LST | | 10 | 260 |
| | Submarines | | 10 | 60 |
| Air Forces | Fighters | | 500 | 820 |
| Reserves (Personnel) | | | 3,040,000 | 7,700,000 |

*Source:* Tae-Yeong Kwon, "Arms Race Trend in Northeast Asia and Course of Korean Security," Korea Research Institute For Strategy, 98.

## Figure 2.2 North and South Korean Military Forces

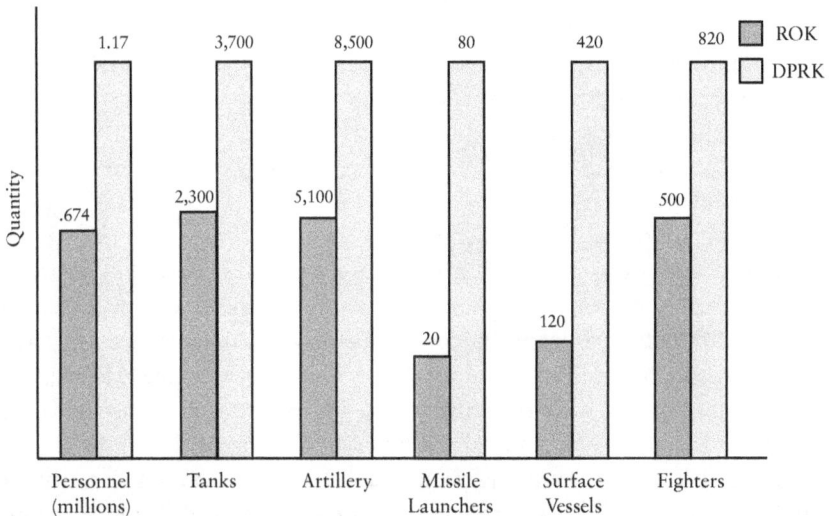

*Source:* Tae-Yeong Kwon, "Arms Race Trend in Northeast Asia and Course of Korean Security," Korea Research Institute For Strategy, 98.

## The Impact on Regional Security of a North Korean Crisis

North Korea now faces the prospect of major change. Top leader Kim Jong Il, 69, is reportedly ill, and there may be a power struggle to determine his successor. Social discipline is becoming increasingly difficult to maintain; defections are on the rise. The country cannot meet basic needs for food and energy from domestic production and, earning less than $1.2 billion annually from exports, lacks foreign currency to purchase them abroad. It will thus likely continue to resort to brinkmanship tactics to induce other states to help supply its needs.

Unable to resolve its fundamental problems, North Korea could experience abrupt, dramatic change. (Some scholars assert that such change has already begun.) I am convinced that North Korea's problems—and the resulting internal instability—cannot be resolved without major change. I define major change in North Korea as political and economic development sufficient to allow the society to support itself without foreign aid. Such change must include opening up to the outside world and instilling a popular motivation for economic achievement. Political change alone will not be sufficient to resolve North Korea's problems—economic change must occur in parallel.

If major change does begin to occur in North Korea, it is difficult to predict how long the regime will be able to maintain social control. Even if social control is maintained, it seems inevitable that the regime itself will have to implement major change. The problem is that the regime does not have the capacity to lead major change and will have to accept substantial external support. Some surrounding countries will likely attempt to use the opportunity to expand their influence, thus increasing external competition over the country.

If social control collapses during such change, competition among surrounding countries to exercise hegemony over North Korea will intensify. In such a scenario, North Korea may lose its sovereignty. One or more countries, perhaps acting collectively, would most likely occupy the country and govern it through a military administration, comparable to the U.S. military occupation of Japan and Korea after 1945. The country or countries would implement the necessary political and economic change in North Korea.

Intervention by surrounding countries in North Korea could undermine stability in Northeast Asia. The most threatening scenario would be if one country sought to gain exclusive authority over North Korea, a situation that could well lead to international conflict. I believe that all of North Korea's neighbors strongly prefer that the North Korean situation does not cause a significant change in the regional balance of power. In other words, they prefer that North Korea successfully reform and open up itself. If this proves impossible, however, all neighboring countries will likely prefer that major change in North Korea be directed by China or the ROK.

To understand how North Korea's neighbors may act in a crisis in the country, it is useful to analyze their basic attitudes and interests.

**ROK:** As fellow Koreans, South Koreans will naturally want to support North Korean efforts at major change. The ROK will also seek the opportunity for peaceful reunification. The ROK would strongly resist Chinese intervention in North Korea.

**China:** The PRC prefers that North Korea remain a pro-Chinese, independent state. Should that not be possible, China will seek to exercise control over North Korea. Since the rapid assimilation of North Korea would evoke numerous challenges, China would incorporate North Korea in a gradual, long-term process, leveraging massive assistance to the society. China would strongly resist North Korea's falling under South Korean control. China would regard such an outcome both as a lost opportunity to absorb North Korea itself and as enhancing U.S. influence on the Korean Peninsula. If, however, the PRC could be assured that the United States would not deploy its forces in North Korea, PRC resistance would be greatly mitigated.

**Japan and Russia:** Japan and Russia desire to maintain the status quo. They would strongly repudiate Chinese control of North Korea as significantly enhancing the PRC's geopolitical and strategic positions and diminishing their own. Japan and Russia would not welcome ROK control of North Korea, but they would prefer that to Chinese control.

**United States:** The United States' main interest will be to secure North Korea's nuclear weapons, but it will also be concerned about the implications of any change in North Korea for the future of regional stability. The United States would support ROK control over North Korea but would have serious concerns about PRC hegemony. If the PRC moved promptly to intervene in North Korea, however, the United States would not risk conflict with the PRC in a confrontation over North Korea unless the ROK itself demonstrated a firm determination to respond and called on the United States for support. The United States will only act as a mediator with the PRC in a crisis scenario involving North Korea if the ROK insists on U.S. support.

### North Korean Crisis Scenarios

Predicting how North Korea will experience major change and how its neighbors will respond is of course fraught with difficulty, but in formulating scenarios I have focused on what I believe to be are two key factors: will the regime be able to maintain internal control and which country will support or lead major change in North Korea?

I believe it will be difficult for the regime to maintain control once major change begins to occur. If it loses control, the pace of change in North Korea will accelerate, as will the responses of surrounding countries. As discussed, competition for hegemony over North Korea may well occur. Without prior coordination and an understanding among the concerned countries, such competition could result in international conflict.

Based on whether the North Korean regime can maintain social control and on which outside country or countries will support or exercise hegemony over a changing North Korea, I have laid out eight possible scenarios in Table 2.7. To summarize:

**Scenario A:** Even if the North Korean regime is able to maintain full internal control, it will require external economic aid to survive and implement necessary changes.

**Scenarios B, C, and D:** If the North Korean regime is no longer able to exercise full internal control, it will require massive external assistance—not only for its economy but also to maintain public order—if it is to continue to survive.

**Scenarios E, F, G, and H:** If the North Korean regime loses control, the regime will lose sovereignty to an external power or powers, which will impose major change on the country.

**Table 2.7 North Korean Crisis Scenarios**

| Scenarios | Internal Control | Surrounding Countries' Responses | |
|---|---|---|---|
| A | DPRK maintains internal control | Limited external support (if DPRK maintains full internal control) | Support from multiple states |
| B | | Massive external support for public order and the economy (if DPRK losses some internal control) | Support from multiple states |
| C | | | PRC support |
| D | | | ROK support |
| E | DPRK loses internal control | PRC hegemony | |
| F | | ROK hegemony | |
| G | | Hegemony partitioned between PRC and ROK | |
| H | | Hegemony exercised by multi-national council | |

*Source:* Author.

## The External Response to a North Korean Crisis

Each country will respond differently to the various scenarios for major change in North Korea based on its assessment of its national interests, including the responses it anticipates other concerned countries will make. To better understand and predict those dynamics, I will analyze how the concerned countries will likely regard each of the eight scenarios. I will employ a numerical index and symbols for each country's view of the degree to which a particular scenario favors its national interest, as shown in Table 2.8.

Table 2.8 Compatibility with National Interests

| Very Favorable | Favorable | Neither Favorable nor Unfavorable | Unfavorable | Very Unfavorable |
|---|---|---|---|---|
| +2 | +1 | 0 | -1 | -2 |
| 😄 | 🙂 | 😐 | 🙁 | 😣 |

*Source:* Author.

Scenario A in Figure 2.3 assumes that the North Korean regime will be able to maintain internal control and that it will eventually implement necessary major change of its own accord, although it will require external economic assistance to do so. This situation could occur either while Kim Jong Il is still leading North Korea or after his departure from the scene. As shown on the map, China, Russia, and Japan would regard this scenario favorably, since it would by definition mean an end to the risk of chaos emanating from an unstable North Korea. If the North Korean regime suspended its nuclear weapons development as part of its major change, the United States would also favor this scenario; if not, the American attitude would be neutral. The only exception would be the ROK, which would regard the scenario as unfavorable to its since it would ensure the long-term survival of another, potentially hostile Korean regime on the peninsula.

Scenario B in Figure 2.4 assumes that the North Korean regime will be unable to maintain full internal control and that the United Nations or multiple states, possibly led by the United States, will deploy peacekeeping forces to help maintain order in the country and provide large-scale economic assistance as North Korea experiences major change. The balance of power in the region would remain unchanged under this scenario. The United States and Japan would regard this scenario favorably. Russia and the ROK would see it as a neutral development in terms of their national interests. The PRC would also view it with relative equanimity, unless the United States led the multinational intervention, in which case the PRC would regard the scenario unfavorably.

**Figure 2.3 (A) Limited Foreign Aid, DPRK Maintains Internal Control**

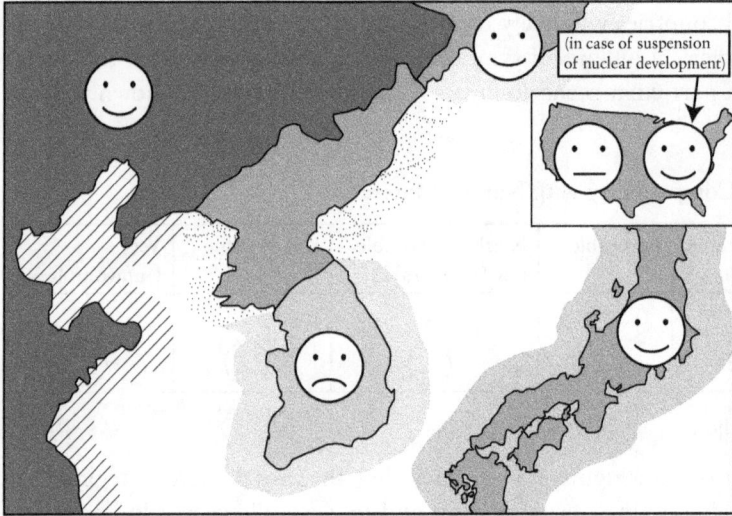

*Source:* Author.

**Figure 2.4 (B) Limited UN/Multinational Intervention**

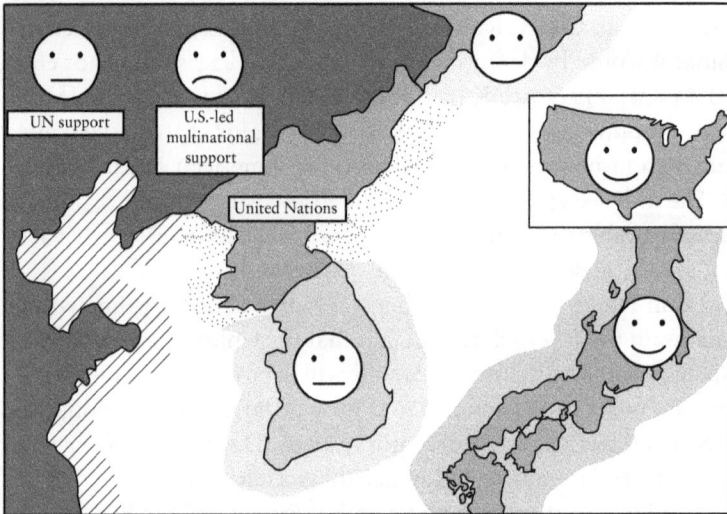

*Source:* Author.

Scenario C in Figure 2.5 assumes that only the PRC will deploy peace-keeping forces to North Korea and provide it with large-scale economic aid to support a regime that is losing internal control as it seeks to cope with major change. Depending on developments, several decades later, the PRC might take full control of North Korea. As a result, the PRC may deploy warships and air forces to North Korea. The balance of power in the region would shift greatly in the PRC's favor. Japan would feel directly threatened. The PRC may preemptively dispatch warships to the waters off North Korea to stave off other foreign intervention, and, depending on developments, the PRC might take full control of North Korea. Russia and the ROK would lose land contact with a sovereign North Korea. The balance of power in the region would shift greatly in the PRC's favor. Only China would view this scenario favorably. Russia would regard it unfavorably, while the ROK, the United States, and Japan would view it as a very unfavorable development.

Scenario D in Figure 2.6 assumes that only the ROK will deploy peace-keeping forces to North Korea and provide it with large-scale economic aid to support a regime that is losing internal control as it seeks to cope with major change. Such ROK action could be taken with the acquiescence and oversight of the major powers in the region. It would entail a relatively small shift in the regional balance of power. The ROK and the United States would view this scenario as favorable to their interests. Russia and Japan would see it as neither favorable nor unfavorable. Only the PRC would regard it unfavorably.

Scenario E in Figure 2.7 assumes that the PRC, reacting to the North Korean regime's loss of internal control, occupies the country and oversees major change there. The PRC would order a large-scale deployment of its ground forces to North Korea and its naval forces in the waters around it. Chinese influence over North Korea would increase, and the PRC would likely eventually assimilate North Korean territory, making it part of China. The PRC would regard this scenario as very favorable to its national interests, but all of the other powers in the region—the United States, ROK, Japan, and Russia—would regard it as a very unfavorable development.

Figure 2.5 (C) Limited PRC Intervention

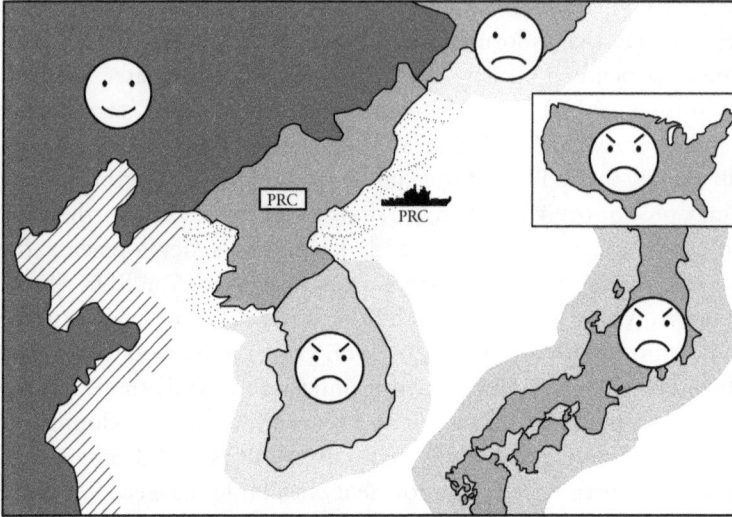

*Source:* Author.

Figure 2.6 (D) Limited ROK Intervention

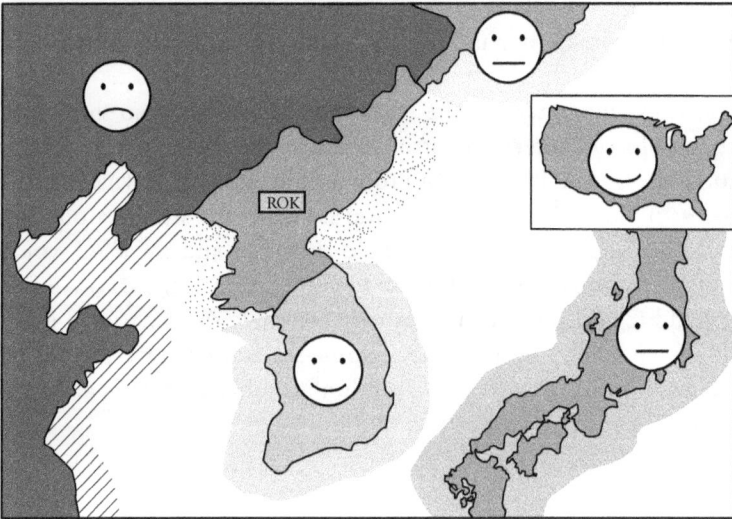

*Source:* Author.

**Figure 2.7 (E) PRC Administration**

*Source:* Author.

Scenario F in Figure 2.8 assumes it will be the ROK that, reacting to the North Korean regime's loss of internal control, occupies the country and oversees major change there. The ROK would be able to act in this regard only to the extent permitted by the other powers in the region, i.e. the United States, PRC, Japan, and Russia. The ROK would regard this scenario as very favorable to its national interests. The United States would regard it as a favorable development; Russia as neither favorable nor unfavorable; Japan as unfavorable; and the PRC as very unfavorable.

Scenario G in Figure 2.9 assumes that, as the North Korean regime loses internal control, the PRC will deploy its military forces to occupy the northern part of the country while South Korea militarily occupies the southern part. The PRC would deploy its naval forces off the East Sea (Sea of Japan) coast of North Korea. The North Korean side of the border between North Korea and Russia would be controlled by the PRC. The balance of power in Northeast Asia would be substantially altered, with the PRC's influence on the region increasing under this scenario. The PRC alone would regard this scenario as very favorable to its national interests. All the other regional powers—the United States, ROK, Russia, and Japan—would regard the development as very unfavorable to their interests.

**Figure 2.8 (F) ROK Administration**

*Source:* Author.

**Figure 2.9 (G) PRC/ROK Administration**

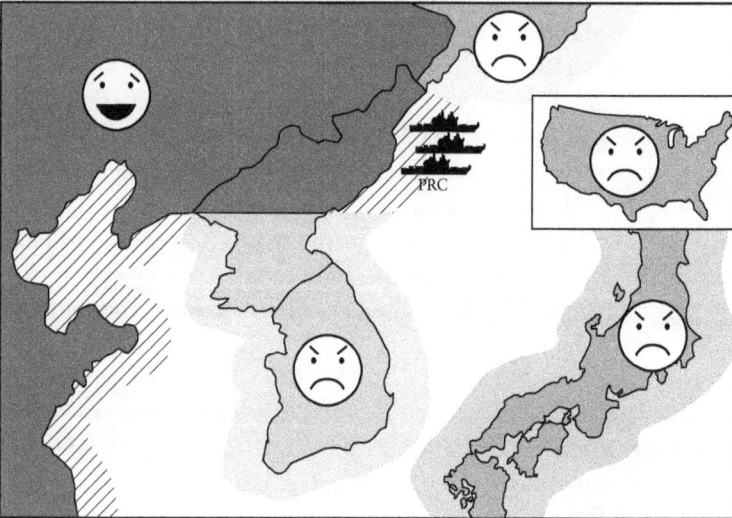

*Source:* Author.

Scenario H in Figure 2.10 assumes that several countries will occupy and administer North Korea when the regime loses internal control. Realization of this scenario would require prior international coordination, and the regional balance of power would not be affected. The United States, Japan, and Russia would regard this scenario as favorable to their national interests. The ROK would view it as neither favorable nor unfavorable, while the PRC would regard it as an unfavorable development.

**Figure 2.10 (H) UN or Multinational Administration**

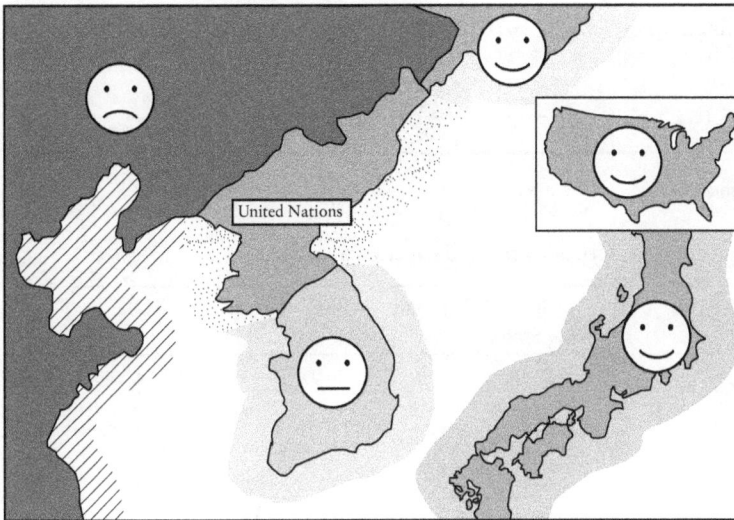

*Source:* Author.

### North Korean Crisis Scenarios and Regional Power Dynamics

The preceding discussion indicates how the countries in the region are likely to regard each of the various North Korean change scenarios. In actuality, however, each country in deciding its course of action will take into account the expected positions of the other countries. Tables 2.9 and 2.10, respectively, provide insight into likely overall regional attitudes toward the first four scenarios, involving limited external support or intervention in North Korea, and the other four scenarios, involving outright foreign administration.

Tables 2.9 and 2.10 highlight that neighboring countries would be most concerned, by far, about unilateral PRC action in North Korea, whether limited intervention or an occupation: all three scenarios involving unilateral PRC intervention result in regional sums of -6. PRC intervention, whether limited or massive, would greatly increase the likelihood that North Korea would fall under the PRC's long-term influence and that the PRC's presence in the East Sea (Sea of Japan) would greatly expand. Such developments would significantly shift the balance of power in Northeast Asia in China's favor, to the detriment of all other states in the region.

Table 2.9 Regional Attitudes toward Limited Intervention Scenarios

| Scenario | United States | Japan | PRC | Russia | ROK | Sum |
|---|---|---|---|---|---|---|
| A: Foreign aid | 0 | +1 | +1 | +1 | -1 | +2 |
| B: UN/Multinational | +1 | +1 | 0 | 0 | 0 | +2 |
| C: PRC | -2 | -2 | +1 | -1 | -2 | -6 |
| D: ROK | +1 | 0 | -1 | 0 | +1 | +1 |
| Total | 0 | 0 | +1 | 0 | -2 | -1 |

*Source:* Author.

Table 2.10 Regional Attitudes toward Occupation Scenarios

| Scenario | United States | Japan | PRC | Russia | ROK | Sum |
|---|---|---|---|---|---|---|
| E: PRC | -2 | -2 | +2 | -2 | -2 | -6 |
| F: ROK | +1 | -1 | -1 | 0 | +2 | +1 |
| G: PRC/ROK | -2 | -2 | +2 | -2 | -2 | -6 |
| H: UN/Multinational | +1 | +1 | -1 | +1 | 0 | +2 |
| Total | -2 | -4 | +2 | -3 | -2 | -9 |

*Source:* Author.

The North Korean change scenario with which regional powers would be most comfortable would be Scenario A, in which the North Korean regime maintains internal control while itself implementing major reforms. Unfortunately, the North Korean regime appears unlikely to be able to stay in power while reforming the system. Indeed, major change within North Korean appears likely to occur in just the next five to ten years.

If, as seems likely, outside intervention or even occupation is inevitable, the scenarios with the least risk of inviting regional instability are B and H, in which the United Nations or a coalition of states takes charge. Such an approach would require close coordination among the concerned countries before a crisis occurs. Unfortunately, differences of interests among the countries mean that prior coordination is unlikely to occur.

The scenarios perhaps most likely to occur in a North Korean crisis are C, E, and G, which involve unilateral PRC intervention or occupation. Unilateral PRC action would, however, greatly increase the risk of instability or even chaos in Northeast Asia. The PRC would install a satellite government in Pyongyang and, if it met little resistance, eventually incorporate North Korea into the PRC. The potential shift in the balance of regional power due to PRC intervention would unsettle other regional powers, which are already mistrustful of China. Moreover, once the PRC intervened in a North Korean crisis, it would be very difficult to induce it to reverse course. Prior international consultation and coordination is thus necessary to prevent PRC intervention and preserve regional stability.

Noted North Korea expert Andrei Lankov's assessment is that neither the ROK nor the United States would be able to respond effectively once the PRC intervened in a North Korean crisis.[5] Lankov insists that the PRC is initially more likely to establish a satellite government in North Korea than annex the territory outright. Annexation would likely hurt the PRC's international image and perhaps result in impediments to its own continued rapid pace of national development. The PRC would inherit the entire burden of economic development in North Korea, and a popular resistance movement might arise in North Korea. Once a satellite government is established, however, Lankov believes that it will very difficult, if not impossible, to limit Chinese options in North Korea, including possibly eventual annexation. Lankov also suggests that North Korean cadres might accept annexation to maintain their own privileges.

Chinese annexation of North Korea would have a profound impact on the ROK and all of Northeast Asia. To South Koreans, it would mean the end to any hope of national unification, which would result in a rapid deterioration of national morale. A pro-China mood would eventually develop among many but not all South Koreans. With public opinion deeply divided, the Republic of Korea could be thrown into internal chaos. In the region, Japan would be the first to react, accelerating its drive to become a stronger military power and challenging China politically, economically, and militarily. A Chinese-Japanese confrontation would not only threaten Chinese and Japanese national interests, but also those of the ROK, the United States, and Russia. To prevent such a destabilizing scenario, all concerned countries need to begin to consult and cooperate now on how to deal with a North Korean crisis.

Compared to scenarios involving unilateral PRC intervention or occupation, regional powers could relatively easily accommodate scenarios D and F, in which the ROK alone intervenes or occupies North Korea. There is no additional hindrance once the understanding of the PRC and the United States is obtained. The evident fact is that the ROK would be unable to proceed with any action that is objected by the PRC or the United States, as well as

Japan or Russia. It should be relatively easy to obtain the acquiescence of the PRC, Japan, and Russia to ROK intervention or occupation of North Korea as long as they are reassured about U.S. intentions.

### Preparing for a North Korean Crisis: Recommendations to the ROK

In a North Korean crisis, the ROK will need the trust and assent not only of the PRC and the United States but ideally also of Russia and Japan, not to mention the cadres and people of North Korea. To prepare for a North Korean crisis, the ROK must begin to collaborate closely now with all the states of Northeast Asia, building up its credibility and reassuring them.

When a crisis does occur in North Korea, the ROK should demonstrate a firm resolve to assume full responsibility for North Korea. While seeking support and assistance from China and the United States, the ROK must make available adequate resources to support the people of North Korea and implement systemic change. By doing so, the ROK would contribute immensely to stability in the region and also increase the possibility of peaceful unification.

It is no exaggeration to suggest that how the North Korean crisis is managed will determine the destiny of the Korean Peninsula in the twenty-first century. South Koreans must thus be firmly resolved to make substantial sacrifices for their brethren in North Korea. Otherwise, the South Korean government will not be able to take these necessary measures.

Given the likelihood of a crisis in North Korea and its complex regional context, it is also essential to maintain the present ROK-U.S. Combined Forces Command until the ROK has been able to successfully implement major change in North Korea and the regional situation has been stabilized. If the ROK and the United States agree to maintain the Combined Forces Command, the two countries will need to cooperate closely to obtain South Korean public support for the budget and other support needed to maintain the system.

To recap: If the ROK is to manage successfully a North Korean crisis, it must:

1. Develop the national resolve to make substantial sacrifices for our North Korean brethren;
2. Obtain the confidence of, and collaborate closely with, the regional powers;
3. Produce a plan to develop North Korea that will win the support of the regional powers;
4. Ensure that ROK military resources and strength are sufficient to support the task of implementing systemic change in North Korea;

5. Enhance the U.S.-ROK alliance and review the decision to end the ROK-U.S. Combined Forces Command in 2012;

6. Support potential leaders among North Korean defectors and refugees, and reassure current North Korean cadres about their position in North Korea in the case of ROK intervention or occupation; and

7. Manage and resolve current North Korean problems in such a way as to promote the prospects for eventual peaceful unification.

If the ROK successfully implements such measures, it will create the conditions for peaceful national reunification and contribute greatly to regional stability.

### Preparing for Crisis in North Korea: ROK Military Requirements

If the ROK wishes to be able to intervene in a North Korean crisis—whether on a limited scale or to reshape the country—it must develop sufficient military power to be able to cooperate with concerned powers and respond to the strategic requirements of the crisis. The ROK's military policy, however, has been focused only on the current North Korean threat. The ROK is implementing Defense Reform 2020, a phased plan ending in the year 2020, to improve the quality of ROK military personnel and equipment while reducing the numbers of both. If the ROK military is to be able to respond to a North Korean crisis, the plan will have to be modified. It should *take into consideration independent defense capacity and dynamic relationship with the allies and other countries*, at the same time it prepares for a potential threat in the future.

Before considering how the defense plan should be supplemented, let me summarize the plan as it currently stands. The then-progressive government of South Korea formulated Defense Reform 2020 in 2004 and adopted it in 2005 in accordance with its emphasis on North-South Korean reconciliation and the development of a "self-reliant national defense." It represented a major departure from the existing national defense policy and military build-up plan.

The intent of Defense Reform 2020 is to build a state-of-the-art, intelligent, science-oriented military with an integrated combat capability. It aims to respond proactively to changes in warfare and develop information science technology. It emphasizes reorganizing the military, procuring high-tech war-fighting systems, and reforming the operation of the national defense system to make it more cost-effective. The plan also stresses supplementing South Korean weapons systems and command and control capabilities to allow the successful implementation of the scheduled transfer of wartime operational control of South Korean forces from the United States to the ROK in April 2012.

Under Defense Reform 2020, the military's war-fighting capabilities are supposed to be modernized while the number of standing uniformed personnel will be gradually reduced. By 2020, uniformed personnel will fall to 500,000 (from 680,000 in 2005) while the ratio of officers and noncommissioned offers to enlisted personnel will rise from 25 percent to 40 percent.

To improve intelligence and command and control (C2I) functions, the ROK will acquire war-fighting capabilities such as early warning airplanes, reconnaissance satellites, high-altitude unmanned aerial vehicles (UAVs), and a joint command and control (C2) system. The acquisition of next-generation weapons, including fighters, guided weapons, 7,000-ton KDX-III Aegis destroyers, and tanks, will improve the ROK military's maneuver and precision-strike capabilities.

The ROK Joint Chiefs of Staff (JCS), which is responsible for military planning and execution, is to establish a JCS-centered operations system that ensures that combat operations will be conducted jointly rather than by the individual services. The interim chain of command and the number of units are to be reduced, bolstering the military's overall operational efficiency and making it better suited to modern warfare.

Among the critical changes to each service that the plan mandates, the ROK army will expand its operations capabilities by reinforcing its intelligence, mobilization, and firepower functions, while reducing the number of its corps and divisions. The ROK navy will enhance its surface vessels, submarines, and air assets, shifting from the existing defense of local waters to a more future battlefield-oriented architecture with a mission that will include the protection of maritime transportation corridors and resources. The ROK marine corps is focusing on acquiring a brigade-level amphibious operations capability, while the ROK air force's goal is to enhance the efficiency of its air operations on the peninsula by introducing new fighters and developing an airborne operations C2 system. Reserve forces will be reduced from the current 3 million to 1.5 million, but their quality is to be upgraded so that they will be equal to standing forces in their war-fighting capabilities.

Formulated in 2005, Defense Reform 2020 needs to be modified to take a longer-term perspective and reflect a changing security environment. Above all, the plan must provide ROK military forces with the ability to adapt to shifts in the Northeast Asian security environment that could be caused by a crisis in North Korea. Specifically, the ROK needs to be prepared for possible military confrontation as inter-Korean tensions rise due to the North Korean nuclear program and internal crisis in North Korea.

The ROK also needs to review the planned sharp reduction in its ground forces in view of North Korea's much larger ground forces and the need for the ROK to be able to collaborate with an international effort in response to a crisis in North Korea. While the main focus of Defense Reform 2020 was on increasing the ROK's "hard power," greater attention to "soft power" is also needed. Soft power is a major factor in constructing military power, and synergies between tangible and intangible combat power can contribute greatly to actual combat power.

Defense Reform 2020 can only succeed if adequately funded. The plan called for the defense budget to increase at an annual rate of 9.9 percent from 2002 to 2010, 7.8 percent from 2011 to 2015, and 1 percent from 2016–2020. During just its first four years of implementation, however, the plan suffered a 3.7 percent budget shortfall compared to the planned expenditure of 106 trillion Korean won. The shortfall will be compounded as the years pass. Moreover, the global economic crisis and the continuing rise in the value of the Korean won in foreign exchange markets pose additional obstacles to the full funding of Defense Reform 2020.

Table 2.11 Funding of Defense Reform 2020 (in trillion Korean won)

|  | 2006 | 2007 | 2008 | 2009 | Total |
|---|---|---|---|---|---|
| Planned Budget | 22.9 | 25.1 | 27.6 | 30.4 | 106.0 |
| Actual Budget | 22.5 | 24.5 | 26.7 | 28.5 | 102.2 |
| Shortfall | -0.4 | -0.6 | -0.9 | -1.9 | -3.8 |

*Source:* Author.

## Korean Security in the Post-Unification Era

The security of a unified Korea should be a vital concern not only to Korea but also to its neighbors and the United States. A militarily weak unified Korea would result in greatly increased tensions and instability in Northeast Asia. Nature abhors a vacuum, but even a "low pressure area" on the Korean Peninsula would put regional security at risk. Neighboring countries would be tempted to compete for influence on the peninsula, and existing disputes over ethnicity, territory, resources, and the environment could escalate into conflict.

Historically, it should be noted, there have been many major regional confrontations involving Korea. These include the Mongol-Koryo alliance's invasion of Japan in 1274 and 1281,[6] Japan's invasion of Chosun-dynasty Korea from 1592 to 1598,[7] and Japan's wars with Qing China (1894-1895) and imperial Russia (1904-1905).[8] These wars all broke out at times when Korea was militarily weak and its neighbors were competing for hegemony over the peninsula. A unified Korea with an appropriate level of military capabilities will have the effect of discouraging its neighbors from competing for hegemony over the peninsula. Moreover, an appropriately-armed Korea can serve as a buffer zone or mediator in the event of conflict among its neighbors.

A key element in the security of unified Korea will be a continuing alliance with the United States. Unified Korea will need to be prepared for potential conflict with any one of its neighbors at any one time. Even a unified Korea, however, will be much smaller economically and militarily than its neighbors; it will thus need the support of a powerful but distant ally such as the United States. Moreover, with appropriate modifications, the ROK-U.S. alliance, together with the Japan-U.S. alliance, can serve as an apparatus to prevent regional conflict in the continuing absence of a regional security consultation mechanism.

Generally speaking, small and middle powers must rely on cooperative security mechanisms such as alliances even more than on their own military capabilities. International security arrangements offer great benefits to smaller powers by enhancing the credibility of their deterrent forces and allowing them to keep their defense budgets under control and thus to continue to develop their economies. As can be seen in the case of Switzerland, however, a country needs to maintain at least minimum independent defense capabilities to maximize its freedom of action in the unpredictable security environment of the future.

Acquiring independent military capabilities offers a country significant advantages. It encourages neighbors to look for diplomatic rather than military solutions to problems, and it makes it easier to find allies, since the overall burden on them is reduced. Independent military capabilities are very costly, however, and countries find it necessary to limit their defense budgets for the sake of economic development. The optimal ROK security policy thus combines limited independent military capabilities, such as Switzerland has, and a continuation of the ROK-U.S. alliance.

For any country, the top security policy goal is to ensure territorial independence and sovereignty. This will be a particular challenge for unified Korea, whose neighbors are the world's most powerful nations. Another security policy priority for unified Korea will be the maintenance of friendly relations with all neighboring states while sustaining a level of military power that will provide deterrence. Maintaining the ROK-U.S. alliance will be another key goal of the defense policy of unified Korea, which will be key not only to unified Korea's security but for that of the region as a whole.

In considering Korea's security needs after unification, I have made use of the following assumptions:

- ROK-led unification will occur sometime before 2030. Regional powers' interests related to North Korea will have been reasonably accommodated in the process.

- Unified Korea will maintain friendly relations with its three neighbors (China, Russia, and Japan) and it will contribute to regional stability by serving as a buffer zone among them. While maintaining an alliance with the United States, unified Korea will focus its efforts post-unification on fully integrating the long-divided societies in the north and the south.

- Relationships among unified Korea's three neighbors will continue to be peaceful and largely cooperative but long-standing territorial, resource, and environmental issues will persist.

- The PRC will attempt to strengthen its overall diplomatic and military position based on its rapid economic development. It will try to exert great influence over the Korean Peninsula and, to that end, will be willing to negotiate with the United States and Japan while seeking strategic ties with Russia.

- Russia will seek to recover its stature as a global superpower. It will also attempt to increase its influence within the region. It will favor peace and stability on the Korean Peninsula as supportive of its efforts for stability and development in Siberia.

- Japan will seek to increase its influence in diplomatic and military spheres commensurate with its economic prowess. As part of this effort, it will strengthen its alliance with the United States to counter the continental powers represented by the PRC and Russia.

- The United States, while maintaining traditional friendly relations with Japan and Korea, will play the role of an active mediator for stability in Northeast Asia, which will also be vital for world peace.

## An "Appropriate" Level of Defense for Unified Korea: Recommendations

What then is the "appropriate" level of military power for a unified Korea? I propose to define it as "the capability to defend most of the nation for one to two months against a conventional military attack from any one neighboring country under any circumstances." Such a level is not absolute. It must be adjusted in a timely way in response to changes in fundamental factors such as the state of the national economy and the ROK-U.S. alliance. It should include the following:

- The primary focus of unified Korea's defense policy should be to deter and defend against a conventional attack. A separate, secondary focus should be to deter and defense against missile and nuclear attack.

- Unified Korea should maintain its tangible combat power capabilities (i.e., hardware) at a relatively low balance vis-à-vis adversaries, while it should dramatically develop its intangible combat power (i.e., software). This will reduce tendencies toward an arms race in the region and maximize the overall balance of unified Korea's combat capabilities.

- The military force structure of the ROK should be reformed along the long-term vision, including by increasing the level of non-enlisted personnel and utilizing civilian employees for some combat service help on a large scale. Also, unified Korea should find the appropriate balance between minimizing the burden of military service on citizens and rebuilding our elite troops at the same time.

The ROK should implement Defense Reform 2020 after adapting it to the long-term vision I have proposed. As noted above, the government will need to obtain public understanding to secure support for the necessary defense budget.

### Balancing Military Hardware and Software

As suggested above, unified Korea will need to achieve the best balance of tangible combat power capabilities or "hardware" and intangible combat power or "software." While it must avoid any absolute inferiority of its tangible forces in various contingencies, I believe it should limit its tangible forces to those required to maintain aggressively defensive operations for one to two months in any conflict with neighboring states. With this in mind, I will first discuss unified Korea's military hardware and then its military software requirements.

Figure 2.11 shows the relationships among five combat functions on the battlefield. In constructing forces, the five functions should be developed harmoniously. Considering the vital role of C2I, however, unified Korea must ensure that it enjoys a solid superiority in those functions. To be able to respond to an opponent, it will of course also need to ensure an appropriate level of capabilities in the maneuver, strike and sustainment functions.

**Figure 2.11 Relationships among Combat Functions**

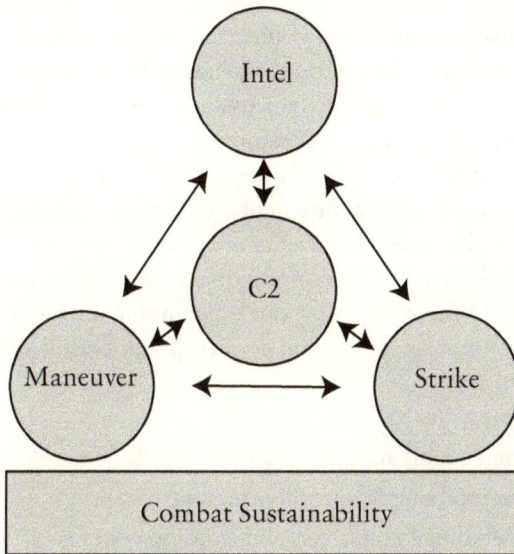

*Source:* Author.

For the intelligence function, unified Korea's focus should be on achieving superior intelligence operating capabilities. While the country will need to acquire independently most of the necessary capabilities, it should also increase interoperability with allied forces to benefit from their intelligence, especially in the areas of strategic and technological information. In addition, linkages between intelligence and C2 systems should be strengthened to lay the foundation for conducting network-centric warfare (NCW).

For the C2 function, the emphasis should be to ensure that unified Korea's decision-making on the battlefield will be more agile than that of its opponent. Korea will need to secure the initiative on the battlefield by developing a mission-oriented command system based on NCW systems.

For the maneuver and strike functions, the focus should be on the coordinated development of maneuverability, terrain acquisition capabilities, and strike capabilities. These measures should be integrated with agility of decision-making to ensure superiority of combat operations. It is important to acquire the capability to force continued attrition and tempo delay on the enemy.

For the sustainability function, unified Korea should put the focus on guaranteeing the survival and activity of its citizenry and combat units. Capabilities to protect basic industry and the populace must be developed, and the timely reinforcement of units, equipment, and materiel must be guaranteed.

Finally, unified Korea must strengthen its deterrence against potential adversaries' use of weapons of mass destruction, including by developing the means and will to retaliate in the event of their use and by encouraging international opinion against their use and possession.

Unified Korea will of course have to creatively apply these concepts and policies regarding its military hardware requirements, taking into account the situation and conditions at the time. However, a unified Korea will likewise need to achieve a dramatic increase in its intangible combat power or military software capabilities. Only in so doing can the country, surrounded as it is by three major powers, overcome its geopolitical vulnerability. It should focus on four key factors:

1.  Enhancing public support for security policies
2.  Nurturing outstanding, expert human resources
3.  Developing Korea-oriented operations theories and systems
4.  Improving unit and personnel education and training systems

The public's willingness to shoulder the financial and manpower service burdens of national security is of critical importance. Public support can be strengthened by civic education about history and security that places emphasis on liberal democracy, national identity, and independence.

Among human resources, the development of an officer corps with outstanding expertise in military operations should be of foremost concern. Successful examples include Germany, Israel, Switzerland, and the United States. Efforts are needed to develop and enhance systems to recruit, develop and manage capable personnel. To avoid discontentment among other regular officers, the current social welfare and professional development programs for them should be improved and everyone must enjoy equal opportunities.

It is also important to develop operations theories and systems that take fully into account the uniqueness of the future situation on the Korean Peninsula and that are adaptable to continuing changes in that situation. This can be done by promoting the use of case studies in military education courses that encourage creative thinking and by improving combat development systems.

Improving education and training systems will help to ensure excellence and rapid response in actual combat. The budget for education and training must be increased, and individuals and units must be assigned to more education and training programs.

I believe that mid- to long-term projects designed to develop such intangible capabilities must be launched in earnest as soon as possible. This is not just the most credible—in fact, it is the only—course of action to ensure Korea's sovereignty and independence in the unpredictable security environment of the future.

## Conclusion

Northeast Asia is assuming a larger role in the international arena as its population grows and its share of the global economy and global trade expands.

While economic cooperation within the region is also increasing, the countries of Northeast Asia remain divided by differences over history, territory, and resources. In recent years, they have increasingly participated in an arms race.

Within the region, the North Korean situation poses an acute security risk. Major change in North Korea is widely viewed as being inevitable—most likely it will be sudden, dramatic change—due to the country's shortage of food, oil, and other basic necessities and its inability to operate a self-sufficient economy. The regime faces a dilemma. To promote economic growth, it must implement major reforms and open up to the outside world, but it fears that doing so would risk internal instability as the people are exposed to outside information. To try to overcome this dilemma, the regime is likely to take radical steps. In this context, the ROK-U.S. alliance's efforts to deter North Korean provocations and aggression have never been more necessary.

Crisis in North Korea! What form will it take? How will it develop? How will North Korea's neighbors react? How destabilizing will it be to Northeast Asia? How serious will be the conflict? These are not just Korean or even regional but also global concerns. In the global effort to peacefully resolve the situation, the ROK must maintain strong military capabilities to play the role expected of it.

After the crisis in North Korea has been successfully managed and the interests of the concerned powers have been accommodated, the opportunity for the peaceful reunification of Korea will arise. Unified Korea will contribute significantly to peace and stability in the region by overcoming the societal differences between the people of northern and southern Korea and by cooperating with neighboring countries.

The state of unified Korea's military capabilities will have a significant influence on the stability of Northeast Asia. If the regional powers regard unified Korea as militarily weak, they will engage in a power struggle with one another for hegemony on the peninsula, destabilizing the region. For the sake not only of Korea but for regional stability as well, unified Korea must maintain sufficient military capabilities to serve as a buffer zone and contribute to the balance of power in the region.

Korea should develop its military capabilities according to a long-term plan that takes into account likely developments in the region. Thus far, the ROK has developed its military capabilities to address the North Korean threat. Henceforth, the ROK should give greater attention to its capacity to manage dramatic change in North Korea, including by enhancing cooperation with neighboring countries. After the crisis in North Korea has been successfully managed, the ROK should rigorously develop a self-defense capability for the post-unification era.

While adjustments to the ROK's existing Defense Reform 2020 plan will be adequate for the short- to mid-term, Korea needs a new long-term strategic vision for the post-unification era, expected to arrive before 2030. I recommend that the vision include:

- An appropriate level of overall military capability, i.e. the capability to defend most of the nation for one to two months against a conventional military attack from any one neighboring country under any circumstances.

- An adequate level of tangible military power, i.e. one that is sufficient to respond to external threats while remaining within national defense budget constraints. In terms of war-fighting functions, Korea should focus on its competitive advantages in an automated C2I system.

- To maximize military capabilities while discouraging a regional arms race and defense budget increases, the ROK needs to promote professionalism in military management or "intangible combat power" by implementing a nationwide project for elite education and professional enhancement.

- A national consensus should be achieved in support of the necessary security budget.

The peace of Northeast Asia depends much more on cooperation among the countries of the region than on military measures. Economic and diplomatic cooperation is vital, and a regional security cooperation organization needs to be established to promote military confidence building. All the countries in the region also need the wisdom to genuinely accept the United States' role in maintaining the regional balance of power and preventing war. Above all, every government and every people in the region needs to understand that war brings devastating losses to all concerned countries and no country ever gains by war. All of us should keep that in mind.

## Notes

1 Europe's historical experience of large-scale warfare—from the religious wars of the sixteenth to seventeenth centuries though World War II—has resulted in a great aspiration for peace there. It is this consensus on which regional security consultation mechanisms such as the North Atlantic Treaty Organization (NATO) are based.

2 Japan's new Basic Policy for National Defense continues to adhere to three principles: an exclusively defense-oriented policy, the need for security arrangements with the United States, and the renunciation of nuclear weapons. However, the new policy is no longer limited to just the defense of Japan; it provides that Japan will expand its role and actively contribute to world peace.

3 The "triad" consists of ICBMs (intercontinental ballistic missiles), SSNs (nuclear submarines), and strategic bombers.

4 Kim Jong Il proclaimed the "military-first policy" to be North Korea's political ideology in the late 1990s. In an international system dominated by imperialism, he argued, socialism and sovereignty can be protected only if the state is based on the military rather than on the working class. In fact, North Korea is no longer a communist state. Rather, it is a distinctly fascist system with a state-controlled economy.

5 Andrei Lankov, professor of Korean history at Kookmin University, Seoul, has frequently commented on North Korean affairs at the DailyNK website ("Andrei Lankov Column") at www.dailynk.com.

6 The Mongol Yuan dynasty in China prevailed on the Korean Koryo dynasty to launch combined expeditions against Japan. Thanks only to a typhoon (the *kamikaze* or "divine wind" of Japanese lore) that decimated the Mongol-Koryo navy during the 1281 invasion, Japan was spared Mongolian rule.

7 In addition to devastating the Korean Peninsula, with great loss of life, the Japanese invasion eventually led to the collapse of the Toyotomi regime in Japan and the weakening of the Ming dynasty in China and its replacements by the Qing.

8 As a result of Japan's victory in these two wars, Korea lost its independence and Japan was set in earnest on a militaristic course that led to the Sino-Japanese War and its ultimate defeat in the Pacific War.

# SOUTH KOREAN AND U.S. POLICY TOWARD NORTH KOREA: A STRATEGY FOR TWO CRISES

## Jongseok Lee

North Korea (the Democratic People's Republic of Korea, or DPRK) presents two contradictory images to the outside world. On the one hand, it is a small and poor country. Its economy is less than 0.05 percent that of the United States and it suffers from severe chronic food shortages. On the other hand, North Korea is also a dangerous country, threatening world peace by developing nuclear weapons. These two images reflect different aspects of the North Korean reality, aspects now dynamically emerging as simultaneous threats to the international community.

Contrary to the self-image portrayed in its own propaganda, much of the international community regards North Korea as a troublemaker engaged in reckless behavior. Among other things, outsiders point to the human rights situation inside the country and the regime's illicit activities to earn hard currency. Above all, of course, North Korea's nuclear problem has contributed to its notorious image abroad and poses the most severe threat to the international community.

However, the nuclear issue has complex roots and will not likely be resolved for some time to come. In the meantime, the recent emergence of a full-fledged systemic crisis in North Korea may well mean that the international community will soon no longer be able to regard the nuclear problem as the sole crucial North Korean issue.

Until recently, North Korea's "systemic crisis" meant only the collapse of its economy due to the functional paralysis of its planned socialist economy and the ensuing famines and food shortages. North Korean absolutist leader Kim Jong Il's (Kim Chŏng-il) apparent stroke in August 2008, however, exposed another potential systemic crisis—its leadership vulnerability.[1] Now two systemic crises, economic *and* political, overlap. History indicates the correctness of the traditional belief that chronic economic crises inevitably weaken leaders and, over the long run, frequently contribute to regime change. In addition, in North Korea today, Kim Jong Il's stroke has exposed the vulnerability of the succession system there, i.e., the lack of a designated successor. In the event of Kim Jong Il's early death or incapacitation, the vulnerability means that political instability will very likely occur.

The range of possible political instability in North Korea includes the complex and extremely dangerous scenario of regime change, which could have severe negative consequences for Northeast Asia, no less so than the North Korean nuclear issue. Given the gravity of the situation, the time has come for the international community to address simultaneously the nuclear issue and the North Korean systemic crisis in order to stabilize North Korea.

In sum, the international community, led by the United States and the countries of Northeast Asia, must seek to achieve two goals simultaneously—the denuclearization of North Korea and the maintenance of political stability there. Unfortunately, the policies needed to achieve the two goals may partially conflict. It is thus all the more important that the international community coordinate to accomplish both goals, especially by establishing an overall strategic framework for dealing with the challenges North Korea poses.

The brunt of the burden will fall on the shoulders of South Korea and the United States, the two countries that have played major roles in dealing with North Korea in the post-Cold War period. American leadership is especially important in dealing with the North Korean nuclear issue. The administration of President George W. Bush pursued a unilateral, inflexible diplomacy toward North Korea without an overall strategy taking into account the complexity of the issues. The Bush administration classified North Korea as a member of the "axis of evil"; it cut off direct dialogue with the regime and attempted to further isolate it. Contrary to the intent of U.S. policy, North Korea actually speeded up its efforts to acquire nuclear weapons during the eight years of the Bush administration. It produced four times as much fissile material as it had previously made and ultimately tested two nuclear devices.[2]

The Obama administration offers hope for a more effective approach toward North Korea. Reacting directly to the Bush administration's missteps, President Obama has championed engagement to deal with the North Korean nuclear issue. This presents a new opportunity to develop appropriate strategies to deal with both the North Korean nuclear problem and the regime's systemic crisis.

Since the inauguration of South Korean President Lee Myung-bak in February 2008 and his administration's approach to North Korea, one at odds with the Obama administration, inter-Korean relations have deteriorated. As a result, North Korea announced that it regarded all previous inter-Korean political and military agreements as nullified. It blamed the "South Korean conservative authorities' reckless moves to escalate the confrontation with DPRK."[3] The historical fact that the earlier improvement in inter-Korean relations facilitated progress in negotiations on the North Korean nuclear program and bolstered peace on the Korean Peninsula underlines the need for urgent efforts to transform the current inter-Korean situation from conflict to cooperation. Moreover, now is the time for South Korea to take the initiative on North Korean issues. The South Korean government needs to develop a new strategy while it still has time to do so.

As noted, with North Korea's increased vulnerability and changes of government in both the United States and South Korea, a new strategy is needed to transform the challenges posed by the current situation from crisis to opportunity. This chapter focuses on shaping the strategic directions of the United States and South Korea to meet the two challenges of North Korea's nuclear weapons development and its internal systemic crisis. Specifically, it describes North Korea's crisis, analyzes the means to deal with it, and considers the future of North Korea. It then examines the North Korean nuclear issue, which stands at a crossroads between peaceful resolution and catastrophe. It concludes with a discussion of strategic goals, principles, and directions, and recommendations to the United States for a policy to achieve North Korea's denuclearization.

## The Deepening Crisis in North Korea

### Battered Economy and Self-Rescue Efforts

The North Korean economy has deteriorated to the point that it threatens the very basis of the regime. The planned socialist economy has collapsed due to the exhaustion of domestic resources and management failures. The factory utilization rate has fallen to as low as 20–30 percent. Except for food, most state rations to the people—symbolic of the socialist system—have been stopped. Since the country suffers from a chronic large-scale food shortage, even food rations are now only partially and intermittently distributed. As a result, hunger has prevailed throughout the country since the mid-1990s, even with outside food assistance. North Korea's gross domestic product (GDP) does not even reach $10 billion, no more than 1 percent of that of South Korea.[4] Of course, North Korea's economic difficulties derive fundamentally from the country's ineffective political and economic system.

To cope with the economic crisis, North Korean authorities in 2002 carried out the July 1 Economic Management Improvement Measures, adjusting wages and prices in an effort to stabilize the economy. The reforms, however, have not resulted in discernible economic progress, perhaps in part, at least, due to increased international isolation as a result of the nuclear crisis. It thus remains debatable whether the steps represented a real change of economic strategy.[5] Seeing the food shortage as a crucial challenge to their regime, North Korean leaders have publicly declared that addressing "the food problem" is their top economic goal and, indeed, they have made every effort to solve it. In the absence of fundamental reform, however, it is difficult to expect a major increase in food production.

At this stage, the food shortage may indeed constitute the most serious threat to the North Korean regime. In exchange for absolute loyalty to the "Dear Leader" (*ch'inae hanŭn chidoja*), the expectation among North Koreans is for a "people's life without lack of food."[6] The anomaly between, on the one hand, a cult of leadership that portrays the top leader as almost omniscient and omnipotent, and a dire food shortage on the other, must be all too clear, despite the lack of free speech in North Korea.

The North Korean regime has defended itself by declaring that the economic difficulties stem from the need to bolster national defense in response to U.S. military moves and economic blockade. Ever fewer North Koreans, however, believe such propaganda. The people have also been losing faith in the ruling ideology of *juche (chuch'e)*, or national self-reliance. The regime had to relax its system of social control considerably from the mid-1990s, when hundreds of thousands of people starved to death. The social control system, based on ideological education and the "unity of the people," is no longer working properly. To meet the new vulnerabilities or challenges, the regime is practicing "military-first politics" (*sŏn'gun chŏngch'i*). The North Korean military is now deeply involved in state operations; it is also being used to enforce social discipline and cope with economic difficulties.

On the other hand, the severe economic difficulties have resulted in an unintentional expansion of the market and broader recognition of private property. From the mid-1990s, when the state could no longer supply food and most other necessities, the people began illegally to privatize wilderness areas, planting them with corn as a self-rescue measure. Private markets, or *changmadang*, arose across the country as places to trade in daily necessities. The marketplaces have grown quite large, replacing traditional legal "peasant markets" that were held only once every ten days. North Koreans now purchase most necessities at these marketplaces, and many are engaged in businesses involving the markets (which traffic heavily in Chinese-made goods).[7]

The marketplaces have played a major role in helping the North Korean people to survive the direst economic circumstances. They have also caused the North Korean people to be more supportive of a market economy. The North Korean authorities, of course, are watching the markets with apprehension. They are concerned that the markets induce people from all walks of life to engage in business and other antisocialist activities. North Korean leaders face a painful dilemma. They know that earlier economic controls contributed to famine and that the markets are essential to cope with economic difficulties. At the same time, the threat to social control posed by the markets may tempt the authorities to reassert control over the marketplaces. The dilemma remains today, with the authorities constantly trying to strengthen control over the markets but unable to end them.[8]

North Korean leaders also seem to be well aware that the international socialist market no longer exists and that they cannot overcome their economic problems without external assistance. They are concerned, however, about the impact of the liberalism and pluralism that would accompany a market economy. North Korean leaders thus cannot help but agonize over whether to open the door to the outside world, and have wandered along the borderline between reform and the status quo. But the status quo, i.e., maintaining the fundamentals of the existing system, means the same as helplessly awaiting regime death.

After 2000, North Korean leaders seemed interested in a limited development strategy combining the Chinese and South Korean models. What North Korean leaders clearly thirst for is a development policy that would allow the coexistence of a market economy and the current political system. In other words, North Korean leaders would like to see a gradual expansion of the market economy while the dictatorship of the Communist Party, specifically the Kim Jong Il regime, continues to function as in the past.

Like China, North Korea has a socialist system in which the Communist Party exclusively controls the entire society. Like South Korea, North Korea is a middle-sized country with a (potentially) excellent labor force but lacking in natural resources. Both South Korea and China have used industrial complexes and special economic zones as hubs for growing their national economies in the primary stage of development.

North Korean leaders seem eager to learn about the Chinese example of economic development while maintaining the dictatorship of the Communist Party. At the same time, they seem to want to copy aspects of the South Korean model, in which authoritarian leader Park Chung-hee (Pak Chŏng-hŭi) successfully led a state-initiated planned economy. Kim Jong Il thus unofficially twice visited representative sites of reform and opening in

China, in 2001 and 2006,[9] including Shanghai. In 2002, a group led by Jang Song Thaek (Chang Sŏng-t'aek), Kim Jong Il's brother-in-law and the first vice director of the Workers Party of Korea, toured South Korean industrial complexes. Also in 2002, the Presidium of the Supreme People's Assembly of North Korea issued a decree establishing the Shinuiju (Sinŭiju) special administrative region, a special economic zone, and adapted supporting legislation.[10] In cooperation with South Korea, North Korea constructed the Kaesong (Kaesŏng) industrial complex and has been operating it since 2003. North Korea also agreed with South Korea to develop a special economic zone in Haeju in western North Korea during the inter-Korean summit talks in October 2007.

Since the eruption of the second North Korea nuclear crisis in October 2002, however, North Korean leaders seem to have drifted away from further consideration of such economic development models. With their thinking having been premised on an inflow of external capital and the opening of areas in North Korea near the demilitarized zone (DMZ) or on the coast, North Korean leaders presumably feel they are no longer in a position to promote development due to an unfavorable external environment, including increased military tensions and economic sanctions. Under the current circumstances, even if they were to adopt such development models, North Korean leaders realize they would not be able to promote them effectively until major progress, at least, was made toward resolving the North Korean nuclear issue.

### Leadership Vulnerability

The most conspicuous characteristic of North Korea's polity and society is its monolithic system, which places a "Dear Leader" holding absolute power at the center of all state of affairs and the people's lives. The system has profoundly influenced North Korea's entire society. While it ensured political stability and continuity through the leadership of the Dear Leader and the existence of his successor, economic collapse weakened the Dear Leader and caused a loosening of social control. Making matters worse, the lack of a clearly designated successor after Kim Jong Il's near-fatal stroke in August 2008 clearly underlined the weakness in the North Korean leadership system.

In North Korea's monolithic system, all parts of the state and society are organized around the leader, analogous to the planets in the solar system revolving around the sun. The system is based on the monolithic ideology, the *juche* idea, and an extreme cult of personality around the Dear Leader. Although North Korea calls its system socialism, it is actually a patriarchal state that is a magnified image of the traditional East Asian family. Indeed, the state portrays itself as an extended family. Trusting and following the Dear Leader is the most important virtue, much like each member of a family must trust and obey the patriarch. The state is also sometimes compared to a human body, in which all the organs work together harmoniously for the good of the whole. The Dear Leader is depicted as the body's brain and the people as the limbs that play their roles in accordance with the brain's direction. The people therefore must display loyalty and filial piety toward the Dear Leader.[11] It is thus not possible to describe North Korea without focusing on the Dear Leader.

This extreme patriarchal, monolithic system has ruled North Korean society for more than four decades, ever since its establishment in 1967. Recently, as noted, the system has weakened as skepticism about the Dear Leader has increased in the wake of chronic food shortages and even famine. Nevertheless, the system still rules the entire society of North Korea.

With Kim Jong Il having wielded exclusive power in North Korea, there is no person or entity—the one officially called the "successor"—who can substitute for him in the event of his sudden death or incapacitation. The role and function of the successor makes the North Korean succession system unprecedented and unique. According to North Korean ideologues, the successor must engage in severe, long-term training to acquire all manner of skills needed to lead the state system, including managing the immediate aftermath of the Dear Leader's death. Kim Jong Il himself prepared to become the successor from 1974 until 1994, when he took office on the death of his father, Kim Il Sung. Of concern here, however, is that until recently (February 2009) there was no indication that a successor had been designated in North Korea, much less that he was being trained.

The Dear Leader's sudden departure from the scene without his successor being in place would therefore likely result in significant confusion and uncertainty. Combined with a battered economy and the presence of 1.1 million soldiers suddenly without a supreme commander, political succession in North Korea could result in severe instability. If this occurs when the North Korean nuclear issue remains unresolved, it is very likely to make the North Korean situation extremely complicated and cause considerable instability in Northeast Asia as a whole.

Such scenarios are premised on the sudden death or incapacitation of Kim Jong Il. However, Kim Jong Il still lives and reportedly is to some extent performing his duties.[12] It is clear that, as long as he is alive and not incapacitated, the domestic situation in North Korea will remain as stable as such a system can be.

What we should pay attention to at this point is that Kim's stroke seems likely to have prompted him to advance the succession project to prepare for his sudden disappearance from the scene. In fact, Kim should already have completed preparations for the succession according to the successor theory laid out by the regime's ideologues.

In view of the characteristics of North Korea's political structure and the successor theory, preparation for the succession will progress focusing on Kim Jong Il's sons. Kim has three acknowledged sons. His oldest son is 37-year-old Kim Jong Nam, born to his late first wife. Kim has two more sons in their late 20s by his late second wife. In 2005, there were moves within the military to support one of Kim's two younger sons as the successor. Kim, however, stopped such moves. Why did he do so, in spite of he himself having been involved in the affairs of the Workers' Party of Korea (WPK) when he was only 25? Perhaps he felt that North Korea's situation was too unfavorable—seriously deteriorated in comparison with the time of his own preparations to succeed Kim Il Sung—to initiate the succession project at the time. In any event, it is likely that he wished to promote the succession project after reviving the economy and resolving the nuclear issue. His sudden illness, however, has changed the situation.

### The Outlook for North Korea after Kim Jong Il

Although North Korean propaganda asserts that the people are overcoming the country's economic difficulties under the Dear Leader's guidance, the reality is that North Korea's current situation is disastrous and, unless serious reforms are implemented, its prospects are also bleak. As long as Kim Jong Il is in power, however, political change cannot be expected. Moreover, Kim's charisma within North Korea and his control of the levers of power also make regime change unlikely. On Kim's departure, however, the situation in North Korea is likely to be different. When Kim does die or becomes incapacitated, uncertainty will likely characterize the situation in North Korea. Of course, if Kim lives long enough to be able to complete the succession process, the uncertainty will be reduced. But the earlier his departure, the greater will be the risk of an internal crisis in North Korea.[13]

As a consequence of his stroke, Kim may wish to promote the succession process in accordance with the "succession system" he himself established. He will probably choose his successor among his sons, most likely one of his two younger sons.[14] It is not clear, however, whether the succession process will succeed. Compared to the period when Kim Jong Il himself emerged as the successor to his father, the situation in North Korea now is extremely bad. Kim's successor will face numerous many high hurdles, including food shortages and economic collapse, the nuclear issue and diplomatic isolation, and the country's absolute inferiority in terms of national power when compared with South Korea. In any event, there may simply not be enough time to fully implement the succession system before Kim departs the scene.

Even if instability surrounding the succession is limited, the new North Korean leadership will be severely tested, owing to the structural problems in North Korea's system and the exhaustion of its domestic resources

Experts have speculated about the consequences if Kim departs the scene soon, leaving no successor or only an unprepared successor. Some anticipate that the military will take power. Others suggest that the military and the bureaucracy will form a collective leadership. Another group of experts believes that a previously designated son of Kim will succeed him.

Among the North Korean cadres, WPK Director Jang Song Thaek seems likely to play a major role in the succession process. Jang enjoys a unique position in this patriarchal state because his wife, Kim Kyong Hui (Kim Kyŏng-hŭi), also a WPK director, is Kim Jong Il's younger sister. Jang thus wields considerably more influence than any other cadre. Although it is inconceivable that Jang himself will emerge as the successor, he will probably try to unite the WPK core group behind Kim's family.

North Korea after Kim is likely to take one of two paths. Political instability could mean regime collapse and a vicious cycle of turmoil and political struggle, or there could be a successful succession resulting in political-social stability. If there is a successful succession, the new leadership, whether a new Dear Leader or a collective leadership, will likely pursue a policy of reform and opening similar to that of China in the 1980–1990s. North Korea's regime after Kim will have a broader range of foreign and domestic policy choices, because the new leadership will be less constrained by Kim Jong Il's policies and dogma.

It is of course possible that some within the leadership may continue to adhere to Kim Jong Il's policies in the initial stages of a new government. It is highly probable, however, that the new leaders will soon turn to a policy of reform and opening, because they will almost certainly realize that the regime cannot survive indefinitely under the existing system owing to the exhaustion of the country's internal resources.

How, then, will the departure of Kim Jong Il affect the situation on the Korean Peninsula and in Northeast Asia? If the succession is successful and domestic stability preserved, the situation will be relatively manageable for South Korea and North Korea's other neighbors. If not, the situation for North Korea's neighbors will be worse than during Kim's period of leadership. Nations sharing a border with North Korea will be concerned about the possibility of enormous inflows of refugees from North Korea. Also, lacking a supreme commander, there may be violent conflict among military factions within North Korea. Outside intervention to bring the situation under control may not be possible due to the continuing existence of massive military forces in North Korea. The result would be a significant rise in tensions on the Korean Peninsula and throughout Northeast Asia.

The nuclear problem is the overriding concern. If the North Korean nuclear issue remains unresolved during the North Korean succession, the outside world will likely be deeply concerned about the status of North Korea's nuclear weapons. If an extremely bellicose faction, intent on keeping nuclear weapons permanently or even on trading them to terrorists or actually using them, gained control over the North's nuclear weapons, the United States and North Korea's neighbors would feel a profound sense of crisis.

## The North Korean Nuclear Issue at a Crossroads

Among all the challenges posed by North Korea, its nuclear program constitutes the most urgent threat to international peace. North Korea appears to have developed nuclear weapons since the 1980s to supplement its declining conventional military strength. When North Korea first began to construct nuclear power plants, it publicly proclaimed its right to enjoy the peaceful uses of atomic energy. The collapse not long thereafter of the USSR, which had supplied North Korea with its initial nuclear technology and thus had a responsibility to monitor North Korea's compliance with international non-proliferation agreements, provided the North with a favorable opportunity to expand the scope of its nuclear activities and develop nuclear weapons.[15] At the time, U.S. influence was minimal due to its extremely hostile relationship with North Korea.

Ultimately, however, North Korea had no choice but to undertake negotiations with the United States due to U.S.-led international countermeasures against its nuclear program, including economic sanctions, diplomatic isolation, and military pressure. North Korea has long remained ambivalent about nuclear weapons. It entered into three agreements[16] to resolve the nuclear problem, only to trample those agreements when it conducted its first test of a nuclear device in 2006.

Will North Korea, then, never abandon its nuclear weapons no matter what it may be offered in exchange? How does North Korea's economic crisis affect the nuclear issue? When and how can we determine conclusively North Korea's intentions regarding nuclear weapons?

We can infer North Korea's intention to denuclearize from an analysis of its tactics. Logically, there are three possible hypotheses about North

Korea's intentions: it may seek continued possession of nuclear weapons; it may aim to abandon nuclear weapons; or its intentions may depend on the circumstances it faces.

Hypothesis I is that it was North Korea's goal from the outset to possess nuclear weapons as a means to ensure its survival. Thus, it would not abandon them under any circumstances. This argument, which we shall call "survival tactics," is advanced mainly by skeptics of North Korea's intentions. It cannot, however, explain why North Korea's possession and test of nuclear devices did not occur during the Clinton presidency. Rather, they occurred after North Korea lifted the freeze on its plutonium program as a consequence of its conflict with the Bush administration over the uranium enrichment issue. Hypothesis I is thus inadequate to explain North Korea's intentions.

Hypothesis II is that North Korea has already decided to give up nuclear weapons in exchange for compensation and is only playing a game to maximize the gains from an eventual settlement with the United States. However, this hypothesis, which we will call the "gains-maximizing tactics," is unable to explain extreme North Korean behavior such as conducting nuclear tests. Such provocative behavior seems to go beyond the realm of mere tactics to maximize gains in eventual negotiations. This hypothesis thus also seems to be an inadequate explanation of North Korean intentions.

Hypothesis III is that North Korea's ultimate decision will depend upon the circumstances. In other words, North Korea has pursued "either-or tactics" since the signing of the Agreed Framework with the United States in 1994. According to this hypothesis, which we shall call "opportunistic tactics," North Korea will abandon nuclear weapons if compensation is sufficient but will not if the proffered compensation is insufficient, particularly in the absence of international solidarity for the denuclearization of North Korea. Given the development of the North Korean nuclear issue since 1994, which has been characterized by the reaching of agreements and deviations from them, North Korea seems to have been pursuing this tactic.

To reiterate, North Korea seems to have pursued opportunistic tactics, and will possess or abandon nuclear weapons depending on the circumstances. We therefore need to take measures that will increase the probability that North Korea will denuclearize, rather than draw an absolute conclusion now as to whether North Korea will or will not discard nuclear weapons.

In seeking to increase the probability that North Korea will decide to discard nuclear weapons, we need to focus on Kim Jong Il's Achilles heel. Kim Jong Il's greatest concern now must be to orchestrate a successful succession. The key to that is a favorable economic and political environment, and only North Korea's abandonment of nuclear weapons would lead to such an environment.

North Korea appears to be standing at a crossroads. It needs to choose whether it will seek economic resurrection or continued possession of nuclear weapons. North Korea's core leadership itself may not know what to choose. Whether North Korea decides to abandon nuclear weapons may depend less on North Korea's intentions now than on the degree of effort by the United States, which has the most influence on the nuclear issue, to shape North Korea's decision.

In conclusion, it is logical to make continued efforts to denuclearize North Korea. There is still clearly a high probability that North Korea can be induced to abandon nuclear weapons if the United States demonstrates leadership by adopting wise policies to increase cooperation among the Six Parties.

We have not yet reached a "moment of truth"—a crossroads or point in time where we have been able to definitively just whether or not North Korea will abandon its nuclear weapons. However, it seems possible to reach such a decisive moment by pursuing a "concentrated approach." By concentrated approach I mean the United States and the other Six-Party participants focusing their attention consistently on the North Korean nuclear issue— something requiring firm policy goals and sophisticated policy direction.

## A Strategic Framework

### Strategic Goals and Existing Agreements

In establishing a strategy, it is important to be clear about its goals and principles.

First, the goal of the strategy for the North Korean nuclear issue, which is also the raison d'être of the Six-Party Talks, must of course be the verifiable denuclearization of North Korea. Like its predecessors, the Obama administration has expressed its strong intention to achieve North Korea's denuclearization.

Recent remarks by some U.S. officials,[17] however, may have given the false impression to North Korea and others that the United States might be prepared to accept North Korea's possession of nuclear weapons. Such statements are harmful because they seem to lend credence to the belief of some that the United States is actually more interested in nonproliferation than in North Korea's denuclearization. In other words, they believe that the United States might be willing to accept North Korea's possession of some nuclear weapons in exchange for guarantees that it will not transfer nuclear materials and technology abroad. The United States government needs to under-line, in clear and consistent language, the absolute importance it attaches to the denuclearization of North Korea. Press leaks and statements that give rise to misunderstanding and concern need to be prevented.

To denuclearize North Korea, it is important to make clear to the people of the United States and South Korea the opportunity costs their countries will incur if North Korea is not denuclearized. It is also very important that the two allies consistently pursue a policy to manage and eventually resolve the North Korean nuclear issue.

Second, another goal of South Korea and the United States must be to stabilize North Korea and thus also induce it to become a less dangerous state. In other words, despite North Korea's systemic and succession crises, South Korea and the United States need to encourage it to follow the path of reform and opening. To reiterate, increased instability in North Korea will constitute a danger not only on the Korean Peninsula but also to all of Northeast Asia, whether it occurs during Kim Jong Il's rule or thereafter. South Korea and the United States need to find measures to reduce the risk of instability in North Korea, particularly after Kim's departure from the scene.

Meanwhile, at this point, the United States and South Korea do not need to agonize about developing a new strategic roadmap for North Korea's de-nuclearization. They already have the Six-Party Talks framework and agree-ments reached there, including the joint statement (September 19, 2005), the initial actions agreement (February 13, 2007), and the second phase actions for the implementation of the joint statement.

To address North Korea's internal crises, there already exist the joint communiqué between the United States and the DPRK of October 2000 and the September 19 joint statement. The joint communiqué in particular provides for high-level bilateral contacts, which might make a breakthrough toward the elimination of North Korea's nuclear weapons.[18]

As for inter-Korean relations, there are important agreements such as the South-North joint declaration (June 15, 2000), the joint declaration (Oc-tober 4, 2007), and the inter-Korean Basic Agreement of 1991. These agree-ments contain provisions to promote inter-Korean peace and economic co-operation, which, if implemented, would greatly encourage North Korea's reform and opening.

The United States does not need to establish new goals or a new strategy toward North Korea. Instead, it should faithfully implement existing agree-ments and work patiently to transform existing, abstract agreements into more concrete forms. The existing agreements already provide a basic roadmap to achieve North Korea's denuclearization and the measures to deal with North Korea's internal crises.

### Principles for Policy Implementation:
### Lessons from the Bush Administration

To achieve the two basic goals of stabilizing North Korea and inducing it to denuclearize, a few key principles of policy implementation need to be applied. The Bush administration's trials and errors in dealing with North Korea highlight the need to pay particular attention to three principles: policy consistency, policy prioritization, and direct dialogue.

These principles are almost matters of common sense. A policy, once established, needs to be pursued consistently and agreements reached with other governments need to be faithfully carried out, even if a change of administration occurs. If we have a number of issues with a particular country, we need to deal first with the most urgent and important problems. If we want to obtain something important from an antagonist, we need to talk directly.

The Bush administration, however, did not follow these fundamental principles. As a result, it failed to earn the trust of its allies as well as those of other concerned countries. Ultimately, it was unable to deter North Korea from testing a nuclear device. It is thus worthwhile to review the Bush administration's North Korea policy to avoid repeating its mistakes.

If a new incoming administration unilaterally invalidates existing agreements with other countries, it will lose credibility, especially with adversaries. Even if it ultimately sits down again at the negotiating table, the other party will not find it easy to trust the new government. The situation is even worse when one administration frequently contradicts its own policies and agreements.

The new Bush administration completely repudiated the Clinton administration's North Korea policy, a phenomenon commonly referred to as "anything but Clinton" (ABC). This happened only a matter of months after the 2000 joint communiqué between the United States and the DPRK that promised "to take steps to radically improve the bilateral relations" between Washington and Pyongyang. Then, in January 2002, President Bush included North Korea in the "axis of evil" in contradiction to the 2000 joint communiqué's provision that the "two governments entertain no hostile intentions toward each other." It is remarkable that the Bush administration denied prior U.S. agreements with North Korea even though North Korea had not violated those agreements. The Bush administration's ABC approach naturally cost it all credibility with North Korea, and subsequently

North Korea's behavior only worsened.

The Bush administration also erred in contradicting another important agreement at a critical moment, in this case even before the ink on the agreement had dried. In the Six-Party Joint Statement (September 19, 2005), the United States and North Korea agreed to take steps to normalize their relations and promote trade and investment. Almost simultaneously, however, the United States Treasury Department imposed financial sanctions on North Korea, accusing it of having used the Macau-based Banco Delta Asia (BDA) to engage in money laundering and the distribution of counterfeit U.S. currency, or supernotes. The policy contradiction made many experts outside the United States doubt that the Bush administration genuinely sought to denuclearize North Korea. Although already largely forgotten today, the BDA problem demonstrates how irresponsible leadership can result in a superpower bungling a vitally important task. The policy contradiction jeopardized implementation of the September 19, 2005 Joint Statement, infuriated North Korea, and eventuated in North Korea's test of a nuclear device.[19]

The BDA episode illustrates the importance of clearly prioritizing the nuclear problem as the most important and immediate North Korea issue, and then acting consistently in accordance with such prioritization. There are of course many other "North Korea problems," including human rights and illicit activities, and they must be addressed. It is important, however, to categorize North Korea issues into immediate, mid-term, and long-term tasks.

If we attempt to deal simultaneously with the nuclear issue and other less immediate problems without prioritizing them, the result will be serious confusion and nothing can be accomplished. We must ensure that less immediate tasks do not interfere with the effort to resolve the North Korean nuclear problem.

While many experts and observers regard direct negotiations between adversaries as natural, it is worth underlining the importance of direct contacts because the issue has been controversial in the United States. Most notably, in the 2008 U.S. presidential campaign, Democratic candidate Barack Obama engaged in a fierce debate with Republican candidate John McCain about the issue. While Obama firmly supported direct talks with adversaries without preconditions, McCain argued that direct contacts served only to legitimize rogue states and their misbehavior. As Obama correctly pointed out in the presidential debates, however, until 2006 the Bush administration had largely refused direct talks with North Korea and had instead attempted to isolate it. This resulted only in an acceleration of North Korea's efforts to acquire nuclear weapons. Thus, we need to make clear that we engage with North Korea not because we trust it but precisely because we do not.[20]

It is very important to pursue consistently the principle of direct negotiations with North Korea. Particularly in the present stalemate, the Obama administration needs to use high-level bilateral contacts to break the deadlock in the negotiations on North Korea's denuclearization.

We are now witnessing the magnitude of the opportunity costs—including North Korea's nuclear test—incurred by the Bush administration in rejecting direct talks with North Korea for most of its eight-year tenure. The Bush administration did not make any progress with North Korea until February 13, 2007, when its shift to direct negotiations resulted in that significant agreement.

Until 2006, the Bush and Roh Moo-hyun (No Mu-hyŏn) administrations fundamentally disagreed about policy prioritization and the need for direct U.S.-North Korean talks. Some critics in both South Korea and the United States blamed the Roh administration for the rift, asserting that President Roh attached greater importance to South Korea's bilateral relations with North Korea than he did to ending North Korea's nuclear program. Critics charged that the Roh administration was nationalistic and pro-North Korean, and that it therefore cooperated only halfheartedly with the Bush administration in efforts to eliminate North Korea's nuclear weapons.

In fact, the rift between the two administrations derived primarily from disagreements about the best policy to end North Korea's nuclear program. The Roh administration consistently urged the United States to give top priority to the nuclear problem among the many North Korean issues and to engage in direct talks with the North Koreans without preconditions. The Bush administration responded that direct dialogue with North Korea would only legitimize the regime and its misbehavior and thus send the wrong message to North Korea and the international community. They insisted that human rights and North Korea's illegal activities needed to be addressed at the same time as the nuclear issue.

The U.S.-North Korean agreement of February 13, 2007, represented a 180-degree shift in the Bush administration's approach to North Korea. Thereafter, the Bush and Roh administrations were rarely in conflict over North Korea policy. This fact demonstrates that the earlier divisions between the two countries were not the result of anti-Americanism or pro-North Korean feelings on the part of the Roh administration—but of policy differences between the two governments.[21]

## *Strategic Directions*

To effectively address the North Korean crisis, the United States and South Korea must establish a common strategy and implement it without delay. Some may argue that there is no need to do so now because the situation will not change until Kim Jong Il departs the scene. Even if that may be the case, if we wait until Kim's departure, it will be too late to accomplish our goals. Under a new strategy, a key focus should be to begin now to minimize risk factors that will arise with Kim's departure.

Above all, South Korea and the United States need to provide substantial support for North Korea to pursue an economic development program combining Chinese-style reforms with South Korean know-how. If North Korea does so, it will become more pro-market and also less threatening to the outside world. This will require that South Korea and the United States expand economic cooperation with North Korea and allow international financial institutions to help the country. It is important that North Korea be made to understand as soon as possible that the benefits of reform and opening will far outweigh the disadvantages.

Economic assistance is a very important factor. It will facilitate the marketization of North Korea's failed socialist economy and help to realize humanitarian justice. It will also serve to change popular attitudes and opinions and strengthen the position of those cadres who support reform.

If divisions occur within the new leadership, the outside world should do all that it reasonably can to help moderates take power.

It is also important for the participants in the Six-Party Talks to draw North Korea into a framework of Northeast Asian multilateral cooperation. This will, among other things, help to change the nature of North Korea from that of a rogue state to a normal state. While there is currently no multilateral cooperation organization in Northeast Asia, the Six-Party Talks have provided an important foundation on which to establish such an international regime. The Six Parties, including North Korea, are already committed to joint efforts for lasting peace and stability in Northeast Asia. In the September 19, 2005 Joint Statement, they agreed to explore ways and means to promote security and cooperation. The Six Parties have also agreed that a permanent peace regime on the Korean Peninsula should be negotiated to replace the existing armistice agreement. Furthermore, in their "Initial Actions for the Implementation of the Joint Statement" from February 2007, the Six Parties agreed to establish a working group on the establishment of a Northeast Asian peace and security mechanism.

To prepare for various North Korean contingencies, nothing is more important than implementing existing agreements, regardless of Kim Jong Il's health. Doing so is in the United States' interests, because the agreements provide a means for the United States to participate actively in multilateral cooperation in Northeast Asia even though, geographically, the United States lies outside the region. The Six Parties should therefore map out a multilateral security regime as soon as possible and otherwise strengthen multilateral cooperation. This is an urgent task for the Northeast Asian countries themselves and will greatly facilitate the resolution of North Korean issues.

Resolution of North Korean issues will also require an early improvement in two bilateral relationships: the normalization of diplomatic relations between the United States and North Korea and the development of relations between South and North Korea. Traditionally, the people of North Korea have regarded the United States as an antagonistic superpower bent on wiping out their country, and they have viewed South Korea also as a dangerous adversary. Thus, improving these two bilateral relationships will significantly reduce North Korea's hostility toward the outside world.

If South Korea and the United States have better bilateral relations with North Korea, it will allow them to play more effective roles in emergencies involving North Korea. If, at the time of Kim's departure from the scene, the core North Korean leadership and the people feel that their situation has improved due to better relations with South Korea and the United States, reform-oriented cadres in North Korea will benefit in any domestic political competition. If not, hardliners will be able to play a stronger hand.

It is necessary now to work consistently to improve inter-Korean relations. As history demonstrates, South Korea played a major role as facilitator in the Six-Party Talks due to the leverage it obtained from improved inter-Korean relations. South Korea must play a leading role in maintaining stability on the Korean Peninsula now as well as in the future, particularly in case of an emergency in North Korea.

Improvements in inter-Korean relations clearly have a positive impact on North Korean popular attitudes. A South Korean Ministry of Unification survey of 3,400 North Korean defectors in 2006 examined attitudes about the improvement in inter-Korean relations after 1998. The survey found that North Koreans who regarded South Korea as an enemy had declined from 49.2 percent in 1999 to only 32.8 percent by 2005, while those who viewed South Korea as a friend had increased from 50.8 percent to 67.2 percent.[22]

In the meantime, however, inter-Korean relations have reached a very low point. To resolve the North Korean crises, the Lee administration should immediately adopt a policy of active engagement with North Korea.

It is important to minimize any conflicts between measures intended to achieve our two main goals of resolving the North Korean nuclear problem and addressing North Korea's internal crisis. Fundamentally, we must address both goals simultaneously and ensure that the measures we adopt to achieve them are mutually supportive. It is of course natural that we should focus for the time being on the North Korean nuclear problem. We should, however, not lose sight of the challenge posed to us by North Korea's domestic crisis. To reiterate: our overall strategic framework must include coordinated measures to achieve both goals.

In fact, the measures needed to achieve our two goals need not be contradictory. Our overarching strategic aim is the stabilization and economic recovery of North Korea. However, since our policies toward the North Korean nuclear problem are conditioned on North Korea faithfully meeting its duty to abandon nuclear weapons, contradictions between our two policy goals can arise if North Korea does not meet its denuclearization obligations while the United States and the other four countries in the Six-Party Talks meet theirs. In that case and as long as North Korea remains within the Six-Party Talks framework, the United States and South Korea should employ other strategic means to achieve their goals toward North Korea rather than abandon their own commitments under existing agreements.

The problem is that North Korea might refuse to abandon its nuclear weapons when we arrive at the moment of truth. If so, the United States and the other four countries in the Six-Party Talks will need to take strong and effective countermeasures against North Korea. By having taken in the meantime a concentrated approach, U.S. leadership will have been bolstered and it will play a vital role, particularly in drawing China into a united front to apply sanctions to North Korea. Under these circumstances, the United States and South Korea may no longer be able to make efforts to address North Korea's internal crisis, because almost all options to deal with the nuclear crisis, except military means, should be on the table.[23] Even so, we will need to maintain the strategic flexibility that North Korea's political situation requires so as to address the more fundamental change in North Korea. Consequently we must wisely coordinate the strategic tasks stemming from these two vital issues to accomplish both targets.

### Recommendations to the Obama Administration

Currently, the most urgent North Korean problem is the nuclear issue. Intensive efforts will be required to resolve it due to its deep roots and complicated nature. Above all, U.S. efforts can make the difference between peaceful resolution and catastrophe.

As previously noted, to resolve the North Korean nuclear problem we need to press matters toward a moment of truth, i.e. the point when we will be able to judge definitively if North Korea will abandon nuclear weapons. How can the United States take a concentrated approach toward North Korea? How can the United States achieve an effective consensus with the other four members of the Six-Party Talks and exercise leadership when the moment of truth has been reached?

In this section, I offer recommendations to the Obama administration for a tailored policy toward North Korea. I have already outlined above my basic thinking, including strategic goals, principles and directions. Here I will offer more concrete recommendations drawn from the experience of the Six-Party Talks.

To counter North Korea's strategy, the United States, in negotiating with North Korea, needs to fully grasp the country's peculiar characteristics. The United States also needs to understand the nature of existing agreements with North Korea if it is to adopt a more effective policy. American policy toward the North Korean nuclear program needs to be carefully tailored to these factors.

First, the United States should take a bold approach based on the "action for action" principle. Since nuclear weapons play a crucial role for North Korea, it will not relinquish them before it receives compensation from the United States and the other members of the Six-Party Talks. This was demonstrated by the failure of the Bush administration's policy of providing compensation to North Korea only after its abandonment of nuclear weapons.

The "action for action" principle means that North Korea and the other five members of the Six-Party Talks must meet their obligations toward one another simultaneously. The Six Parties officially agreed to the principle in the September 19, 2005 Joint Statement.

The United States also needs to understand that the measures it and the other four Six-Party countries should take are reversible, while North Korean steps ultimately are not. For example, the United States' removal of North Korea from its terrorism blacklist, the normalization of relations, and economic assistance can all be withdrawn or suspended at any time if North Korea fails to meet its commitment to give up nuclear weapons. Once North Korea has abolished its nuclear weapons program, however, North Korea cannot restore it. This indicates that the "action for action" principle is actually more advantageous to the United States and other Six-Party participants than to North Korea.

Second, the United States needs to avoid making ambiguous agreements with North Korea. It should use bilateral contacts with North Korea within the Six-Party Talks framework to clarify agreements on the North Korean nuclear problem.

Negotiating with North Korea, unlike friendly countries, is a very delicate matter. Agreements with North Korea must be spelled out in the clearest possible language. The United States should avoid situations in which it will later have to contend with North Korea over the interpretation of an agreement.

It is important to recall that North Korea, skilled at finding pretexts to deviate from agreements, has taken advantage of ambiguous language to do just that, especially from agreements with South Korea and the United States. Of course, negotiations with a difficult counterpart such as North Korea inevitably tend to result in ambiguous agreements. However, ambiguity should be avoided if at all possible, and resorted to only if necessary to achieve a breakthrough or avoid catastrophe.

Generally, ambiguity in international agreements is the result of an impatience for results and a desire for domestic political gain. But ambiguity naturally leads to disputes over the interpretation of agreements and complicates further negotiations. Therefore, as parties approach final agreement, the more important it becomes to clarify and eliminate remaining ambiguities.

In negotiations on North Korea's denuclearization, North Korea is on the defensive while the United States is on the offensive. In general, the party on the defensive prefers ambiguity, which offers it an opportunity to back away from an agreement due to a disputed interpretation of its meaning. We have experienced this several times with North Korea.

How can the United States make progress in implementing agreements with North Korea while avoiding protracted disputes over their interpretation? In addition to using only the clearest possible language in agreements with North Korea, the United States needs to confirm the interpretation of agreements between United States and North Korea within the Six-Party Talks.

Even an agreement concluded between only the United States and North Korea needs to be officially confirmed in the Six Party-Talks if it is related to the nuclear problem. Doing so allows all of the Six Parties to know the contents of the agreement and share a common interpretation. Then, if North Korea violates an agreement, the United States in particular will receive strong support from the other participants. The Bush administration's neglect of this essential procedure gave rise to frequent disputes over its agreements with North Korea.[24]

Third, the United States should scrupulously fulfill its commitments to North Korea. This is vital to ensuring that North Korea implements its own commitment to give up nuclear weapons, as it will allow North Korea no excuse to deviate from existing agreements. The Bush administration, however, frequently did not meet its obligations in a timely manner, due primarily to resistance from domestic hard-liners. This provided ready pretexts to North Korea to deviate from its agreements.

In regard to fulfilling its commitments, the United States needs to take a bold approach toward the provision of a light water reactor to North Korea. The United States should make good on its agreement in the September 19, 2005 Joint Statement to "discuss, at an appropriate time, the subject of the provision of light water reactor [sic] to the DPRK." If the United States does so, it will strengthen its leadership in the Six-Party Talks and increase its solidarity with the other four participants to press North Korea to fulfill its commitments to the letter.

The issue of providing North Korea with light water reactors will inevitably emerge as a key problem when the Six-Party Talks resume. As suggested by the text of the September 19, 2005 Joint Statement, North Korea will not easily abandon nuclear weapons unless it receives light water reactors. Moreover, in determining North Korea's ultimate intentions, i.e. to arrive at the "moment of truth," the issue of the provision of light water reactors, along with the normalization of U.S.-DPRK relations, is likely to be key. If the United States refuses to discuss the provision of light water reactors, the United States will be denying the Joint Statement, to which it is a party.

The United States thus needs to agree to implement the provision in the agreement. It should comprehensively review its position on light water reactors. It should, for example, consider whether to resume the terminated, but still salvageable, light water reactor project pursued under the Agreed Framework and examine how the resulting nuclear waste would be disposed. If, however, the United States does not intend to provide a light water reactor to North Korea, it should offer the latter another means of meeting its energy needs within a reasonable period of time. Whether that means conventional power plants or some other energy source, the time has come for the United States to decide its position on the issue.

Fourth, the United States should enhance the role of its new Special Representative for North Korea Policy. While the new administration faces even more acute and significant problems such as Iraq, Iran, and Afghanistan, the North Korean nuclear issue remains a major concern to the United States.[25] It is currently the most important threat to the security of Northeast Asia. In South Korea, the problem not only threatens security but it has produced severe domestic political conflict and hindered economic development. The United States needs to address the North Korean nuclear problem so that it does not suddenly emerge as a major foreign policy crisis. Another North Korean nuclear test, for example, could threaten U.S. diplomatic and strategic arrangements in Northeast Asia.

The Obama administration's decision to create the new position of Special Representative for North Korea Policy to deal exclusively with the North Korean nuclear problem rectified the situation in the Bush administration, in which the Assistant Secretary of State for East Asian and Pacific affairs also served as the chief U.S. negotiator in the Six-Party Talks. The North Korean problem was so time consuming that the assistant secretary found it difficult to deal with other major issues in the region.

The role of the special representative should not be limited to negotiating with North Korea. In fact, what the United States most needs is a policy coordinator. Unlike its status in the Middle East and Pakistan-Afghanistan issues, the United States is a core stakeholder in the North Korean nuclear issue. Coordinating the U.S. response to developments in the Six-Party Talks and to North Korea's violation of agreements requires frequent, major U.S. policy decisions. Over the years, U.S. policy toward North Korea has suffered from interagency disagreement and inadequate internal coordination. Given that the Obama administration has already designated a special representative, it should enhance the role of the position to include not only negotiating with North Korea but also coordinating United States policy toward it.

## Conclusion

As we have seen, the challenges North Korea poses to the international community are gradually becoming even more complicated. The increasing North Korean internal crisis will likely make the situation even more difficult and delicate. While the North Korean nuclear problem remains the most serious issue, the United States and South Korea must establish a strategic framework that deals with both North Korea's internal crisis and the nuclear issue. In this chapter, I have recommended that our strategic goal to accomplish these ends should be North Korea's reform and opening. Specifically, I have recommended that we support a North Korean economic plan that combines China's development model with South Korean know-how.

Regarding the North Korean nuclear issue, I have urged that we take steps to arrive at a moment of truth—the point when we can confirm North Korea's ultimate intentions about the possession of nuclear weapons. Furthermore, I recommended specific policies I believe are required to test North

Korean intentions. I acknowledge that my recommendations are simple, perhaps nothing more than common sense. Unfortunately, the Bush administration took another approach. I argue that we do not need a brilliant new approach but the careful and consistent implementation of a policy based on historical experience and good sense.

If the Obama administration pursues the concentrated approach I have recommended, U.S. leadership toward North Korea will be enhanced and we can proceed quickly toward the moment of truth when the regime's intentions will become clear. If North Korea then does not abandon nuclear weapons, the United States will be able to pursue a much wider range of options to deal with North Korea. Of course, no one can say with confidence that North Korea will ultimately abandon its nuclear weapons ambitions. I believe, however, that it will be very difficult for the regime to retain nuclear weapons if its neighbors and the United States apply pressure based on diplomatic and moral solidarity. The key to resolving the North Korean nuclear problem and meeting the future challenges a distressed North Korea poses will be to pursue a concentrated approach in a strategic framework.

## Notes

1 Steven Erlanger, "Doctor Confirms Kim Jong Il Stroke," *New York Times*, December 12, 2008.

2 "Transcript of first presidential debate," September 26, 2008, http://www.cnn.com/2008/POLITICS/09/26/debate.mississippi.transcript/.

3 Korea Central News Agency, "DPRK to Scrap All Points Agreed with S. Korea over Political and Military Issues," January 30, 2009.

4 Jong Seok Lee, "Re-evaluation of North Korean National Income," *Current Issues and Policies* (2008-3), 2.

5 Un-Chul Yang, "Structural Change of Market and Political Slack in North Korea," in *North Korea in Distress*, edited by Haksoon Paik and Seong-Chang Cheong (Seoul: Sejong Institute, 2008), 61–93.

6 In other words, a standard of living that at least does not mean starvation.

7 Jong Seok Lee, "North Korea's Strategy Transformation toward South Korea," in *Is North Korea Changing?: 1997 vs. 2007*, edited by Seong Chang Cheong (Seoul: Sejong Institute, 2008), 213–218.

8 According to a reliable source, North Korean authorities issued a decree in fall 2008 that strictly regulates marketplaces. Enforcement was to have begun in January 2009 but has been postponed. Research Institute For North Korean Society, *North Korea Today* (260, January 6, 2009), http://goodfriendsusa.blogspot.com/2009/01/north-korea-today-no-260.html.

9 Korea Central News Agency, "Kim Jong Il Pays Unofficial Visit to China," January 20, 2001; Korea Central News Agency, "Kim Jong Il Pays Unofficial Visit to China," January 18, 2006.

10 Korea Central News Agency, "Decree on setting up Sinuiju Special Administrative

Region issued," September 19, 2002; Korea Central News Agency, "Basic Law of Sinuiju Special Administrative Region," September 20, 2002.

11 Jong Seok Lee, *The Understanding of Contemporary North Korea* (Seoul: Yoksabipyongsa, 2000), 216–221.

12 Wang Jiarui, director of the international department of the Chinese Communist Party Central Committee who met Kim Jong Il in January 2009, said that Kim appeared to be in good health during their meeting. Masami Ito, "Kim Jong Il in good health, reports visiting Chinese official," *Japan Times Online*, February 21, 2009.

13 In this chapter, I do not directly address the issue of concrete policies related to the North Korean crisis. Rather, I deal with the strategic direction needed to avoid a North Korean crisis that could result in turmoil on the Korean Peninsula. I will also propose a strategy to take the initiative to successfully manage a major crisis in North Korea.

14 See Seong-Chang Cheong, "Kim Jong Il's Illness and Prospects for Post Kim Leadership," *East Asian Review* 20, no. 4 (Winter 2008).

15 Looking at it from a different perspective, North Korea may have promoted the development of nuclear weapons as a self-rescue measure in response to the collapse of the communist camp.

16 Agreed Framework (1994), September 19 Joint Statement (2005) and February 13 Initial Actions agreement (2007).

17 The following two reports, which described North Korea as a nuclear weapons state, gave rise to confusion and doubt about the United States' will to denuclearize North Korea: U.S National Intelligence Council, *Global Trends 2025: A Transformed World* (Washington, DC: US Government Printing Office, 2008), and Secretary of the Defense Task Force on DOD Nuclear Weapons Management, *Phase II: Review of the DOD Nuclear Mission*, (Washington, DC, December 2008).

18 The Atlantic Council also recommended that the Obama administration reaffirm the "Joint Communiqué." The Atlantic Council of the United States "A New US Diplomatic Strategy toward North Korea," Issue Brief (Washington, DC: February 2009), 5.

19 See Haksoon Paik, "North Korea's Pursuit of Security and Economic Interests: Chasing Two Rabbits with One Stone," in *North Korea in Distress: Confronting Domestic and External Challenges* (Seoul: Sejong Institute, 2008), 121–25.

20 U.S. Asia Pacific Council, "Top Advisors Illuminate the U.S. Presidential Candidates' View on Asia Policy," *Washington Report* 5 (September 2008), 5.

21 Why, then, did the Roh administration adhere so strongly to this policy rather than make concessions to the U.S. perspective? Basically, the Roh administration was confident in the rationale of its policy and concerned that mishandling the North Korean nuclear crisis could lead directly to war.

22 Jong Seok Lee, "North Korea's Strategy Transformation toward South Korea," *Is North Korea Changing?: 1997 vs. 2007* (Seoul: Sejong Institute, October 2008), 214.

23 A military option should not be used because it would very likely trigger war on the Korean Peninsula. Moreover, in an extreme situation, the international community could bring about the gradual collapse of the North Korean regime simply by applying full-scale economic sanctions against it, assuming that the United States policy leadership allows it to take the moral initiative to the extent that China would cooperate.

24 See, for example, the conflict between the United States and North Korea over

the interpretation of the "U.S.- North Korea Understandings on Verification" (October 11, 2008).

25 See Jong Seok Lee, "Why the Obama Administration Should Designate a High Policy Coordinator on the North Korean Nuclear Issue," *Current Issues and Policies* (2009-1).

# SOUTH KOREA'S RELATIONS WITH ITS NEIGHBORS

# CHINA'S PLACE IN
# SOUTH KOREA'S SECURITY MATRIX

## *Jae Ho Chung*

Over the years, many foreign observers have marveled at the pace at which South Korea and China expanded bilateral cooperation in economic, cultural and diplomatic realms. The volume of Sino-South Korean trade increased from $19 million in 1979 to $168 billion in 2008, an 8,859-fold increase over 29 years, and a rate that is virtually unparalleled. Pundits are nearly unanimous in their appraisals of the close level of diplomatic coordination between Seoul and Beijing in coping with the North Korean nuclear problem through the Six-Party Talks framework since 2003.[1] Nearly six million people visited between China and South Korea in 2007. And, as of 2008, 830 flights linked the two countries on a weekly basis. Furthermore, South Koreans account for the largest number of foreign students in China while Chinese take up the lion's share (78 percent) of foreign students residing in South Korea.[2]

Behind such sustained cooperation, close coordination and frequent exchanges lay the rise of mutually positive and favorable perceptions between South Korea and China for much of the last three decades. Cultural affinities are often mentioned as an important factor in drawing South Koreans and Chinese closer by way of cultural phenomena like the "Korean wave" (*hanliu*) and "China fever" (*hwap'ung*).[3] Growing mutual benefits reaped from close economic cooperation further reinforced these mutually positive views. Unlike Japan, Taiwan and Australia, until recently South Korea has rarely expressed security-related concerns regarding the rise of China. In fact, during President Lee Myung-bak's (Yi Myŏng-bak) state visit to China in late May 2008, South Korea and China even agreed to upgrade the bilateral relationship from a "*comprehensive* cooperative partnership" to a "*strategic* cooperative partnership" in efforts to move it beyond economic and diplomatic cooperation.[4]

Where, then, is China currently placed in South Korea's security matrix? In order to answer this complex question, it is first necessary to make the following observations. Irrespective of ongoing debates on offensive or defensive realism or on soft power, neighbors that share history and borders with China are bound to be wary of China's ascent.[5] Or, if realism is any practical guide at all to understanding international politics, being wary of an emerging great power has been a norm for enhancing national security in the self-help system of anarchy. For geopolitical reasons, the rise of China became manifest in East Asia much earlier than it did on a global scale. And the shadow of China's rise was cast much more extensively and faster over South Korea in particular. In fact, neither Seoul nor Washington and Tokyo fully understood the long-term strategic implications of Sino-South Korean rapprochement when it was happening during the 1990s.[6] Only in recent years has South Korea gradually awakened to the clear and present impact of China's ascent.

The pertinent literature suggests that South Korea's mode of response to a rising China has been a proactive engagement while at the same time seeking to sustain its military alliance with the United States as a strategic counterweight.[7] Despite the generally positive perceptions of China, the specific combination of South Korea's modes of dealing with China—including an amalgam of appeasement, balancing, bandwagoning, and binding—has not yet been fixed but rather evolving over the years, particularly since the watershed year of 2004. As the shadow of China's rise grows larger, South Korea's threat perceptions have also been changing accordingly, though subtly. Some of these threat perceptions have been real while others more imagined—i.e., unavoidable effects of China's ascent as a great power.

This chapter consists of four sections. The first discusses the background for the "premature" demise of the honeymoon phase in Sino-South Korean relations. The second examines the environment in which China is increasingly depicted as presenting multiple—economic, normative and traditional security-related—sources of concern in the eyes of South Koreans. The third section then explores the curious case of "strategic cooperative partnership" established between South Korea and China in May 2008. The last section offers some concluding observations on Seoul's strategic posture toward Beijing given its changing views and perceptions of China in recent years.

## A Honeymoon That Was Only Too Brief

It is by now established that the rapprochement and diplomatic normalization between China and South Korea were accomplished through a long and arduous process of clandestine contacts and secret negotiations in consideration of North Korea and Taiwan, respectively.[8] Naturally, both Seoul and Beijing cherished their newly normalized relationship and the various practical benefits accrued to it. Until 2000 (if not 2004)—that is, at least for eight years since the diplomatic normalization in 1992—China and South Korea enjoyed a sort of honeymoon period, during which both were more than willing to accommodate and tolerate each other.[9]

The honeymoon did not last long, however. The eruption of the East Asian financial crisis in 1997, which had a particularly harsh impact on South Korea, completely altered China's view of South Korea as a useful model for emulation. Worse yet, China and South Korea engaged in a fierce trade dispute over the import of Chinese garlic in 2000. While Seoul certainly had its own share of blame, the garlic episode revealed that China was apparently much less tolerant and more willing to retaliate when it came to business transactions and the national reputation related to them. The "garlic battle" constituted a watershed in transforming China and South Korea's mutual images of each other.[10]

On the surface, these events seemed catalytic. Below the surface, however, the incongruence of expectations and outcomes led to the evolving and unstable perceptions and relations in the post-honeymoon phase. In normalizing relations with South Korea, China's primary goal was two-fold. One was economic in nature (that is, expanding trade with and soliciting investment from South Korea), which was accomplished beyond Beijing's initial expectations.[11] The other was a geostrategic goal of "separating" South Korea from its closest ally, the United States. While assessments may vary on this particular score, it can be argued that Korean-American relations today are not what they used to be in the past, regardless of the official rhetoric issued from Washington and Seoul.[12] Whether due to the changing dynamics of South Korea's domestic politics or to Beijing's success with its wedging strategy, China's second goal was also rather successfully accomplished, at least during the first half of the 2000s.

What were South Korea's goals and expectations as they were related to the normalization of relations with China? It appears that Seoul also had two major expectations. For one, South Korea wished to diversify its key economic partners, and China at the time seemed a perfect one to utilize in reducing its heavy dependence on the United States and Japan. While this goal of diversification was fairly successfully accomplished, it is at the same time ironical that South Korea's increasingly heavy dependence on China is becoming an intricate problem in Sino-South Korean relations (details below).

As for the other, South Korea wished to pull China away from North Korea for a couple of reasons. Diplomatically, if successful, such an act would greatly enhance Seoul's international status relative to Pyongyang's.[13] Militarily, given the historical precedent of the Korean War and the geopolitics of the Cold War thereafter, diluting the alliance relationship between China and North Korea would certainly provide additional security for South Korea. Drawing China closer to its side had two additional benefits for South Korea. First, such a change could make it difficult for Beijing to actively and explicitly oppose a type of reunification in which South Korea could absorb a failing North Korea. Second, it could also create some room for South Korea to utilize Beijing as a diplomatic counterweight, if needed, against Tokyo and even Washington.[14] In retrospect, however, South Korea's efforts to pull China away from North Korea were not that successful. Despite the ebbs and flows, Beijing still sustains its alliance relationship with Pyongyang (at least in theory), steering the mid-course whenever necessary and possible. It is not all that clear if China would ever stand on the side of South Korea for key strategic issues if that meant a strained relationship with North Korea.[15]

Then there came the 2004 history controversy concerning the Dynasty of Goguryeo (Koguryŏ, C. Gaogouli) (37 BC–AD 668). The South Korean media began in 2003 to report heavily on the so-called Northeast [History] Project (*dongbei gongcheng*, K. *dongbuk kongjŏng*)—i.e., China's systematic efforts to incorporate Goguryeo as part of Chinese local history. In the summer of 2004, when the Chinese Foreign Ministry deleted the Goguryeo section on its official website, the whole issue erupted as a political-diplomatic problem in Sino-South Korean relations.[16]

If the 1997 financial crisis changed China's positive view of South Korea and if the "garlic battle" in 2000 transformed Sino-South Korean relations from a "special relationship" to a normal partnership, the Goguryeo controversy brought about a "reawakening" to South Koreans—intellectuals in particular—in their views of China and Sino-South Korean relations. Some pundits even went so far as to project that the "history war" would become a critical turning point or watershed in Sino-South Korean relations.[17] By the fall of 2004, it appeared that the end of the honeymoon phase had arrived.

## The Ascent of China as Sources of Concern: Horizon-Gazing

As noted elsewhere, South Korea's perceptions of China had been largely positive and favorable for many years since the two countries began their clandestine contacts in the early 1980s.[18] In tandem with China's swift rise, however, certain concerns and worries have arisen in South Korea, particularly during the 2000s. By and large, China is being depicted as a new source of economic, normative and security threats to South Korea. Below is a preliminary attempt at horizon-gazing.

## China as an Economic Concern

Some critical and even negative views of China have lately gained a growing audience in South Korea. The vanguard of such views was first found in business communities that have become increasingly concerned about the prospect of South Korea losing out to China in overseas markets. While the share of South Korean products in the American market declined from 3.7 percent in 1990 to 2.4 percent in 2007, that of China rose from 3.1 to 16.4 percent in the same period. The number of China's global bestselling products was 1,029 while that of South Korea was only 58 in 2007, a decrease of 434 from the year 2000.[19] Grave concerns were also expressed repeatedly regarding China's rising competitiveness vis-à-vis South Korea in a wide range of key industries, including such advanced sectors as the semiconductor, automobile, and shipbuilding industries.[20]

Table 4.1 South Korea's Trade Dependence on China, 1985–2007

| Year | China portion of South Korea's total trade (percent) |
|---|---|
| 1985 | 1.9 |
| 1990 | 2.8 |
| 1995 | 6.4 |
| 2000 | 9.4 |
| 2003 | 15.3 |
| 2007 | 19.9 |

Source: http://stat.kita.net.

There were also worries about South Korea's rapidly increasing trade dependence on China. As Table 4.1 shows, South Korea's trade dependence on China skyrocketed from 1.9 percent in 1985 to nearly 20 percent in 2007 (22.2 percent in the case of export). Some even go so far as to suggest that the figure may rise to 30 percent by 2012, while others argue that it is not the speed but the relative dependence that really matters. Given that China's trade dependence on South Korea for 2007 was only 6.7 percent, the widening gap in terms of relative dependence has become a source of concern on the part of South Korea despite the huge surpluses Seoul has been reaping from the trade with Beijing.[21]

A new dimension to this thread—i.e., China as a source of economic threat—concerns the prospect that South Korea may soon begin to score trade deficits with China. Since diplomatic normalization in 1992, Seoul has never recorded a deficit with Beijing on a yearly basis. However, the rate of increase in South Korea's export to China has been declining rapidly, from 42 percent in 2004 to 24 percent in 2005 and 13 percent in 2007. The total trade surplus against China also decreased from $21 billion in 2006 to $19 billion in 2007, the year when South Korea emerged as number one importer of Chinese goods. Some even project that South Korea may have trade deficits with China beginning in 2012.[22] Given the pivotal position that the China trade has occupied in South Korea's foreign economic relations for so many years, how the changing trade structure would affect the perceptions and dynamics underlying the bilateral relationship remains uncertain.[23]

### China as a Threat to Values/Norms

Normative considerations often weigh in heavily in formulating South Korean perceptions of China. Human-rights concerns in particular have recently loomed large in generating negative perceptions of China in South Korea. On several occasions since 2000, China extradited "refugees" ("escapees" or *tuobeizhe* as the Chinese officially call them) to North Korea without any assurance of their physical safety upon returning. The South Korean media has often expressed human rights concerns regarding the worsening situations in Tibet and the problem of forced migrants in China. As South Koreans' human rights awareness has been considerably enhanced in recent years, their view of China as "uncivil" has also amplified accordingly.[24]

Some analysts in South Korea have also harbored serious doubts as to whether China really possessed the will to prevent North Korea from developing nuclear weapons and related technologies. While China's official position on this issue has certainly changed compared to the first crisis of 1993-94 when it largely sat on the fence, many South Korean experts believe that Beijing is not genuinely committed to pressuring Pyongyang to abolish its nuclear weapon-related facilities and technologies. They even put the Chinese official thesis of "responsible great-power diplomacy" (*fu zeren de daguo waijiao*) into question so far as the North Korean nuclear conundrum is concerned.[25]

The aforementioned Goguryeo controversy dealt a major blow to South Korean views of China. South Korean intellectuals reflected on this unfortunate episode by asking themselves, if China treats us like this today, how is it going to deal with us after its rise? Immediately after the eruption of the controversy, the Korean Broadcasting System (KBS) took a nationwide opinion poll, finding that 58.2 percent of the respondents did not have an affinity toward China.[26] As far as the South Korean views of China were concerned, as Table 4.2 indicates, the Goguryeo controversy generated highly negative impact. While the perceptions of China prior to the summer of 2004 had been very positive—even to the point of surpassing those of the United States—South Koreans' view of China clearly plummeted thereafter.

Table 4.2 Impact of Goguryeo Controversy on South Korean View of China

| Year | Poll question | (percentage) China | United States |
|------|---------------|-------|---------------|
| 2002[a] | Which of the four major powers do you feel most favorably toward? | 41 | 30 |
| 2003[b] | Where should South Korea's foreign policy focus be placed? | 48 | 33 |
| 2004[c] | Which country should South Korea regard most important? | 61 | 26 |
| 2005[d] | On which country should South Korea's foreign policy focus be placed? | 29 | 55 |
| 2005[e] | Where should South Korea's foreign policy focus be placed? | 11 | 46 |
| 2006[f] | Where should South Korea's foreign policy focus be placed? | 12 | 50 |
| 2006[g] | Which country should South Korea regard most important? | 24 | 47 |
| 2008[h] | Which country do you feel most favorably toward? | 15 | 45 |

Sources: (a) Sisa Journal, March 2002; (b) Joong-ang Ilbo, February 12, 2003; (c) Dong-A Ilbo, May 4, 2004; (d) Dong-A Ilbo, November 7, 2005; (e) Joong-ang Ilbo, December 22, 2005; (f) Joong-ang Ilbo, May 18, 2006; (g) Munhwa Ilbo, September 16, 2006; (h) Kyunghyang Sinmun, August 15, 2008.

### China as a Traditional Security Concern

Does China matter to South Korea militarily? This is a question that South Koreans have managed to avoid for a long time. Either due to the economic foci of Sino-South Korean relations or to Seoul's calculated ambiguity on the subject, few South Korean security experts, let alone the government, talked publicly (and negatively) about the military implications of the rise of China. Considering that China was South Korea's military adversary nearly sixty years ago, it is all the more interesting to hear a wide range of calls for the expansion of bilateral military cooperation, resulting most recently in the establishment of hotlines between the navies and air forces of the two countries.[27] A Chinese scholar even went so far as to argue that Korea has wished to expand military ties with China mainly because to highlight constraining China as the principal function of the Korean-American alliance would be the last thing Seoul would want.[28]

Seoul has to date maintained a sort of strategic ambiguity as to whether and under what circumstances China is likely to pose a military threat and as to how to cope with such contingencies.[29] Officially, of course, such ambiguity is still well maintained. Yet, certain changes, though subtle, are being felt lately. Three issues in particular have been catalytic in generating security-related concerns in South Korea regarding China. First, the half-blown—and potentially alarming—dispute between South Korea and China in 2006 over the Socotra Rock (K. Ieodo [Iŏdo], C. Suyanjiao), south of Jeju (Cheju) Islands and northeast of Shanghai, raised security concerns in South Korea. The media's loaded attention to this episode also contributed significantly to the rise of nationalistic—anti-Chinese—sentiments in South Korea (and anti-Korean sentiments in China as well).[30]

Second, the so-called North Korean contingencies generated growing concerns with China's geo-strategic ambitions toward the Korean Peninsula. The logic of the most popular version goes like this:

1.   With the mounting economic difficulties and the uncertainties of political succession, the likelihood of North Korea's "collapse" (e.g., the loss of power by Kim Jong Il [Kim Chŏng-il] and his protégés) is rising.

2.   In case of extreme turmoil, China will be more than tempted to move in to "manage" the post-Kim Jong Il situation in its favor.

3.   China's dominance is deemed necessary in this regard since Beijing has been deeply concerned with the possibility that a unified Korea might reclaim its territorial rights to Southern Manchuria (K. Gando [Kando]; C. Jiandao).

4.   China's "Northeast Project" and recent efforts to increase its economic influence over North Korea are designed to accomplish the same goal of positioning China favorably in case of such strategic uncertainties in North Korea.[31]

Third, more recently, with the inauguration of the Lee Myung-Bak administration, Seoul's foreign policy priority has been re-assigned to the strengthening, if not recovering, of the Korean-American alliance, above everything else. While both Seoul and Washington have repeatedly stated that the alliance was not directed against China or its rise, it appears that some in the Korean military establishments have begun to present a new logic for the alliance—i.e., constraining China if it were to become a source of instability by challenging the U.S.-dominated order.[32]

## China in Lee Myung-Bak's Foreign Policy:
## The Curious Case of "Strategic Cooperative Partnership"

Given these changes in South Korea's view of China, we would naturally expect that Seoul's China policy might have changed quite a bit for the period under discussion and particularly since Lee Myung-Bak's inauguration as president in February 2008. Interestingly, however, at least on the surface, there is no apparent sign that the Lee administration is less pro-China, although it may be certainly more pro-American. In retrospect, it is not quite clear whether the Roh Moo-hyun (No Mu-hyŏn) administration was particularly more pro-China compared to the preceding ones. It might have in fact been the Roh administration's non-pro-American policy stance that made it appear as if it were more pro-China than it really was.[33]

Even if it were indeed pro-China, the actually executed policy of the Roh administration did not seem that pro-China particularly after 2005. Sino-South Korean coordination and cooperation through the Six-Party Talks framework notwithstanding, the latter part of the Roh's tenure was as pro-United States as it was pro-China. The free trade agreement was granted to Washington before Beijing despite that it was China with which Seoul first began pertinent feasibility studies and informal negotiations. Furthermore, in January 2006, after several years' delay, the Seoul government officially accepted the concept of "strategic flexibility" for the American forces stationed in South Korea.[34]

Throughout the year of 2007 during which his popularity rating was second to none, presidential candidate Lee Myung-Bak repeatedly stressed that, once elected, he would make maximum efforts to mend the ties between Seoul and Washington. As soon as the election result was out, Beijing immediately inquired about the possibility of dispatching a special envoy. In January 2008 China sent Wang Yi, deputy foreign minister, to Seoul as the special envoy to congratulate President-elect Lee. The dispatch of the special envoy in itself was an extraordinary arrangement for Beijing, since it was the first time the Chinese government had ever sent a special envoy to meet with a president-elect of another country.[35]

In President-elect Lee's audience with Wang Yi on January 14, 2008, some sort of "upgrading" of Sino-South Korean relations was allegedly proposed.[36] Unfortunately, there are different versions available regarding who first made the proposal as such. The Korean side has argued that it was Wang Yi who first mentioned the possibility of enhancing the bilateral relationship to a strategic partnership while the Chinese side has contended that it was President-elect Lee who first commented on the need for upgrading South Korea's relations with China to a higher—though unspecified—level.[37]

This author's interviews made it possible to reconstruct what happened and it resembles the following. In his meeting with Ambassador Wang, President-elect Lee said many things to the effect that China was an important partner to Seoul and it was crucial to maintain good relations with Beijing. Yet, Lee did not make a direct reference to the term strategic partnership. Towards the end of the meeting, Wang asked the following question in the course of summarizing Lee's remarks: "[S]o, Mr. President-elect, what you're saying is basically that the two countries need to upgrade their bilateral relations?" Since there was no objection at the time from Lee or his aides to this verbal summary, Wang returned home and reported as such—i.e., as if it was Seoul who first proposed the upgrading of bilateral relations to a strategic partnership.[38]

When the foreign ministers of the two countries had lunch together prior to President Lee's state visit to China in May 2008, China's Foreign Minister Yang Jiechi made a statement that "in accordance with South Korea's proposal, China agrees to establish a strategic cooperative partnership." South Korea's Foreign Minister Yu Myung-hwan (Yu Myŏng-hwan) did not take issue with the remark at the time and, therefore, on the record, South Korea became the party that first proposed it.

This author's interviews with government officials and experts during the second half of 2008 suggest that the establishment of a strategic cooperative partnership with China, at least in the beginning, did not have much substantive meaning for the Lee administration. That is to say, it is not quite clear if serious thoughts and due preparation were given to the task of establishing the strategic partnership, considering the administration's pronounced pro-U.S. policy stance and relatively low policy priority assigned to China.

At least four reasons account for this assessment. First of all, the establishment of a strategic cooperative partnership with China was initially interpreted by officials in Seoul as more "symbolic" than substantive. A close reading of the communiqué from the Lee-Hu summit in May 2008 suggests that no concrete details were embedded in the upgrading of the bilateral relationship to a strategic cooperative partnership. In this respect, a comment by an interviewee (of the Ministry of Foreign Affairs and Trade) is worthy of citation: "We [the government] were looking for an appropriate prefix to replace 'comprehensive' and were unable to come up with something other than 'strategic.'" In fact, most of the interviewees in Seoul were not able to differentiate the real meaning of "strategic" that is fundamentally different from "comprehensive."[39]

Second, if Seoul had really been so serious about the strategic partnership that it was about to establish with Beijing, it should have studied the precedents and their implications more closely and carefully. Yet, there is no concrete evidence to support that the South Korean government did that. Given the fact that, as noted earlier, Seoul offered to establish a strategic partnership with China twice earlier, the lack of research and preparation was all the more surprising, clearly indicating that it was more rhetorical than substantive.[40] It was even surprising that some government officials and mainstream media mistook the strategic partnership (*zhanlue hezuo huoban guanxi*) South Korea established with China to be the same as the one agreed between China and Russia (*zhanlue xiezuo huoban guanxi*).[41]

Third, what South Korea and China agreed to establish was the same as those maintained between China on one hand and India and Pakistan on the other.[42] A question begs to be answered at this juncture: why the same ones with India and Pakistan? While Pakistan has long been a close strategic partner of China since 1964, the same cannot be said of India perceptually as well as policy-wise.[43] Where do Seoul and Beijing want the South Korea-China strategic cooperative partnership to be located? More toward Islamabad or New Delhi?[44]

Fourth, a related question concerns why the Seoul government did not propose to establish a category of its own. That is to say, given the convention that Korean affairs have been generally treated as "special," why didn't the Lee administration propose a designation of partnership that is applicable only to South Korea-China relations, as were the cases with Sino-Russian and Sino-Japanese relations? Why invite unnecessary suspicion and criticism on the part of the United States and others? Again, it appears that due attention and proper preparation were not given to the task of establishing a strategic partnership with China. In a nutshell, it was more symbolic and rhetorical than substantive.

Was it merely symbolic from China's viewpoint as well? A negative answer may be found in the official commentaries by Qin Gang, the spokesman of China's Foreign Ministry, made on the day of President Lee's state visit to China. In a reply to a foreign correspondent, Qin commented, "The Korean-American alliance is a product of historical processes.... Times have changed and situations in each country have also become radically different.

Therefore, military alliances of the Cold-War era are inadequate to cope with diverse security challenges that the region is currently facing."[45] Subsequently, the Korean media was flooded with critical reports on these comments and even South Korea's Foreign Ministry said that there was a misunderstanding. Qin Gang, however, rebutted by saying that his comments were well thought-out ones that were officially approved by the Ministry."[46]

At this juncture, let us go back to the issue of who first proposed the strategic cooperative partnership newly established between South Korea and China. As noted earlier, on the record, it was South Korea and therefore, it seems, China may think that it is eligible to make such a statement, tacitly asking where Seoul wishes to place itself on the continuum between India and Pakistan. After all, what was deemed largely symbolic to Seoul might not have been merely symbolic and rhetorical to Beijing.[47]

## Conclusion

Pinpointing China's place in South Korea's security matrix is a task neither as easy nor as straightforward as it may seem. Intermittent public opinion surveys provide some concrete figures but they do not always or automatically translate themselves into real policy impact. The perceptions and views of policy elites are much more important but, at the same time, equally difficult to tap into, let alone be substantiated empirically. Besides, the appearance of South Korea's policy and view of China being totally fixed may not be in Seoul's best interest. If flexibility is shorthand for pragmatic diplomacy, fixed views and petrified policies are hardly desirable for South Korea, which is more of a dependent variable than an independent one in the international politics of Northeast Asia.

For much of the period since the diplomatic normalization in 1992, the pillars of South Korea-China relations were largely economic, thus rendering the bilateral relationship more of a positive-sum dynamic. In tandem with China's ascent in East Asia, Seoul hastened to assign strategic-military importance to its relations with China, particularly during the Roh Moo-hyun administration, thereby introducing elements of zero-sum games. Ironically, the Lee administration appears to be adopting the same stance by adding the prefix "strategic" to its partnership with China. While, admittedly, artificial differentiation of "economic" and "strategic" may no longer be possible, proactively assimilating Sino-South Korean relations to U.S.-Korean relations may not be ideal for Seoul in the long run given the volatility of U.S.-China relations.[48]

Some argue that it is imperative for Seoul to maximize the overlapped area between Korea-U.S. relations and Korea-China relations. While it may sound reasonable theoretically, there is a missing link. Whether Seoul can expand the overlapped area between Korea-U.S. relations and Korea-China relations depends on South Korea's diplomatic capability to handle intricate issues related to both the United States and China. Or, alternatively, will Washington and Beijing perceive Seoul as such a player? A worst-case scenario would project an outcome where South Korea's efforts toward hedging and a maximum-winning coalition may end up in a policy impasse and distrust of Seoul by both Beijing and Washington.

Uncertainties will continue to loom large in determining China's place in South Korea's security matrix. Assuming that the capabilities of the United States and China may eventually converge, which of the two will be viewed as more benign is likely to constitute a crucial variable. In the years to come, a "popularity competition"—or a soft-power race—will become a key issue to watch. As a smaller middle-level power, South Korea undoubtedly prefers to remain symbiotic with China but, given the role of asymmetry in international politics, it is perhaps more up to China whether the relationship can remain so. One thing is for certain: Seoul's view of and policy toward Beijing continues to evolve.

## Notes

The research for this article on which this chapter was based was supported in part by the John and Catherine MacArthur Foundation's Asia Security Initiative grant (08-92783-000-GSS) on "Managing Sino-Korean Conflicts and Identifying the Role of the United States" for 2009–12 (http://masi.snu.ac.kr) .

1 Such an appraisal came under fire, however, as China's position on the Chon'an sinking and the Yonpyong shelling in 2010 was more defensive of North Korea than neutral between the two Koreas.

2 See *Chosun Ilbo* [Chosun Daily], August 22, 2007 and September 25, 2008; and *Dong-A Ilbo* [Dong-A Daily], August 29, 2008 and June 22, 2009.

3 On the importance of cultural factors in Sino-South Korean relations, see Xu Derong and Xiang Dongmei, "Zhonghan jianli mianxiang 21shiji hezuo huoban guanxi de Beijing fenxi" [Analyzing the background of China and South Korea establishing a cooperative partnership for the 21st century], *Dangdai hanguo* [Contemporary Korea], no. 22 (1999): 34; and Zheng Chenghong, "Hanju keyi dadong Zhongguo" [Korean dramas can move China], *Shijie zhishi* [World Affairs], no. 4 (2005): 17–19.

4 *Chosun Ilbo*, May 28, 2008; and *Renmin Ribao* [People's Daily], May 28, 2008.

5 For the nature of these debates, see Youngnam Cho and Jong Ho Jeong, "China's Soft Power: Discussions, Resources, and Prospects," *Asian Survey* 48, no. 3 (May/June 2008): 453-472; and contributions by Zhu Feng and Tang Shiping in *China's Ascent: Power, Security, and the Future of International Politics*, eds. Robert S. Ross and Zhu Feng (Ithaca: Cornell University Press, 2008), ch. 2 and 6.

6 For Washington's exemplary assessment as such, see the Office of Research (Department of State), "For South Koreans, China's Draw Is Mainly Economic," *Opinion Analysis*, M-127-03 (September 30, 2003).

7 Victor A. Cha, "Engaging China: The Views from Korea," in *Engaging China: The Management of an Emerging Power*, ed. Alastair I. Johnston and Robert S. Ross (London: Routledge, 1999), 40–42; Taeho Kim, "South Korea and a Rising China: Perceptions, Policies and Prospects," in *The China Threat: Perceptions, Myths and Reality*, ed. Herbert Yee and Ian Storey (London: Routledge, 2002), 175–176; Jae Ho Chung, "South Korea between Eagle and Dragon: Perceptual Ambivalence and Strategic Dilemma," *Asian Survey* 41, no. 5 (September/October 2001: 777–796; Jae Ho Chung, *Between Ally and Partner: Korea-China Relations and the United States* (New York: Columbia University Press, 2007), ch. 8–9; and David Kang, *China Rising: Peace, Power and Order in East Asia* (New York: Columbia University Press, 2008), 104–125.

8 Chung, *Between Ally and Partner*, ch. 4–6.

9 See, for instance, Chae-Jin Lee and Stephanie Hsieh, "China's Two-Korea Policy at Trial: The Hwang Chang Yop Crisis," *Pacific Affairs* 74, no. 3 (Fall 2001): 321–41.

10 For the demise of the honeymoon phase, see Jae Ho Chung, "From a Special Relationship to a Normal Partnership: Interpreting Sino-South Korean 'Garlic Battle,'" *Pacific Affairs* 76, no. 4 (Winter 2003–2004): 549–568; and Song Chengyou, "Zhonghan jianjiao 16 nian—liangguo guanxi fazhan guiji de huigu" [Sixteen years since the normalization of Sino-South Korean relations: retrospect of the developmental trajectory of the bilateral relations], paper presented at the Korea-China Forum (*zhonghan guanxi luntan*) organized by the Center for Korean Studies at Peking University (December 18, 2008).

11 For instance, the 2008 target for bilateral trade—$100 billion—was met in 2005, three years ahead of the original schedule. Whether the 2012 target—$200 billion—will also be met earlier remains to be seen.

12 Norman D. Levine, *Do the Ties Still Bind? The US-ROK Security Relationship after 9/11* (Santa Monica: RAND Corporation, 2004); and Ralph Cossa et al., *The United States and the Asia-Pacific Region: Security Strategy for the Obama Administration* (Washington, D.C.: Center for New American Security, February 2009), 67–68.

13 For such mindsets held by both Seoul and Pyongyang, see Byung-Chul Koh, *The Foreign Policy Systems of North and South Korea* (Berkeley: University of California Press, 1984), ch. 1.

14 The now-defunct concept of "strategic balancer" pronounced by the Roh Moo-hyun administration and its middle-of-the-road, if not pro-China, position were perhaps reflective of such lines of thinking. For China's positive response to the concept, see Li Dunqiu, "Lu Wuxuan: zuo junhengzhe [Roh Moo-Hyun to perform as Northeast Asia's balancer]," *Shijie zhishi* [World Affairs] 11 (2005): 30–33.

15 Even after the many years since diplomatic normalization in 1992, China still does not inform South Korea of its high-level exchanges with North Korea. Several Chinese officials, diplomats and analysts are alleged to have been successively purged since 2006 for "leaking" such sensitive information to Seoul. See *Chosun Ilbo*, June 24, 2010.

16 For a detailed discussion of this episode and its implications for Sino-South Korean relations, see Jae Ho Chung, "China's 'Soft Clash' with South Korea: The History War and Beyond," *Asian Survey* 49, no. 3 (June 2009): 468–483.

17 See Scott Snyder, "A Turning Point for China-Korea Relations?" *Comparative*

*Connections* 6, no. 3 (October 2004): 115.

18 See Jae Ho Chung, "Dragon in the Eyes of South Korea: Analyzing Korean Perceptions of China," *Korea: The East Asian Pivot*, ed. Jonathan D. Pollack (Newport: Naval War College Press, 2005), 254–259.

19 *Dong-A Ilbo*, July 14, 2001 and August 19, 2008; and *Chosun Ilbo*, November 17, 2008.

20 See Korean Chamber of Commerce and Korea International Trade Association (eds.), *Chungguk kyŏngje ŭi pusang kwa Han'guk ŭi chŏngch'aek taeŭng* [The Rise of China and Korea's Policy Responses] (Seoul, October 2004); *Chosun Ilbo*, November 19, 27 and 28, 2001; and *Dong-A Ilbo*, June 16, 2002, May 9, 2007 and September 5, 2008.

21 The Chinese ratio was calculated on the basis of *Zhongguo tongji nianjian 2008* [Statistical Yearbook of China 2008] (Beijing: Zhongguo tongji chubanshe, 2008), 707.

22 Samsung Economic Research Institute, *Han-Chung muyŏk kujo ŭi pyŏnhwa wa sisajŏm* [Changes in the Structure of Korea-China Trade and Their Implications] (Seoul: SERI, February 11, 2008); *Chosun Ilbo*, February 12, 2008; and *Dong-A Ilbo*, August 19, 2008.

23 South Korea's Ministry of Planning and Finance published a report that was explicitly wary of Seoul's diminishing influence because of China's rise: see *Chosun Ilbo*, April 14, 2009.

24 See *Dong-A Ilbo*, October 13 and 18, 1999 and June 18, 2002; *Chosun Ilbo*, January 27, 2000 and June 24, 2002; *Wŏl'gan Chosŏn* [Chosun Monthly], June 2000, 458–472; *New York Times*, May 31, 2000; Mark O'Neil, "Jilin Uses Strike Hard to Force out Starving Koreans," *South China Morning Post*, July 25, 2001; and *Joong-ang Ilbo* [Joong-ang Daily], January 17, 2007.

25 See, for instance, Hong Chun-ho, "Pukhaek idaero Chungguk e matkyŏ to toena?" [Can we still leave the North Korean nuclear problem to China?], *Chosun Ilbo*, February 16, 2005; Nam Man-gwŏn, "Pukhaek kwallyŏn Chungguk yŏkhal ron e taehan ŭigiuim" [Doubts about the role played by China in the resolution of the North Korean nuclear problem], *Tongbuk-a chŏngse punsŏk* [Northeast Asia strategic analysis] by the Korean Institute for Defense Analysis), April 15, 2005; Ku Cha-ryong, "Chungguk i Pukhan e kkok haeya hal mal" [Things that China must tell North Korea], *Dong-A Ilbo*, February 16, 2009; Pak Sŏng-jun, "Chungguk ŭn t'aedo rŭl punmyŏnghi hara" [China needs to clarify its position on North Korea], *Chosun Ilbo*, March 19, 2009; and "Ho Kŭm-do ŭi taebuk chase uryŏ toenda" [Growing concerns with Hu Jintao's position on North Korea: editorial], *Dong-A Ilbo*, April 4, 2009.

26 See http://find.joins.com/joinsdb_content_f.asp?id=DY01200409140125.

27 See *Chosun Ilbo*, November 25, 2008. The naval hotline was set up between Pyongaek (P'yŏngt'aek) and Qingdao (Shandong), while the air force hotline was established between Daegu (Taegu) and Jinan (Shandong).

28 Liu Ming, "Hanguo de diyuan weizhi yu qi waijiao he anquan zhengce" [Korea's geographical location and its diplomatic and security policy], *Yatai luntan* [Asia-Pacific forum], no. 3/4 (1999): 37.

29 See, for instance, Eric A. McVadon, "Chinese Military Strategy for the Korean Peninsula," in *China's Military Faces the Future* eds. James R. Lilley and David Shambaugh (Armonk, NY: M. E. Sharpe, 1999): 271–294.

30 See "Iŏdo nombon ŭn Chungguk hŭksim mwŏn'ga" [China's territorial ambition over the Socotra Rock], *Chugan Han'guk* [Hankook Weekly], October 3, 2006, 58–59;

and Jiang Xun, "Han zhanling suyanjiao bengju zhonghan shenjing" [South Korea's occupation of the Socotra Rock getting on China's nerve), *Yazhou Zhoukan* [Asia Weekly], December 3, 2006, 24–27.

31 Lee Jin-woo, "China Distorts History to Prepare for North's Collapse," *Korea Times*, October 11, 2006; Yoon Hwy-tak, "China's Northeast Project: Defensive or Offensive Strategy?" *East Asian Review* 16, no. 4 (Winter 2004): 100–101; Zhang Zhirong, *Zhongguo Bianjiang yu Minzu Wenti* [Problems of Borders and Ethnicities in China] (Beijing: Beijing daxue chubanshe, 2005); Mark Byington, "A Matter of Territorial Security: China's Historiographical Treatment of Goguryeo in the Twentieth Century," in *Nationalism and History Textbooks in Asia and Europe* (Seoul: The Academy of Korean Studies, 2005); and *Weekly Dong-A*, October 21, 2008.

32 No documentary sources are available on this but interviews are indicative of the emergence of such views. For a view that lists potential conflicts with China as a factor for South Korea's recent increase of military spending, see John Feffer, "Ploughshares into Swords: Economic Implications of South Korean Military Spending," *KEI Academic Paper Series* (February 2009), 5.

33 See Jae Ho Chung, *Chungguk ŭi pusang kwa hanbando ŭi mirae* [The Rise of China and the Future of the Korean Peninsula] (Seoul: Seoul National University Press, 2011), ch. 12.

34 If one of China's core strategic goals is to constrain America's military movement in the East Asian region, this was indeed a big score for Washington. For an unusual reference to the Chinese mindset as such, see Zhang Yushan, "Zhonghan quanmian hezuo huobanguanxi de huigu yu zhanwang" [Retrospect and Prospect for China-South Korean Comprehensive Cooperative Partnership], in *Yafei congheng* [Cross-Currents in Asia and Africa], no. 4 (2007): 6.

35 When Qian Qichen was dispatched to Washington as a special envoy to congratulate on George W. Bush's re-election in the winter of 2004, Bush was already the president of the United States.

36 Discussions here draw from the author's extensive interviews in Seoul in the second half of 2008.

37 When President-elect Lee met with Ning Fukui, China's ambassador to South Korea, a few days after the election, he commented on upgrading Korea-China economic relations but did not mention the possibility of establishing a "strategic partnership." See Korea Times, December 21, 2007. For a media report that points to China as the party that first proposed the establishment of "strategic cooperative partnership," see *Chosun Ilbo*, May 28, 2008.

38 According to the author's interviews, South Korea proposed to establish a strategic partnership with China twice earlier, first in 1998 and second in 2006, both rejected by Beijing. It is possible, therefore, that China might have simply interpreted President-elect Lee's reference to upgrading as that to a strategic partnership.

39 Some take pains to argue that the main difference lies in "going global" but they all fail to elaborate on what South Korea will and can do together with China on a global scale, particularly in security-military terms.

40 Some attribute this problem to the lack—if not absence—of China hands inside the Lee administration's foreign policy team. Then, again, there were few, if any, inside the Roh administration either.

41 See, for instance, *Chosun Ilbo*, May 29, 2008.

42 See the Policy Research Bureau of the Foreign Ministry of the People's Republic of China (ed.), *Zhongguo waijiao 2007* [China's Foreign Affairs 2007] (Beijing: Shijie zhishi chubanshe, 2007), 128, 190, 201.

43 See, for instance, John W. Garver, "China's Influence in Central and South Asia," in *Power Shift: China and Asia's New Dynamics*, ed. David Shambaugh (Berkeley: University of California Press, 2005), 213–217, 220–223.

44 For a critical view along this line, see Byung-kwang Park, "Sino-Indian and Sino-Pakistan Strategic Cooperative Partnerships: Implications for Korea-China Relations," paper presented at the conference on "Assessing the Korea-China Strategic Cooperative Partnership," organized by the Institute for China Studies at Seoul National University on June 10, 2009. Also see Vidya Nadkarni, *Strategic Partnerships in Asia: Balancing without Alliances* (London: Routledge, 2010), ch. 5.

45 See http://article.joins.com/article/article.asp?ctg=10&total_id=3162775. Author's translation.

46 *Chosun Ilbo*, May 30, 2008.

47 For a Chinese take that interpreted Seoul's "proposal" for a strategic cooperative partnership as South Korea's "balancing diplomacy," see *Jiefang ribao* [Liberation Daily], May 27, 2008.

48 The hasty establishment of strategic relationship with China was forewarned in Jae Ho Chung, "Pragmatic Realism: A Key to Managing Relations with China," *Korea Herald*, February 19, 2008.

# JAPAN:
# SOUTH KOREA'S STRATEGIC ASSET

## *Benjamin Self*

From the perspective of the United States, unfortunate disputes between South Korea (the Republic of Korea, or ROK) and Japan over
history and territory have hindered the formation of a "virtual" alliance that would serve all three countries' strategic interests. In Tokyo there
is a completely different picture, in which the security partnership between
Tokyo and Seoul has endured and even blossomed, despite regular diplomatic spats and shifting geopolitical realities, since it first emerged some
four decades ago.

Both pictures offer glimpses of a complex reality. We can use these two
perspectives to triangulate the truth of how South Korea has benefited from
security cooperation with Japan over the past forty years. Japan has a great
deal to offer as a security partner for the future as well. There is an element
of truth to the argument that Japan's utility as a strategic partner for the
ROK is limited by its inward-looking strategic culture. Enduring apologist
views of Japan's history of imperial expansion, however annoying, do not
undermine its reliability. While stopping short of a full embrace of Tokyo,
Seoul should at a minimum take the necessary steps to ensure its cooperation with Tokyo can continue to serve as a strategic asset.

## South Korean Relations with Japan

Within South Korea, as in much of East Asia, relations with Japan remain
controversial. This controversy arises from a tension between the costs and
benefits of closer ties with Tokyo. The costs tend to be a matter of domestic politics—Japan has a negative image among the peoples of the region,
stemming from its history of imperialist expansion, colonialism, and war.
Particularly in cases where regime legitimacy faces real challenges, a pro-
Japanese posture can be a significant liability, whether in multi-party elec-

tions, intra-party competition, or the special inter-state struggle between the two Korean regimes.

Ties with Japan have been especially controversial in the South Korean case for three reasons. First, the period of Japanese colonial rule in Korea created severe social, cultural, and economic disruption, with uneven consequences for the Korean people. Postwar cooperation with Japan resonates with the internal legacy of colonial-era collaboration, a problem not eased by Japanese leaders' frequent claims that Japan effectively caused South Korea's modernization.

Second, North Korea's (nearly) complete isolation from Japan made its claims of legitimacy through resistance plausible, at least to some, and thus made any open efforts at reconciliation with Tokyo by Seoul more hazardous or costly in South-North competition for image. Third, shared anti-Japanese sentiment can provide glue for relations with other victims, notably China. Under Jiang Zemin, the Chinese Communist Party (CCP) buttressed its domestic legitimacy by playing up its image as liberator from Japan's brutal occupation, and also stressed the common struggle against Japanese imperialism in its foreign relations.[1]

This last factor may have eclipsed the others in significance, since the inter-state struggle for legitimacy with North Korea is no longer salient and the domestic political costs of ties with Japan seem to have faded somewhat over time. Not that any South Korean politician can remain silent in the face of something like the Tamogami scandal,[2] but the Kim-Obuchi declaration of 1998 and the joint hosting of the 2002 Soccer World Cup are signs that the relationship is less politically controversial among the South Korean public than it once was.[3]

Certainly we have seen signs that China's influence on South Korea includes a greater emphasis on common experience of anti-Japanese struggle, and not only in response to provocation from the unrepentant Japanese right wing. China's growing power and deepening bilateral trade relations have tempted Seoul into positions as extreme as the espousal of a "strategic balancer" role in future Northeast Asia. One must be careful not to see Chinese machinations behind every outburst of anti-Japanese Korean nationalism, but there can be no doubt that in the post-Cold War Sino-Japanese struggle for preeminence in the region, South Korea is the most coveted prize. Any increase in Japan-Korea tensions—over historical issues, the names of bodies of water, or disputed territories—benefits Beijing.

During the Cold War, South Korea allied with the United States and aligned with the capitalist democracies against communist totalitarianism. As a result its society prospered and it achieved both economic growth and, eventually, democratization. In the post-Cold War era, however, South Korea faces a more ambiguous choice. China is rising, and although China does not share South Korea's liberal political system, it has substantially opened its economy and established strong trade and investment relations with the outside world, including South Korea. Seoul has no wish to return to the Cold War, and fears that clear alignment with Tokyo and Washington would be costly in terms of its relationship with China and thus harmful to its economic and long-term national security interests.

## Asymmetries and Their Impact

In international relations, states tend to prefer to develop close relations with other states that seem similar—the "like likes like" theorem of alliance formation.[4] Conversely, states (and societies) tend to make rivals of states that are different, and also to categorize their enemies as "other."

Frequently we see efforts to emphasize similarities as states seek rapprochement, and likewise an emphasis on difference as a precursor to confrontation. The point bearing emphasis here is not that the similarity (or dissimilarity) of type of regime or other characteristic in and of itself drives states' behavior, but rather that the images held within a given state of itself (which is to say its identity) and of its counterpart tend toward affinity or aversion. When China and the Soviet Union were cooperating they emphasized their ideological solidarity, but after they broke into confrontation they each accused the other of being "deviationist" or "revisionist." The process of envisioning another state as "like" and the development of intimacy are mutually reinforcing. Moreover, the process can spill over into identity formation—the tendency to see or create in oneself the traits that one admires in one's partner—and from there even into the institutions of the state; the Cold War democratization of many U.S. allies was thus a process of both push (from America) and pull.

Obviously there are many partnerships of convenience, such as the U.S. security commitment to Saudi Arabia, in which the shared characteristic is little more than the existence of a common threat. Even in these cases an effort is made to justify the relationship, if vaguely, through reference to "freedom" or "stability." This implies that the existence of a security partnership is a force for affinity or identification. From this stems the principle that the seeds of such affinity must exist as a prerequisite for alliance. Even in the extreme case of the United States and Saudi Arabia, there has to be a tolerance for the influence of American values—and when the costs of that in terms of domestic control became too great, Riyadh attenuated its relationship with

Washington, vastly reducing the presence of U.S. troops in the kingdom.

In the case of Korea and Japan, there are two parts of this affinity aspect of security alignment that demand attention. First, the extent to which actual asymmetries in the bilateral relationship have hindered the formation of a security partnership, and second, the degree to which perceptions of asymmetry or "otherness" continue to militate against the sense of commonality—that is, the dominance of alienation over identification.

To establish a baseline for the relationship before examining images and identities, we should begin with a review of the structural asymmetries that exist between South Korea and Japan. One of them is size. Japan has almost three times the population and some four to five times the economy of South Korea. While Japanese tend to think of their country as small and resource-poor, they compare themselves implicitly to the United States, China, Russia, and other relatively enormous countries. South Korea is much smaller. If both Koreans and Japanese have long viewed their countries as small in a world of great powers, Japan has disdained Korea and Korea has feared the much larger Japan.

South Korea's economy trailed Japan's in almost every respect, but the gap has closed in recent years. Not only have incomes increased dramatically, raising South Korean standards of living almost to Japanese levels, but also South Korean companies have entered the global top tier, competing against big-name Japanese firms in both "First World" and developing world markets.

In raw military power, the imbalance is much less than economy or population alone would indicate. This is mainly because of Japan's internal constraints on defense capabilities, limiting its defense budget to one percent of gross domestic product and its military systems to "defensively-oriented defense." Of course Japan's geography and alliance with the United States provide the material basis for this policy choice. South Korea faces a very different threat environment, and despite its alliance with the United States has had to devote much greater levels of resources to the military. As a result the asymmetry is opposite what their size would lead one to expect: South Korea can play a combat role in international security operations, and Japan can not.

Another dimension of asymmetry emerges from their geographic difference: Japan, as an archipelago, was peripheral to the pre-modern Sinocentric world order and remains at distance, whereas peninsular Korea was not only within China's orbit but also was actually protected from Japan by China at the end of the sixteenth century.[5] This experience informs each state's perspective on the question of bandwagoning with China versus balancing against it.

Structure only goes so far in explaining how states perceive themselves and their neighbors. For all their similarities as wealthy, maritime trading nations allied with the United States, South Korea and Japan confront territorial and, more than anything else, historical disputes that have seriously divided them. It is in the area of historical asymmetry that we will find the most serious obstacles to affinity-based security cooperation.

### History is the Key Divisive Factor

One obvious dimension of their asymmetrical history is that Japan was an imperial power and Korea was its colonial victim. Rather than peer competitors like many of the European states that, despite centuries of warfare and enmity, have evolved into the European Union, Japan and Korea had a highly hierarchical relationship that shapes their attitudes toward each other to this day. Japanese remain condescending toward Korea, an outlook that is ironically exacerbated by Korea's careful emulation of Japan's miraculous economic success. Koreans, conversely, remain resentful of Japan more than sixty years after the end of the colonial era, and somewhat fearful despite its demilitarization.

The difference in views is illustrated by the repeated failure of Japanese to understand the degree to which they are resented by Koreans. Opinion polls show that Japanese believe that bilateral relations are good when Koreans think they are bad, and Japanese basically trust Korea but Koreans emphatically do not trust Japan.[6] The key reason for that mistrust is the history issue. Trust is about expectations of future behavior, but it is of necessity based on the experience and shared understanding of the past, which allows affinity to emerge. International conflict over history issues is implacable because views are central to identity and cannot be sacrificed to diplomatic considerations; domestic contestation over history is so controversial precisely because it threatens collective national identity.

Trust is a critical element in any security relationship. Even in negative relationships, adversaries seek to reduce the risk of war through confidence-building measures, and the stability provided by deterrence rests on a kind of trust—the certainty of intervention or retaliation. Much more important, though, is the role of trust in alliances. According to the famous dilemma, allies must always be fearful of entrapment or abandonment, and relying for their security on another nation requires a great deal of trust.

## Different Alliances

Aside from the various aspects of their geography and troubled history that divide them, South Korea and Japan differ in their respective alliances with the United States. Although the expectation in Washington has long been that it can act as the hinge to bring its two Northeast Asian allies together, the relationships are not similar enough to grant the United States sufficient leverage. The U.S.-ROK Alliance was born in the Korean War, when the United States came to the rescue of South Korea after the North invaded in June 1950, while the origins of the U.S.-Japan Alliance lie within the Occupation and the need to keep Japan inside the Western camp in the global struggle against the Soviet Bloc. For its first eight years, the U.S.-Japan Security Treaty did not oblige the United States even to defend Japan, but instead gave it the right to intervene in case of domestic turmoil. The extension of the Treaty in 1960, despite revision to correct the infringements on Japanese sovereignty, provoked severe backlash as the bulk of the public felt it was embroiling Japan in the Cold War.[7]

The differences in the alliances go deeper, as well, to connect with fundamentally divergent attitudes about the appropriate role of the military in national security, politics, and society. The Japanese Imperial Army and (somewhat less so) Imperial Navy received the brunt of the blame for Japan's disastrous war against the United States, and therefore the military was delegitimized in postwar Japan. The American-written constitution forbade Japan to use force to resolve international disputes, or to maintain forces for that purpose. As such, it has been understood that Japan's constitution prevents it from exercising its right of collective self-defense. Japan cannot defend the United States, its only treaty ally. South Korea, by contrast, was forced to fight for its survival from a tender age. The military has been a pillar of the nation, and if its role in the history of politics and democracy in South Korea is problematic, still the military as such does not lack legitimacy. Seoul can contribute and has dispatched forces to U.S.-led missions around the world, from South Vietnam to Iraq to Afghanistan.

Japan in recent years has begun an incremental transformation toward "normal nation" status, and as such has contributed non-combat troops to UN Peacekeeping Operations and to multilateral U.S.-led coalition missions. The process of moving the national security apparatus out of the shadows and into the mainstream is well under way, if far from complete, but in the postwar era the defense establishment was of near-pariah status.

The domestic political structure of Japan's problem of historical denial was the amalgam of centrist pragmatists and right-wing nationalists united against the socialist/communist left in the 1950s to form the Liberal Democratic Party (LDP), which ran the country (with only a brief interruption) from its creation in 1955 until its ouster in 2009. The practical result was that Japan hewed to a pacifist policy (avoiding revision of the war-renouncing Article IX of the postwar Constitution) but harboring extreme and unreconstructed nationalist views, which frequently erupted as rhetoric that damaged Japan's ties with its neighbors.[8] The pragmatic centrists were often displeased at the impact of the right-wing nationalist statements but had little choice but to maintain the overall framework in the context of the Cold War, the political party structure, and left-right ideological confrontation.

## South Korea-Japan Security Cooperation during the Cold War

While Japan has long recognized the strategic importance of Korea ("a dagger aimed at the heart of Japan") since the advent of the modern international system in Asia and even before the Meiji era, Japan's range of options in the postwar years was quite restricted. At the start of the Korean War, Japan was still under U.S. occupation, and had no say in the use of its territory in support of U.S. combat operations in Korea. Even after 1960 and the revision of the treaty to include a clause on prior consultation, the United States maintained control of Okinawa and there was a blanket assumption that it would be able to use bases throughout Japan in the event of renewed hostilities on the Korean Peninsula. Japan hosted the American forces that would be critical to ensuring Korea's security, but Japan itself could take no direct role.

Japan rejected the establishment of a Northeast Asia Treaty Organization, although the United States was promoting the creation of regional alliances on the NATO model. This was due to both Japan's decision to abjure military tools in its quest to regain great power status and also to Japan's hierarchical perspective: it could not ally as equals with its former colonial subjects Korea and Taiwan.

In part due to this enduring hierarchical perspective, and also in part to the low status of the Self-Defense Forces and the Japan Defense Agency, even after the normalization of Japan-ROK relations in 1965 there was no military component to the relationship. (Of course Korean sensibilities must have been the dominant factor, but had Japan possessed a "normal" military in the 1960s it seems likely that some standard military-to-military relationship would have begun, even if slowly, by the 1970s at the latest.) Instead, Japan and South Korea engaged in bilateral governmental talks led by bureaucrats and politicians. As such, when the two sides agreed on the importance of South Korean security and prosperity to Japan's own security, the nature of Japan's contribution toward that goal was non-military. Still, as argued by Azuma Kiyohiko, the Japanese fully understood the strategic purpose of economic cooperation with South Korea, including financial support for the South Korean defense industry.[9] Even before, but especially after, the Nixon Doctrine, Japan was active in supporting South Korea's national power base in terms of trade and industry, helping the South catch up to the more industrialized North and surpass it.

Again, during the so-called Second Cold War of the 1980s, large-scale economic cooperation between Japan and South Korea under the Nakasone cabinet can be understood as one of the strategic contributions Japan made to the Western camp.

## After the Cold War

The well-known humiliation suffered by Japan during the first Gulf War brought about a long-term process of becoming a "normal nation." The Japanese defense establishment, studying the successes of Europe and the practices of nations it understood as peers, began to emphasize security dialogue and defense exchange as components of overcoming its legacy of imperialism and contributing to the creation of a stable international security environment. The outcome was the inauguration of a range of bilateral and multilateral processes, including bilateral defense exchanges and security dialogues with South Korea. From 1994 the two sides began reciprocal visits of defense officials, including ministers, and naval confidence building measures such as joint search-and-rescue exercises, although exchanges between the air forces did not begin until 2000. By the late 1990s, the Japanese side was quietly affirming the closeness of the bilateral military-to-military relationship, but for reasons of enduring sensitivity within Korea the rapprochement was kept rather quiet.

This militarization of the bilateral security relationship is often mistakenly seen as the very birth of South Korean-Japanese cooperation in security affairs. The Cold War era economic cooperation was seen as clearly strategic by both sides. Nonetheless, by excluding the military dimension, the two sides failed to sow the seeds for public trust and mutual respect. Japan's economic support for Korea could be understood as reparations for colonization rather than strategic assistance, and because of its unidirectional nature it did nothing to erase the asymmetries discussed above. As they began military confidence building in the 1990s, Seoul and Tokyo were in some ways starting from scratch.

For this reason, the United States began to view its role as hub in the hub-and-spokes security framework as the useful basis for contributing to consolidation of the wheel's rim. Reaffirming its alliances in Northeast Asia, the United States has also sought to strengthen relations among all its Pacific allies. A good case can be made that Washington effectively brokered the new security relationship between Australia and Japan, and certainly it sought to do the same between South Korea and Japan. The United States also found ways to include Japan in multilateral exercises, such as RimPac and Cobra Gold, so as to hasten the region's acceptance of Japan as an active military contributor to regional security.

Trilateral military exercises and security cooperation have been hindered, though, by the same political constraints that undermine ROK-Japan bilateral defense relations. Statements by Japanese leaders about the colonial or wartime eras, territorial disputes, and education policy have all instigated severe uproar in Korea (and elsewhere). This has forced interruption of high-level (high-profile) bilateral defense exchanges, including cancellation of defense ministerial visits. Lower level exchanges and joint participation in multilateral processes continue, but while these can strengthen trust between the two military establishments, the very fact that they can continue despite diplomatic tension reveals that they are insulated from the mainstream of national public opinion.

## The Rise of China

> The future influences the present just as much as the past.
> —Friedrich Nietzsche

The rise of China has left South Korea balanced on the edge of a geopolitical divide once again. In seeking to maintain its good ties with China while avoiding the possibility of being dominated by surging Chinese power, Seoul maintains its close alliance with Washington. But in keeping Japan at arm's length, it may be missing a chance to contribute to regional stability without becoming provocative.

America's strategic goal in the post Cold War Asia-Pacific security environment has been fairly clear: prevent the emergence of any challenge to the existing regional order. This requires a mix of accommodating and constraining the only power capable of upsetting that order, the People's Republic of China. Since all countries in the region (with the possible exception of North Korea and Burma) have derived tremendous benefit from the existing order, there seems little controversy in U.S. efforts to maintain it, but the reaffirmation of the U.S.-Japan Alliance in 1996 in particular, coming as it did in the midst of the worst crisis in the Taiwan Strait since the 1950s, fed suspicion in Beijing. The rude awakening from China's dream-vision of emerging global multipolarity (and thus greater freedom of action for itself) would by itself have made the alliance reaffirmation somewhat unpalatable. Its timing, and the implicit decision by Japan to support American hegemony as a means of containing China, sparked an ongoing rivalry between Tokyo and Beijing.

Sino-Japanese relations have been tense and difficult ever since, as repeated efforts to patch things up and paper over differences have failed to last. Even the United States, a major beneficiary of the strategic competition between Japan and China because it gains leverage over both of them, has expressed concern that mutual antipathy is burning too hot. How much more must South Korea, caught precisely between the two, suffer from their competition?

Of course being courted by both sides has its advantages, as Seoul is able to exert influence disproportionate to its strategic weight. As long as it avoids making excessive commitments to one side or the other, South Korea preserves an advantage in not being taken for granted. It is able to form a trilateral group with Tokyo and Beijing—the +3 of ASEAN+3—that is gradually beginning to establish a framework for cooperation. In this sense, maintaining a "balance" between its relations with Japan and China has its own persuasive logic. Certainly Seoul wants all the influence it can get in Beijing, both because of China's growing wealth and power in general and because of China's important role in dealing with North Korea in particular.

Yet over the longer term, China's rise will create ever greater pressure for accommodation of its interests, although most likely not for mimicry—in a word, Finlandization. Korea's history of bandwagoning with a strong China sets the stage for this course, but it would be preferable for South Korea to cooperate with Japan to retain its own independence.

## Convergence

South Korea can viably increase its reliance on Japan because of growing convergence between the two nations. Certainly the asymmetries discussed above still exist, but they are shrinking in absolute size and in relevance. In terms of population and economy, both Japan and South Korea are mature; they confront relative decline in the context of Chinese growth but less and less threat from each other.

In terms of military capabilities, South Korean naval modernization is closely mirroring the structure of Japan's Maritime Self-Defense Forces.

While some see this as a sign that South Korea views Japan as a potential threat, others see this increasing symmetry as both reassuring and promising: reassuring because as the less powerful state South Korea would more likely seek to cope with a rival's military through asymmetrical means (as North Korea increasingly does toward the South and China has been doing towards the United States); promising because the harmonization of U.S. and Japanese naval forces offers a "plug and play" option for South Korea to contribute to the same framework of cooperation, as Seoul adjusts to the shift of the U.S.-ROK Alliance to a regional role.[10]

Japan's gradual move toward "normal nation" status will ease the asymmetry of national security establishments and paradigms. Both countries remain committed to civilian control and rule of law. Both must cope with population aging, and a thus military more reliant on high-tech equipment rather than large-scale manpower. Both depend on open global markets. Increasingly, they are similar nations in similar circumstances.

The asymmetry of history will never disappear, but the postwar history of economic growth, democracy, and social freedom is becoming more and more salient to both peoples. Thanks to South Koreans' tenacity and determination, they have outcompeted their rival to the north and achieved a prosperous, modern, free society. This has won them genuine respect and affection within Japan, spurring the increasing popularity of Korean cultural products there.

Japan's own views of history are also in flux, and the political structure of historical denial—the fact that the ruling LDP was an umbrella covering both pragmatic centrists and right-wing nationalists—has been shattered. The new political framework emerging in the wake of the 2009 victory of the Democratic Party of Japan (DPJ) is that the pragmatic center has split, and now the possibilities exist for a coalition with moderate leftists or moderate rightists, without the necessity of extreme nationalists or ideologues to taint the government position on history. This new, still-evolving political environment offers hope that Japan will avoid the provocations that have so inflamed Koreans in the past.

As hopeful as that picture may be, bilateral disputes continue to fester and will never vanish. This is the nature of nation-states; even within the European Union there are resentments and lingering negative stereotypes. In the United States, many Southerners still resent the North nearly 150 years after the Civil War, and historical interpretation remains inflammatory to this day. Certainly there are fissures and disputes within South Korean society as well. So, while a complete absence of friction between South Korea and Japan is not possible, neither is it necessary for the bilateral relationship to build a stronger framework of security cooperation. Japan can continue to be a strategic asset for South Korea.

## Notes

1 For example, during Jiang Zemin's 1995 state visit to Seoul he joined President Kim Young-sam in rebuking Japan for its refusal to recognize that WWII was a war of "aggression." See B. C. Koh, "South Korea in 1995: Tremors of Transition," *Asian Survey* 36, no. 1 (January 1996): 53–60.

2 The issue is explained thoroughly by Tobias Harris, "The Tamogami Affair," *Observing Japan* (blog), November 5, 2008, http://www.observingjapan.com/2008/11/tamogami-affair.html.

3 Kim Tae-Hyo, "Korea's Strategic Thoughts toward Japan: Searching for a Democratic Alliance in the Past-driven Future," *Korean Journal of Defense Analysis* 20, no. 2 (Summer 2008): 41–154.

4 Democratic Peace is the most famous example of this class of theories that stress regime affinity. See the seminal Michael Doyle, "Kant, Liberal Legacies, and Foreign Affairs," *Philosophy and Public Affairs* 12 (Summer and Fall 1983): 205, 207–8.

5 Hideyoshi's invasions and attempted conquest of Korea from 1592 to 1598 prove to many Koreans that Japan's twentieth century colonization was not an aberration but the continuity of something fundamental in Japan's character.

6 "Joint Survey Shows Japan-ROK Gaps," *Yomiuri Shimbun*, April 18, 2010.

7 See George R. Packard, *Protest in Tokyo: The Security Treaty Crisis of 1960* (Princeton: Princeton University Press, 1966), 332.

8 Wakamiya Yoshibumi, *Sengo Hoshu no Ajiakan* [The postwar conservative view of Asia] (Tokyo: Asahi Shimbunsha, 1995), 11–22.

9 See Azuma Kiyohiko, "Nikkan anzen hosho kankei no hensen: Kokkou seijouka kara reisengo made" [Vicissitudes of Japan-ROK security relations: from normalization of relations to after the Cold War], *Kokusai Anzen Hosho* [International security] 33, no. 4 (March 2006), esp. 94–95.

10 My thanks to Michishita Narushige for this point.

# RUSSIA AND SOUTH KOREA: NEW HORIZONS FOR STRATEGIC PARTNERSHIP

## Alexandre Y. Mansourov

In 2010, Russia and the Republic of Korea (ROK, or South Korea) marked the twentieth anniversary of the establishment of diplomatic relations between Moscow and Seoul. Former Cold War enemies are now friendly neighbors who adhere to the values of liberal democracy, free markets and open societies, share many economic interests and security concerns, and are rapidly expanding their political, economic, military, and cultural relations in the direction of "strategic partnership," regardless of what political group may be in power in the Kremlin and the Blue House at any given time.

Usually the North Korean question tends to crowd out all discussions about Russian policy toward the ROK. Geopolitical pressures and the current security context inevitably push the coordination of issues related to the denuclearization of the Democratic People's Republic of Korea (DPRK, or North Korea) and provision of economic and humanitarian assistance to North Korea to the top of the bilateral agenda. Nonetheless, it is important to remember that the Russian-ROK relationship is multifaceted, thick, and dynamic. Despite long distances, it is driven by pragmatic interests and underpinned by shared values and concerns. It has an intrinsic value for both nations. This chapter will explore it on its own merits.

## Declaratory Framework for Russian Policy Toward the Republic of Korea

The Concept of Foreign Policy of the Russian Federation, dated June 28, 2000, states that Russia is striving to have "equal participation in the resolution of the Korean problem" and "to maintain balanced relations with both Korean states."[1] Russia wants "stability and involvement on the Korean Peninsula."

In summer 2007, the Russian Foreign Ministry published an interagency-drafted white paper, "A Survey of the Russian Federation Foreign Policy,"[2] which devoted a whole chapter to the Asia-Pacific region. It regards the Korean Peninsula problems as both posing "a serious challenge to security and stability in the region" and creating "a window of opportunity for the creation of a permanent dialogue mechanism on security and cooperation in Northeast Asia."[3]

Moscow's relations with Seoul are guided by the Russian-ROK Treaty on Basic Relations, signed in November 1992 during President Yeltsin's visit to Seoul. In addition to the basic treaty, Russian-ROK relations are framed by the Joint Statement signed at the Kim Dae-jung (Kim Tae-jung)–Putin summit in Seoul on February 26-28, 2001; the Joint Declaration signed at the Putin-Roh Moo-hyun (No Mu-hyŏn) summit in Moscow, September 20-23, 2004; the Joint Action Plan adopted at the Roh Moo-hyun–Putin summit in Seoul on November 19, 2005; as well as the Joint Statement signed at the Medvedev–Lee Myung-bak (Yi Myŏng-bak) summit in Moscow on September 28–30, 2008.

## Political Relations

After the establishment of diplomatic relations in 1990, Russian and ROK leaders had twenty summits. According to *Chosun Ilbo*, the Korean and Russian presidents will likely meet alternately in Seoul and St. Petersburg every year starting 2010, the 20th anniversary of diplomatic relations. During President Lee Myung-bak's visit to St. Petersburg on September 30, 2008, Korean and Russian leaders agreed to hold annual bilateral summits from 2010 on.[4]

Russian and South Korean prime ministers exchanged visits once, respectively, in October 2006 and October 2000, something that had not happened during Yeltsin's years. In February 2008 Premier Viktor Zubkov paid a working visit to Seoul and attended the inaugural ceremony of President Lee Myung-bak.

The Russian government maintains a rather active dialogue with the ROK at the foreign ministry level. Russian and ROK foreign ministers are used to having consultations at the annual Asia-Pacific Economic Cooperation (APEC) meetings and UN General Assembly meetings. Foreign Minister Igor Ivanov paid an official visit to Seoul on July 26, 2002, and in 2008 Russian Foreign Minister Sergei Lavrov met the ROK's Minister of Foreign Affairs and Trade (MOFAT) Yu Myung-hwan (Yu Myŏng-hwan) three times—on the sidelines of the ASEAN Regional Forum in Singapore (July 23), in Moscow (September 9–11) and in Astana (October 16). The Russian Ministry of Foreign Affairs (MOFA) conducts regular interministerial consultations with its ROK counterpart (between the head of the First Asian department of the Russian MOFA and the head of the Third Department [Russia and the Commonwealth of Independent States (CIS)] of the ROK MOFAT) on the basis of biannual bilateral protocols on interministerial consultations. In accordance with the agreement reached during the Moscow 2008 summit, Russia's First Deputy Foreign Minister Andrei Denisov held the first round of Strategic Dialogue on Foreign Policy and Security Issues with his ROK counterpart Kwon Jong-rak in Seoul on December 18, 2008. Russian ambassadors in Seoul (Konstantin V. Vnukov [October 2009–present], Gleb Ivaschentsov [June 2005–August 2009], Teymuraz Ramishvili [August 2001–April 2005], Evgeny Afanasiev [1997–2001], and Georgy Kunadze [1994–1997]) all have played indispensable roles in shaping the implementation of Russian policy toward South Korea on the ground.

In addition to top-level and high-level exchanges, the Russian government engages the ROK government at the ministerial level within the framework of bilateral intergovernmental committees and interdepartmental commissions. The Russia-Korea Joint Committee on Economic, Scientific and Technological Cooperation was set up in 1999. It is cochaired by one of the Russian deputy prime ministers and his ROK counterpart, and composed of senior officials of mainline ministries and agencies under the Russian Cabinet of Ministers and its ROK counterparts. The Russian-ROK intergovernmental commission usually meets once every year. The Joint Committee includes ten sectorial committees and subcommittees. During preparations for the Russia-ROK summit, an expanded meeting of the vice chairmen of National Sides of the Inter-Governmental Committee was held in Seoul in September 2008. Also, the two governments set up the Russian-Korean Committee on Siberia and Far East in 2001, and encouraged the formation of the Russian-ROK Business Council and Russian-Korean Academic Forum.

Furthermore, Moscow cannot ignore the opinions of regional and municipal elites in Khabarovsk, Chita, Tomsk, Omsk, Novosibirsk, Irkutsk, Vladivostok, Yakutiya, Nakhodka, Sakhalin, and Kamchatka, who are actively engaged in interregional and cross-border trade, investment projects, and cultural exchange with various entities in the Republic of Korea. Sometimes, regional and local officials got ahead of the center or found themselves at cross-purposes with Moscow, especially on immigration and local infrastructure development issues.

In general, Russia and the ROK share a number of principled approaches to key international issues, including building an equitable multipolar world order under the central role of the United Nations, non-acceptance of coercion in interstate relations, nonproliferation of weapons of mass destruction and protection of global energy security. These common approaches set a good basis for bilateral cooperation in the UN and at other international forums.

A traditional agenda for bilateral political dialogue is focused on the problems of denuclearization of the Korean Peninsula and inter-Korean reconciliation. In its discussions with Seoul, Moscow emphasizes the need to preserve stability and promote regional socioeconomic development in Northeast Asia by preventing any escalation in military tensions on the Korean Peninsula that could stem from a humanitarian emergency or any military contingency. From Moscow's perspective, the preservation of peace is more important than prevention of WMD proliferation, promotion of democracy, and observation of human rights in North Korea. Furthermore, from a geopolitical point of view, although Russia does not want to see an unchecked increase of any foreign domination in Korea, which would endanger its interests, it does not aim per se to increase its own influence in the area. Russia seeks more say in the decision-making process in Korean affairs in order to protect its national interests. Moreover, Moscow encourages Seoul to help its northern brother transform its internal and external policies, not to threaten it with punishment for its odd behavior at home and perceived provocations abroad. Finally, according to Georgy Toloraya,[5] "Russia generally supports North-South reconciliation and cooperation with a distant goal of eventual reunification in a form agreed upon by North and South. Such a development would not contradict Russian interests if it would result in the creation of a united, peaceful, and prosperous Korea that is friendly to Russia. Such a country would be one of Russia's most important partners in Asia, helping to build a more balanced system of international relations in the Far East."

The September 2008 Moscow summit between President Medvedev and President Lee Myung-bak opened new broad horizons in further upgrading Russian-South Korean relations in the direction of strategic partnership. First, Lee's talks with Medvedev and Premier Putin confirmed the continuity of the ROK's strategy aimed at broadening and intensifying bilateral relations with Russia. Although Lee holds different positions on many international issues from his predecessors, this does not concern relations with Russia. Moscow believes that the ROK's political elites (both neoconservatives and liberals) share a national consensus about the desirability of developing a full-fledged partnership with Russia. Second, the Russian-South Korean summit took place in the wake of the Russian-Georgian War, when the West accused Moscow of excessive use of force in the Caucasus. The Kremlin was particularly appreciative of Seoul's intention to upgrade bilateral relations to the level of strategic partnership at the time of what was perceived as an active anti-Russian diplomatic campaign in some Western capitals. Seoul's independent position on the problem of South Ossetia and Abkhazia raised its prestige in Moscow's eyes and contributed to strengthening the ROK's influence in regional and global affairs, as far as Moscow was concerned.

All in all, Lee Myung-bak's official visit to Russia in September 2008 gave a new impetus to further development of the whole gamut of complex bilateral relations. Moscow and Seoul agreed to cooperate on such important issues as new challenges and threats, the global financial crisis, climate change, energy and food security, combat against trans-border crimes (including financial and cyber-crimes), as well as piracy. Russia now considers its relations with South Korea, as "positively developing towards a strategic partnership" and as one of the priorities of Russian foreign policy in the Asia-Pacific region.[6]

## Economic Relations

Economic exchanges with the ROK are by and large left to market forces, and they tend to develop autonomously, regardless of the minor vacillations in the rather stable political temperature in bilateral relations. In general, one often hears Russian relations with its South Korean neighbor described as "warm politics, warm economics."

To promote commerce with the ROK, the Russian Ministry of Economic Development and Trade maintains a Trade Representative Office (TRO) at the Russian Embassy in Seoul. In formulating Russian foreign economic policy toward South Korea, it has to balance the priorities of the Russian Ministries of Industry and Energy, Regional Development, Natural Resources, and Finance, as well as the interests of major Russian exporters of oil and gas (Gazprom, Rosneft, Transneft, Lukoil, former Yukos, Roszheldor), electricity (RAO UES), timber (Rosles), minerals and ores (RUSAL, Norilsk Nickel, Bazovy Element, Severstal) and wholesale importers of autos, textiles, consumer electronics, manufactured goods (such as Renova Group), in addition to the plans of Russian domestic industries and manufacturers, as contrasted with priorities of foreign investors. Table 6.1 lists the existing general trade and investment agreements signed by the Russian government with its ROK counterpart.

Table 6.1 Trade and Investment Agreements, Russian Federation and ROK

| Intergovernmental agreements | Interdepartmental agreements |
| --- | --- |
| Joint Action Plan in the Field of Trade and Economic Cooperation (November 19, 2005) | Interdepartmental memorandum of understanding on collaboration and cooperation between Russian Federal Agency for Managing Special Economic Zones and ROK KOTRA (October 17, 2006) |
| Intergovernmental Declaration on Facilitating the Development of Trade and Economic Cooperation and Science and Technology Cooperation (September 28, 1995) | Intergovernmental agreement on the establishment of Russian-Korean Industrial Complex in Special Economic Zone "Nakhodka" (October 2000) |
| Intergovernmental Trade agreement (December 14, 1990) | Interdepartmental memorandum of understanding on industrial cooperation (October 2000) |
| | Intergovernmental agreement on promotion and mutual protection of investments (December 25 1990) |

*Source:* Author.

Further, on November 19, 1992, Moscow concluded an intergovernmental agreement on avoidance of double taxation with respect to income taxes with the ROK; on the same day, to facilitate trade, the Russian Federal Customs Service concluded an intergovernmental agreement on cooperation and mutual aid in customs affairs with the ROK. In addition, the Russian Ministry of Natural Resources on October 17, 2006, signed an interdepartmental memorandum of understanding with the ROK on cooperation in forestry between the Russian Federal Forestry Agency and the ROK Forestry Administration. President Medvedev's Ministry of Agriculture inherited an intergovernmental agreement on cooperation in fisheries with the ROK, signed on September 16, 1991.

At present, Russia is the eighth largest trading partner of the Republic of Korea. In the past ten years, Russian-ROK trade increased nine-fold from $2.23 billion in 1999 to $18.09 billion in 2008. In 2008, Russian exports equaled $8.34 billion—imports were $9.75 billion—and were projected to grow to $30–40 billion in the next five years. In 2007, crude oil and oil products occupy a whopping 90 percent share of Russian exports to the ROK, with the rest going to aluminum and marine products. Russian imports from the ROK consist of industrial machinery and equipment, and transportation vehicles (63 percent), chemical products (20 percent), consumer electronics (10 percent), textiles (4 percent), and foodstuffs.[7]

Notwithstanding the lion's share of crude oil in Russian exports to South Korea, one should not consider Russia only as a raw materials supplier for the ROK's market. For example, more than sixty percent of all civilian helicopters used in the ROK were made in Russia. More than a third of nuclear fuel used at the ROK's atomic power plants comes also from Russia.[8] Russian and South Korean companies are engaged in numerous negotiations involving multi-million dollar commercial contracts on joint scientific research and design as well as on production of Russian licensed high-tech goods in the ROK.[9]

Inter-regional and cross-border trade between Russian Siberian and Far Eastern regions (Maritime and Khabarovsk regions, Amur and Magadan oblasts, Kamchatka) and South Korea account for nearly thirty percent of bilateral trade with the ROK.[10] Of particular significance is the Republic of Sakha (Yakutia), because of its size, geographic location, natural resource endowment, and its important role as one of the locomotives of socioeconomic development in the Russian Far East. Republic of Sakha (Yakutia) President Shtyrov's October 2007 visit to the ROK laid a solid foundation for the participation of ROK companies in the economic development of the region.[11]

Especially promising, albeit controversial, is Russia's cooperation with South Korea in the energy sector, the main directions of which are set forth in the international section of the government document called "Energy Strategy of the Russian Federation up to the Year of 2020"[12] and in a state program of energy infrastructure development in Siberia and the Far East developed by Gazprom, the Ministry of Economic Development and Trade, and the Ministry of Industry and Energy in 2003.[13] Energy cooperation is directly related to the energy security of the ROK and has the potential to affect the regional economy and geopolitics in many positive and negative ways.

Cooperation in the energy sector includes region-wide shipments of crude oil and oil products by Rosneft and Lukoil; gas supplies via current liquefied natural gas (LNG) deliveries from the Sakhalin platforms (1.5 million tons of LNG for the ROK in the next twenty years) and future gas pipelines; potential gasification of the DPRK with Gazprom's and KOGAS's technical assistance; potential cross-border surplus electricity transfers via North Korea;[14] possible multilateral cooperation in the construction of nuclear power plants in North Korea; supply of fuel for nuclear power plants in the ROK[15] and reprocessing of their spent nuclear fuel in Russia; possible cooperation in the uranium ore trade;[16] potential cooperation in the modernization and expansion of the Soviet-built hydro-electric power plants and heavy fuel oil (HFO) fired power plants in the DPRK; construction of oil and gas pipeline systems (Eastern Siberia-Pacific Ocean and Russia-China),[17] and so on.

Russia annually earns a multibillion petrodollar windfall via energy sales in the region. All sides want long-term price stability—but the question is at what level. Given rising energy prices around the world, the Russian government strives to lock in the formula and rates equivalent to those used in Russian energy trade with Western Europe in its new long-term energy contracts with major Asian consumers, while Korea, as Japan and China do, appears to prefer for now the traditional formula and deliveries based on spot market prices, hoping that one day the prices will come down to the more affordable levels seen in the late 1990s. Moscow is rather subtle in flexing its energy muscles in political bargaining with Seoul, but it often uses its energy cards in playing Seoul off against Tokyo and Beijing, which is particularly evident in the Russian-Chinese-Japanese-South Korean negotiations on the construction of the Pacific oil and gas pipeline system.

In addition to the energy sector, Russia promotes cooperation with the ROK in the transportation sector, including Russian-ROK cooperation in the modernization of the North Korean railroads and connection of the Trans-Siberian railways with the Trans-Korean railways. On May 20, 2008, Russian Railways Chairman Vladimir Yakunin visited Seoul and held bilateral talks with the representatives of the ROK government and KORAIL regarding the question of possible South Korean participation in a trilateral Russian-DPRK-ROK project designed to modernize the 55-kilometer Khasan-Rajin railway and container terminal in the DPRK port of Rajin. In principle, Seoul confirmed its intention to take part in the pilot project by agreeing to establish a joint Russian-ROK logistics company, RuKoLogistics. But, the agreement implementation talks with Korean forwarders have not produced any concrete results yet. Table 6.2 lists all existing intergovernmental and interdepartmental agreements in the energy and transportation sectors between Russia and ROK at present.

Moscow also promotes cooperation with South Korea in science and technology, including the communications and information technology sectors, peaceful use of space, nuclear science research, nanotechnology,[18] environmental protection, and other areas. In 2007, the Russian-Korean Committee on Scientific and Technological Cooperation held its ninth session in Seoul and outlined the main prospective directions of further cooperation between R&D centers and academic universities of the two countries. They also began to negotiate a bilateral intergovernmental Protocol on Principles of Protection and Allocation of Intellectual Property Rights in the Area of Science and Technology.

**Table 6.2  Russian Federation-ROK Intergovernmental Agreements, Energy and Transportation Sectors**

| Energy |
| --- |
| MOU between OAO Gazprom and KOGAS on organizing gas supplies from the Russian Federation to the Republic of Korea (September 29, 2008) |
| Intergovernmental agreement on cooperation in gas industry (October 17, 2006) |
| Interdepartmental agreement between Tatneft and LG on designing, equipment supplies and construction of an oil processing and petrochemical complex (worth $3 billion) in Tatarstan (September 21, 2004) |
| Interdepartmental MOU between the government of Tatarstan and Korean Export-Import Bank concerning the opening of a $1.3 billion credit line for Tatneft (September 21, 2004) |
| Intergovernmental agreement on cooperation in the energy sector (October 2000) |
| **Transportation** |
| Trilateral Russia-ROK-DRPK consultations on connecting Trans-Korean railroads with Trans-Siberian Railroad |

*Source:* Author.

Of particular significance is Russian-South Korean cooperation in joint outer space exploration. On September 21, 2004, during President Roh Moo-hyun's visit to Moscow, the Russian and South Korean governments signed an intergovernmental agreement on cooperation in the exploration and use of outer space for peaceful purposes. Subsequently, Russia launched the ROK "Arirang" satellites from its satellite launch base at Plesetsk in 2007. Russian Federal Space Agency Director Perminov visited Seoul in October 2007. On April 8–19, 2008, a Russian Soyuz spaceship transported the first Russian-trained South Korean cosmonaut Yi So-yeon to the International Space Station from the Russian Space Center Baikonur. Russia assisted in the construction of the ROK Naro Space Center on the island of Waenaru in Goheung, South Jeolla Province. Russian and South Korean space agencies and their subordinate organizations (Khrunichev Space Center, Scientific-Production Association EnergoMash, and Transport Machine-Building Design Bureau, from the Russian side) are cooperating in designing and manufacturing (including ground infrastructure) a joint Russian-South Korean rocket, KSLV-I, capable of carrying a 100 kilogram payload into the Earth's orbit.[19]

For many years, the Russian government sought to attract foreign direct investment to Russia, and the efforts produced substantial fruits. In particular, ROK investments in Russia reached $620 million in 2006 and $894.6 million in 864 business projects (the total amount of announced investments is $1.54 billion) in 2008. These include the Hyundai auto assembly plant in Ulyanovsk; an LG stake in the new oil-processing and petrochemical complex that it built for Tatneft in Tatastan; the construction of a Lotte hotel and shopping mall in downtown Moscow; LG Electronics' consumer electronics plant in Rusa (Moscow area); and the (slow-going) construction of the Russian-Korean Industrial Complex in Special Economic Zone Nakhodka.[20] It is noteworthy that South Korean automakers are intent on expanding joint production in Russia. Hyundai Motor invested a total of $500 million in its first Russian full-cycle car assembly plant in St. Petersburg, commissioned in September 2010; it initiated mass production of four-door sedans in January 2011 and began to export its Accent model within the CIS region shortly after in April. Hyundai anticipates increasing the plant's annual capacity to 150,000 units in 2012. [21]

In contrast, Russian capital outflows to the ROK remain miniscule. Russian investments in the ROK economy amounted to $75.6 million, including only $260,000 in direct investments in 2007. To enable direct credit and payment for foreign trade transactions, banking and investment services, on September 29, 2008, the Foreign Economic Bank of Russia (Vnesheconombank) signed a framework agreement between the State Corporation Bank of Development and External Economy (Vneshekonombank) and the Export-Import Bank of the Republic of Korea.

Following the general line of the Putin administration aimed at reducing overall Soviet/Russian government debt and curtailing future external government borrowing, the Russian Ministry of Finance negotiated major debt settlement agreements in the region. In particular, on September 15, 2003, Moscow signed an intergovernmental agreement with Seoul on restructuring the debt (principal and interest equal to $2.24 billion) of the former USSR, whereby $660 million in interest was written off, $300 million was to be paid in armaments deliveries in 2003–2006, and the repayment of the principal of $1.26 billion was restructured and extended until 2025.[22] This agreement entered into force on March 9, 2004. In June 2007, the Russian Finance Ministry announced that Moscow had started repaying its outstanding debt of $1.33 billion to South Korea. The repayment process is expected to take nineteen years. Russia intends to repay $70 million in cash annually, starting in 2007, under the 2003 debt settlement accord.

In the pursuit of WTO membership, after hard bargaining for a few years, the Russian Ministry of Economic Development and Trade (under former Minister German Gref) on behalf of Russian government signed the WTO accession protocol with the ROK on September 21, 2004.[23]

## Military-to-Military Relations, Military-Technical Cooperation, and Cooperation in Other Security Areas

The Russian military-industrial complex and national security establishments have long-standing interests in Northeast Asia. The Russian Ministry of Defense, General Staff, Russian Security Council, Siberian and Far Eastern military district commands, Pacific Fleet command, and other power organs and intelligence services have a rather keen interest in and contribute substantively to the formulation of Russian defense and security policy toward Northeast Asia in general and the Korean Peninsula in particular. Also important is the intensive lobbying of policymakers by the state monopoly Rosvooruzheniye (formerly known as Rosoboronexport), state concern Roskosmos, MIG Corporation, Sukhoi Corporation, Uralvagonzavod State Production Association (Nizhniy Tagil), Admiralty Shipyard Association (St. Petersburg), Baltic Plant Joint Stock Company (St. Petersburg) and other military industrial enterprises. In the 1990s, their primary motivation was industrial survival. These days, they are driven mostly by the considerations of profit and market share, as well as by Russian geopolitical interests.

In general, Russian military doctrine does not regard the Far Eastern strategic direction as posing any large-scale military threat to Russia at present and in the next ten to fifteen years, despite persistent tensions on the Korean Peninsula and in the Taiwan Strait.[24] The Russian military's approach toward the ROK is relatively apprehensive and tentative, because the latter is one of two main U.S. military allies in the region.

For a long time, the fact that the ROK was regarded as a staunch military ally of the United States—with 37,000 U.S. troops on its soil—had prevented any substantive development in Russian-ROK military-to-military relations. The first dent in this wall was made when General Kim Jang-soo, Director, Operations, Joint Chiefs of Staff, of the ROK Ministry of National Defense (MND), visited Moscow on May 15, 2001, and the two ministries decided to set up a joint consultative group on defense issues at the department head level.[25] In 2002, the two governments signed an intergovernmental agreement on prevention of dangerous military activity. On April 10, 2003, then Russian Defense Minister Sergei Ivanov made the first ever defense minister's visit to Seoul where he met with his ROK counterpart Cho Young-kil (Cho Yŏng-gil), paid a courtesy call on President Roh at the Blue House and visited several military bases in the ROK. It is interesting to note that while expressing general support for the ROK's policy of peace and prosperity and agreeing that close cooperation between South Korea and Russia was crucial to seeking a peaceful settlement of the North Korean nuclear issue, Ivanov surprisingly stated that "Russia is willing to guarantee North Korea's security," which may have been designed to send a message to the United States and its allies not to try a military solution on the peninsula, despite the escalating North Korean nuclear crisis and America's emerging euphoria from its quick and decisive battlefield victory in Iraq.[26]

Ivanov's Seoul visit led to the first meeting between chiefs of the Air Forces in July 2003, and in August 2003 the ROK Navy participated in a combined maritime search and rescue exercise hosted by the Russian Pacific Ocean Fleet. As a goodwill gesture, a detachment of three naval vessels of the fleet under the command of Admiral Fyodorov visited Incheon in February 2004.[27] In August 2004 an inaugural meeting of the Joint Military Committee was held in Moscow to discuss the implementation of a 2002 agreement on prevention of dangerous military activity. On April 24, 2005, ROK Minister of Defense Yoon Kwang-woong (Yun Kwang-ung) paid a reciprocal visit to Russia where he held productive talks with his Russian counterpart. During his visit, the Russian Ministry of Defense and the ROK Ministry of National Defense signed an interdepartmental memorandum of understanding on the transfer and joint development of weapons technology, and a memorandum of understanding on setting up a hotline to exchange aviation information. As a sign of rising mutual trust and improving military relations, Russia agreed to pay part of its debt to the ROK from 2003–2006 in the form of $300 million worth of armaments deliveries (T-80U tanks, BMP-3 armored personnel carriers, patrol boats, and Igla air defense rocket complexes). In 2007, Russia delivered military equipment worth about $50 million to South Korea.

As of December 2010, Russia has almost completed fulfillment of its obligations under previous foreign military sales (FMS) contracts. Bilateral military-technical cooperation now involves mostly R&D on commission, shipments of spare parts and post-sale maintenance of Russian armaments and military equipment.

In December 2007 Moscow and Seoul signed a Memorandum of Understanding on Military-Technical Cooperation, stipulating the development of a joint long-term program of military-technical cooperation, which will include the mutually agreed upon list of armaments and military equipment to be delivered from Russia to South Korea and the R&D topics in the military-technical area to be jointly developed on a commercial basis and as a partial repayment of the old Soviet debt to the ROK.

The two militaries also maintained active exchanges in 2007. Colonel General Nikolai Frolov, Commander of the Russian Army's Anti-Air Artillery Forces, and Major General Oleg Kolyada, Chief of Staff of the Flight Support Service of the Russian Air Force, led two Russian military delegations to Seoul. Admiral Song Young-moo (Song Yŏng-mu), Chief of Staff of the ROK Navy, and Army General Kim Tae-young (Kim T'ae-yŏng), Commander of the ROK's First Field Army and later Minister of National Defense, led two ROK military delegations to Russia. A group of battleships from the Russian Pacific Fleet made a port call to Incheon. Russian and Korean military historians held official consultations. However, Russian Defense Minister Serdyukov has not visited the ROK yet, despite Seoul's official invitation.

The Russian Federal Security Service (FSB) continues its cooperation with the National Intelligence Service (NIS), aimed at joint collaboration in the fight against international terrorism, narco-trafficking, and trans-border organized crime through joint anti-terrorist exercises and mutual consultations on the above issues. The NIS delegation took part in the Sixth International Conference of the Chiefs of Special Services, Security Services, and Law Enforcement Agencies, organized by the FSB in Khabarovsk in September 2007. The FSB Border Service and the ROK's Coast Guard conducted a number of joint maritime search and rescue exercises.

## Cultural Exchange

The Russian government devotes much attention to promoting Russian cultural and civilizational influence in Asia in general and on the Korean Peninsula in particular. It encourages self-organization of the Russian diaspora in the ROK, which has grown from 10,000 to 50,000 since the collapse of the USSR; promotes study of the Russian language, which is growing in Korea (via Roszarubezhtsentr-sponsored programs like "Russian Language, 2006-2010"), and backs the advances of the Russian Orthodox Church in the region. It also organizes and lends financial support to nationwide cultural festivals designed to promote cultural ties with its neighbors, like the "Days of Moscow in Seoul" and "Days of Seoul in Moscow" in 2004, the "Russian Nights in Seoul" festival in September 2006 and the "Seoul Nights in Moscow" festival in August 2007.

In 2007–2008, the Russian government allocated 25 federal stipends for prospective South Korean students to study in Russian universities. It also finances the education and training of 150 Russian students in ROK universities. About sixty Russian professors are employed in various ROK universities on the basis of long-term employment contracts.

As Russian living standards rise, tourism becomes an important venue of interaction between Russians and their Asian neighbors. To promote tourist exchange, the Russian Federal Tourism Agency and Ministry of Economic Development and Trade signed an intergovernmental agreement on cooperation in tourism with the ROK on February 27, 2001. Moscow and Seoul also signed an intergovernmental Agreement on Facilitation of Visas for Short-term Visits by their Nationals on September 29, 2008.

Although it is difficult to estimate the exact amount of travel transactions between Russia and South Korea,[28] it appears that Russian travel expenditures in the ROK exceed Russian revenues from ROK-originated travel and, therefore the Russian balance of payments carries a certain deficit in travel services with the ROK. In the absence of easily accessible hard data on cash expenditures, one possible set of statistics pointing toward this conclusion is contained in Table 6.3, which shows the number of outbound trips made by the citizens of the Russian Federation traveling to the ROK in 2006, and in Table 6.4, which shows the number of inbound Russia trips made by the citizens of ROK in 2006.

It appears that the mutually restrictive visa regimes inhibit the intensification of people-to-people diplomacy and "shuttle trade" between Russia and South Korea. To facilitate people-to-people exchanges, Russia maintains one consulate-general in Pusan, ROK, at present.

Although the Russian Orthodox Church is officially separated from the Russian state, under President Putin's watch the Russian government never shied away from supporting and promoting the interests and activities of the Russian Orthodox Church in the Far East in general and on the Korean Peninsula in particular, at both the political and logistical levels. Russian Orthodox Church advances in the Far East face some common problems, including a lack of official recognition and state registration; frequent prosecution by state authorities; low numbers of adherents; lack of revenue-generating assets and a poor financial base; competition with Greek Orthodox Church and Russian Orthodox Church Outside of Russia; as well as suspicions of engaging in espionage for the benefit of Russia.[29]

**Table 6.3 Outbound Trips by Russian Federation Citizens to the ROK, 2006**

| Purpose of Visit | Number |
|---|---|
| Official Government at All Levels | 23,972 |
| Tourism | 28,911 |
| Business | 24,583 |
| Permanent Emigration | 187 |
| Seamen and Technical Personnel | 40,081 |
| Military Personnel | 1 |
| Total | 117,735 |

*Source:* Russian Federal Tourism Agency, Moscow. See "Incoming and Outgoing Tourism: Results of 2006," spravka, Federal Tourism Agency of the Russian Federation, Moscow, http://www.russiatourism.ru/files/analiz-2006.doc.

**Table 6.4 Inbound Trips by ROK Citizens to the Russian Federation, 2006**

| Purpose of Visit | Number |
|---|---|
| Official Government at All Levels | 13,704 |
| Tourism | 42,951 |
| Business | 10,719 |
| Permanent Emigration | 212 |
| Seamen and Technical Personnel | 17,054 |
| Transit | 26,148 |
| Total | 110,788 |

*Source:* Russian Federal Tourism Agency, Moscow. See Table 6.3 for details.

Despite the presence of a significant Christian population, the Russian Orthodox Church has no foothold in South Korea at all. In the future, it will probably recognize and join efforts with the Russian Orthodox Church Outside of Russia in the ROK, which has about one hundred believers, a St. Anna Church in Samcheok, Gangwon-do (Samch'ŏk, Kangwŏn-do), one priest, one sub-deacon, and one reader. This church is in poor financial shape and cannot compete with the much wealthier and more established Greek Orthodox Church in Korea.[30]

The Russian public appears to hold relatively favorable opinions about the ROK.[31] In a sample public opinion poll taken in Russia in February 2001, 58 percent of respondents answered positively when asked if South Korea was friendly toward Russia. Nevertheless, Russians know little about the ROK.[32] 61 percent of them said they knew nothing about it.[33] Russians were most likely to speak about the high-quality goods the South Koreans produce, mainly electronics and household appliances (11 percent): survey comments included "this country specializes in electronics;" "engineering, my razor;" "radio equipment from Korea;" "a positive evaluation for our TV set, which was made there, it's working well in our home." Of the respondents, 10 percent considered South Korea to be a rich, comfortable nation ("a little dragon that is gaining strength;" "Koreans are good people—they managed to make sweet stuff from nothing in only thirty years;" "this is an Asian miracle;" "great progress"). According to 5 percent of respondents, Koreans who managed to make such great progress in economic development in quite a short period are very hard working ("this is a hard-laboring nation and people;" "they aren't wasteful people: everything is used, they lose nothing;" "people work best there, like bees;" "they are hard-working people"). Only 5 percent of those surveyed mentioned the nature and climate of the country, and its geographical setting: "splendid blossoms and summer;" "it's a peninsula;" "it's exotic, with hot weather." And another 5 percent mentioned historical events associated with Korea in the twentieth century: "the American intervention in the '50s;" "the war...in 1953;" "the war between South and North Korea." When answering the question on what comes to their mind when they think of South Korea, some Russians said that it would be better if South and North Korea were united into one state: "when South and North Korea get together, my mind will be more calm;" "South Korea is going to meet North Korea halfway, and I would like their people to unite like the FRG did with the DDR in Germany. This is a civilized process."

## Conclusion

A strong Russia is back on the Korean Peninsula, and former President Putin deserves credit for it. The geopolitical picture in the region is quite promising for Moscow. Both Koreas again court Moscow for favor, looking forward to Moscow's intermediation in the denuclearization of the peninsula and Moscow's blessing for Korean reunification. Putin's pragmatic and flexible diplomacy with respect to the two Korean states made Russia's balancing act on the peninsula somewhat easier, and is now carried forward without any amends by President Medvedev.

For historical reasons, Russia and the ROK have different traditional allies and tend to be preoccupied with different problems in international affairs. However, Russia does not seek any privileges in South Korea, nor does it intend to compete for influence with anyone on the Korean Peninsula. Moscow does not regard its relations with Seoul through the prism of its relations with any other capital—whether it is Washington, Beijing,

Tokyo, or Pyongyang. Russia views its partnership with South Korea as self-sufficient and a necessary element of the multipolar world, based on geopolitical checks and balances, the equality of states and mutual respect of their national interests. They both jointly build a more democratic, fair, and safer world order.

## Notes

1 "The 2000 Concept of Foreign Policy of the Russian Federation," June 28, 2000, http://www.mid.ru.

2 "A 2007 Survey of Russian Federation Foreign Policy," http://www.mid.ru/.

3 Ibid.

4 "Regular Korea-Russia Summits Planned," *Chosun Ilbo*, February 17, 2009, http://english.chosun.com/w21data/html/news/200902/200902170002.html.

5 For a more detailed explanation of Moscow's positions, see Georgy Toloraya, "Continuity and Change in Korea: Challenges for Regional Policy and U.S.-Russia Relations," (Center for Northeast Asian Policy Studies: The Brookings Institution Press, Working Paper 31, February 2009), http://www.brookings.edu/~/media/Files/rc/papers/2009/02_korea_toloraya/02_korea_toloraya.pdf.

6 Gleb Ivaschentsev, "Russia and Korea: New Horizons for Partnership," *Mezhdunarodnaya Zhizn* [International Life] (November 2008).

7 Ministry of Foreign Affairs of the Russian Federation, "Trade and Economic Cooperation between Russia and Republic of Korea," spravka, 17 September 2007, http://www.mid.ru/. Also, Korean Customs Service, "Korea's exports to Russia soar," press release, October 8, 2007.

8 In April 1997 the Russian firm Elemash signed an agreement with South Korea to supply nuclear fuel for South Korea's nuclear power plants. For details, see Alexander Rubtsov, "Russian Nuclear Power Engineering Manufacturers Have to Count on Foreign Contracts," *BizEkon News*, April 15, 1997.

9 Ministry of Foreign Affairs of the Russian Federation, "Relations between Russia and ROK," informational spravka, February 19, 2009, accessed March 12, 2009, http://www.mid.ru/.

10 Russian Ministry of Foreign Affairs—First Asian Department, "Inter-regional Ties between the Russian Federation and the Republic of Korea," spravka, September 17, 2007, http://www.mid.ru/.

11 Ivaschentsev, "Russia and Korea."

12 Ministry of Energy of the Russian Federation, "Energy Strategy of the Russian Federation up to the Year of 2020," adopted by the decree (*rasporyazhenie*) #1234-p of the Government of the Russian Federation, August 28, 2003.

13 For details, see "State Program of Establishing a Unified System of Extraction and Transportation of Gas and Gas Provision in Eastern Siberia and the Far East, Taking into Consideration Possible Export of Gas to the Markets of China and Other Countries in the Asia-Pacific Region," *Gas Forum*, Gazprom, (March 2003), http://www.gasforum.ru/concept/gasprom_atr_0303.shtml.

14 In August 2006 the DPRK government confirmed its interest in a proposal from "VostokEnergo" (a subsidiary of RAO UES, "Unified Energy Systems of Russia") to

conduct a feasibility study regarding the construction of a 380 kilometer high-voltage (500 kWt) transmission line from the Russian Far East to the port of Chongjin and the northern provinces of the DPRK.

15 See Rubtsov, "Russian Nuclear Power."

16 According to Russian Minatom officials, the DPRK reportedly offered Russia exclusive rights to its natural uranium deposits in exchange for support at the stalled talks on Pyongyang's nuclear ambitions. The two countries have been in talks since 2002 on a deal for Russia to import uranium, which Moscow wants to enrich and sell as nuclear fuel to China. See The Associated Press Tokyo, December 3, 2006.

17 At the 12th prime ministerial talks held in Moscow on November 5-6, 2007, the two governments agreed to complete the construction of an oil pipeline connecting China and Russia by the end of 2008. For further details, see "China, Russia pledge to enhance co-op in various fields," Xinhua News Agency, November 6, 2007, http://news.xinhuanet.com/english/2007-11/06/content_7023010.htm.

18 On September 29, 2008, Moscow and Seoul signed a Memorandum of Understanding and Cooperation between the state corporation Russian Corporation of Nano-Technology and the Ministry of Education, Science and Technology of the Republic of Korea. In October 2008 of Russian Corporation of Nano-Technology Chairman Anatoliy Chubais visited Seoul and held productive talks with his ROK counterparts.

19 For further details, see Kim Tong-hyung, "Home-Made Satellite to Be Put Into Orbit Next Year," *The Korea Times*, October 19, 2008, accessed March 10, 2009, http://www.koreatimes.co.kr/www/news/biz/2008/10/123_32918.html.

20 Ministry of Foreign Affairs of the Russian Federation, "Trade and Economic Cooperation between Russia and Republic of Korea," spravka, September 17, 2007, http://www.mid.ru/.

21 "Hyundai Starts Up St. Petersburg Car Assembly Plant," Russia-Briefing.com, http://russia-briefing.com/news/hyundai-starts-up-st-petersburg-car-assembly-plant, and "Russia: Hyundai begins exports from St Petersburg," AutomotiveWorld.com, http://www.automotiveworld.com/news/emerging-markets/86591-russia-hyundai-begins-exports-from-st-petersburg.

22 See "South Korea to write off part of Russia's debt," Itar-Tass, September 10, 2003.

23 See "Russia and ROK signed protocol on completion of negotiations on Russian accession to WTO," newsru.com, September 21, 2004, http://www.newsru.com/arch/russia/21sep2004/vto.html.

24 See Ministry of Defense of the Russian Federation, "Military Doctrine of the Russian Federation," Presidential decree #706, April21, 2000, http://www.mil.ru/849/11873/1062/1347/1818/index.shtml; Ministry of Defense of the Russian Federation, "Naval Doctrine of the Russian Federation up to 2020," approved by Presidential decree, July 27, 2001, http://www.mil.ru/849/11873/1062/1347/1819/index.shtml; and Sergey Ivanov, "Aktualnye Zadachi Razvitiya Vooruzhennykh Sil RF" [Immediate Tasks of Development of the Armed Forces of the Russian Federation], October 2, 2003, 20-24.

25 Ministry of Defense of the Russian Federation, "On the Meeting between Deputy Chief of the General Staff Colonel-General Manilov and General Kim Jang-soo, Director of Policy Planning Bureau of the ROK Ministry of National Defense," press release, May 17, 2001, http://www.mil.ru/.

26 Kyodo News, "South Korea, Russia agree on peaceful end to nuke issue," April 10, 2003.

27 Ministry of Foreign Affairs of the Russian Federation, "On the Upcoming events devoted to the 100th anniversary of the sinking of destroyer 'Varyag' and escort vessel 'Koreyets,'" press release, February 6, 2004.

28 Traditionally there have been two main methods for compiling international travel estimates of expenditures by nonresidents during their journeys in the reporting country and expenditures of residents during their journeys abroad. The first is direct reporting mechanisms of international transactions. This is based primarily on reports from banks on purchases and sales of foreign currency, combined with information on turnover on credit cards, eurocheque cards, etc. Sometimes this data is supplemented by other information, for instance, from tour operators on external payments or accommodation statistics (number of tourists, country of residence, number of nights stayed). The second main method is sample surveys, either frontier or border surveys (which can collect both credits and debits) or household expenditure surveys (which can only collect debits). Administrative data are regularly used to supplement both methods. For further explanation of the assessment methodology involved, see "Bilateral Comparisons of Travel Transactions," BOPCOM-02/23, Office of National Statistics, UK, Fifteenth Meeting of the IMF Committee on Balance of Payments Statistics Canberra, Australia, October 21–25, 2002.

29 For an insightful analysis of the related issues, see A. V. Popov, *A History of Russian Orthodox Church in the Far East* (China, Korea, and Japan) (Vladivostok: Far Eastern State University, 2000), 149-154.

30 Fr. Justin Kang, Tae-Yong, "Brief history and present status of Russian Orthodox mission in Korea," last updated May 1, 2005; for more details, see the official website of the mission at http://www.korthodox.org/eng/KOM.html .

31 A comprehensive examination of Russian strategic thought and elite opinions on Northeast Asia can be found in Gilbert Rozman, Kazuhiko Togo, and Joseph P. Ferguson, eds., *Russian Strategic Thought Toward Asia* (New York: Palgrave Macmillan, 2006).

32 For a detailed examination of Russian elite opinions regarding Moscow's policy toward the Korean Peninsula, see Alexander Vorontsov, "Current Russia—North Korea Relations: Challenges and Achievements," (Center for Northeast Asian Policy Studies working paper, The Brookings Institution: Washington, D.C., February 2007).

33 The Public Opinion Foundation, Moscow, conducted a Russia-wide poll of urban and rural populations. Nationwide home interviews were conducted on 10-11 February 2001 in 100 localities in 44 regions. A sample size was 1500 respondents. There were additional polls of the Moscow population, with a sample of 600 respondents. The margin of error did not exceed 3.6 percent. Detailed analysis of the polling results by Tatiana Yakusheva, researcher at the Public Opinion Foundation, can be found at http://www.fom.ru/.

# NONTRADITIONAL CHALLENGES TO SOUTH KOREA'S SECURITY

# ECONOMIC CHALLENGES TO
# SOUTH KOREA'S SECURITY

## *Kyung-Tae Lee*

After graduating from college in 1970, instead of entering the job market or going on to graduate school, I dutifully joined the military and became a ROTC cadet. At that time late North Korean leader Kim Il Sung (Kim Il-sŏng) had allegedly threatened South Korea by saying he wanted to celebrate his sixtieth birthday in Seoul. I spent the next two years in the 7th infantry division of the Republic of Korea (South Korea, or ROK) army, stationed along the barbed-wire fences on the southern border of the Korean Demilitarized Zone (DMZ).

Compared to that period when the Korean Peninsula was filled with much tension, it seems Koreans now enjoy complete peace. The possibility of a North Korean military invasion is extremely slim for three reasons. The first is the total collapse of the former Soviet bloc; the second is the comprehensive reform of China in the direction of a market economy, which impresses upon China the importance of keeping peace in the region; and the third is the ever-widening economic gap between South and North Korea.

North Korea's attempts to develop nuclear weapons do not seem to stir up serious security concerns among ordinary Koreans. Some think that North Korea's nuclear program can be averted with either engagement or containment. Others think that its nuclear weapons do not aim at South Korea; they argue that the North wants to have nuclear weapons as assurance to protect the security of its regime and as leverage for negotiation with the United States.

North-South relations have turned more contentious under the Lee Myung-bak (Yi Myŏng-bak) government. North Korea has repeatedly sent warning signals that it would retaliate against the South militarily if it were not to abandon its alleged hostile stance against the North. More recently, the North tested another nuclear weapon and fired missiles. More surprisingly, it boldy announced that it is enriching uranium for the purpose of making nuclear weapons, something it had previously vehemently denied. So far, though, there seems to be no visible negative impact on the South's security environment.

I think the reason for this blasé response by South Koreans toward the North's nuclear program and its verbal threats is the huge economic gap between the two countries. South Koreans are convinced that economic power gives them the upper hand to stop any military provocation from the North. Is this really justifiable? If so, I will go on to clarify the relationship between economic superiority and military security. If the case can be made that economic superiority strengthens military security, then I will try to identify the potential risks that might damage the South's current economic superiority.

Economic power affects security indirectly via the ability to respond to security threats such as terror, natural disaster, disease, crime, climate change, etc. Although the kind of security related to these factors is distinctively different from the traditional type of military security, it is an issue gaining more attention since the end of the cold war. As the possibility of a hot war diminishes, security concerns are moving from the political and military domains towards other areas such as human rights, welfare, and socio-economic development. With greater economic power comes more human and material resources to deal with non-military security concerns. Thus, the second subtopic in this paper is to investigate the relationship between economic power and non-traditional security concerns.

In addition to the relative size of the South and North Korean economy, economic integration in Northeast Asia and East Asia bears significant implications on the security of the Korean Peninsula, and so will be touched upon below.

## Economic Superiority and Military Supremacy

Economic strength can be closely related to military strength: a strong economy allows a nation to better provide the material resources necessary for its military supply chain. Thus, if South Korea were to have a significantly stronger economic capability than the North, it would be safe to say that military superiority lies in the South.

Military tension on the Korean Peninsula was high after the Korean War until the mid-1970s, and probably climaxed in 1968 when thirty-one North Korean commandoes almost succeeded in raiding the Blue House—the presidential office and residential compound—in Seoul.

At that time, the size of the North Korean economy was estimated to be bigger than that of the South. Moreover, North Korea invested a greater portion of its economic resources in building up military capacity and making its defense industry self-sufficient. However, South Korea began surpassing the North economically in the late 1970s. Simultaneously, the North Korean economy began a spiraling decline, culminating with the Great Famine in the early 1990s.

The widening economic gap between South and North Korea resulted in the gradual mitigation of military tension on the Korean Peninsula. The economy of South Korea has overwhelmingly outpaced that of the North. As of 2007, the per capita income of South Korea was close to $20,000, in stark contrast to North Korea's $1,000. South Korea was the 11th largest trading nation in the world with its trade volume amounting to $857 billion in 2007. On the other hand, North Korea's trade volume was negligible, with a mere $2.7 billion in the same year.

South Korea is the world's biggest ship builder and the biggest dynamic random-access memory (DRAM) producer; as a global producer it is ranked fifth in automobiles, sixth in steel, and second in mobile phones.

However, the gap in military power may be far smaller than that in economic power. According to South Korea's "Defense White Paper 2008," it is not clear which side holds superior military power.

Table 7.1 Military Forces: South Korea and North Korea, 2008

|  | South Korea | North Korea |
|---|---|---|
| **Army** | | |
| Troops (1,000) | 522 | 1,020 |
| Tanks | 2,300 | 3,900 |
| Artillery | 5,200 | 8,500 |
| S-S missiles | 30+ | 100+ |
| **Navy** | | |
| Troops | 65,000 | 60,000+ |
| Submarines | 10+ | 70+ |
| Combat Vessels | 120 | 420 |
| Landing Vessels | 10+ | 260 |
| **Air Force** | | |
| Troops | 65,000 | 110,000+ |
| Fighters | 490 | 840 |
| Helicopters | 680 | 310 |
| **Reserve forces (1,000)** | 3,040 | 7,700 |

*Source: Defense White Paper*, ROK Ministry of National Defense, 2008.

Based on the figures in Table 7.1, one might assess that North Korean armed forces are stronger than those of South Korea. North Korea arguably holds sufficient military muscle to strike the South by mobilizing long-range artillery deployed along the DMZ or by air. Such an attack would bring about enormous economic insecurity, not only by the destruction of production facilities but also by the damage done to the mindsets of domestic and foreign investors.

To prevent such a disastrous calamity, it is essential for South Korea to convince the North that any military attack—even one of a hit-and-run nature—would be met by fatal retaliation. Taking the economic superiority of South Korea into account, North Korea's military power and its wretched economy fall far short of the level needed for waging an all-out, sustained war against the South. Thus, except for the case of suicidal attacks, the possibility of a large-scale military provocation from the North can be discounted as long as South Korea maintains economic superiority.

Since the beginning of the Lee administration, the South-North relationship has been changing for the worse. Economic cooperation projects such as Mount Kumgang (Kŭmgang) tourism and the Kaesong (Kaesŏng) Industrial Complex were either closed or curtailed. Official dialogue channels were cut off. The South has repeatedly said that the door for bilateral talks is wide open, but the North has been stepping up propaganda campaigns and has not hesitated from warning the South of military action—in fact, it was reported that the North is preparing for a missile test in the immediate future.

Would a North Korean military provocation inflict substantial damage on the South Korean economy? Looking back upon the history of military provocations by the North gives some clues.

For example, in 1998 North Korea test fired the Taepodong-I (Tacp'odong-I) long-range ballistic missile. The Korean stock market (KOSPI) rose 1.76 percent on the same day, pushing up the KOSPI index to 310.16. For about a month thereafter, the KOSPI index fluctuated around 300 points. Exchange rates stayed stable without added volatility. In 2002, North Korean naval vessels attacked South Korean counterparts in the Yellow Sea. The incident occurred near the Northern Limit Line (NLL), an area that has been a point of conflict between the two for a long time. The stock and foreign exchange markets both demonstrated resilience. Stock prices went up the following day, with foreign exchange rates remaining stable. In 2006, the North surprised the world by testing a nuclear bomb. The Korean stock market closed that day with a 2.4 percent drop. But the fall was short-lived. After one week, stock prices recovered to the pre-test level and after one month, well above the pre-test level. The Korean won fell 1.6 percent against the dollar immediately after the test but was stronger than the pre-test level just one month later.

On May 25, 2009, the North announced its second nuclear test. The KOSPI index fell moderately by 29 points the next day, and another 10 points the day after, but recovered strongly by 30 points. For one month thereafter, the stock price fluctuated around the before-test level, without showing lasting effects. A similar story is told in the foreign exchange market. Before the test, some argued that the North's nuclear test in the midst of the global economic crisis would dampen investors' sentiments much more seriously than during a healthy economy. But that argument turned out to be false.

All these incidents did not significantly disrupt the South Korean economy. It seems that both domestic and foreign investors did not take North's military provocations too seriously, as long as they were on-and-off incidents. Even the nuclear tests by the North apparently were not perceived as serious security threats to the South. The market insensitivity can be attributed to the reliability of the U.S. nuclear umbrella.

## Challenges to South Korea's Economic Superiority

Economic superiority is a necessary, though not a sufficient, condition for assuring the national security of the Republic of Korea. Sustained economic growth close to the full growth potential is essential for maintaining and expanding its dominance over North Korea. There are several challenges that might undermine the economic superiority of the South, such as declining growth potential, the catching up of China, the current global economic crisis and Korea's vulnerability to it, and deteriorating income distribution.

### Declining Growth Potential

South Korea has achieved tremendous economic progress over the last three and a half decades, but growth has slowed down in recent years. Looking forward, most forecasters expect potential growth to decline substantially. The Korea Development Institute (KDI) reported the 2003–2007 potential growth rate of Korea as 5.4 percent but predicted that it would slow down to 5.1 percent between 2008 and 2012.

In the process of overcoming the 1997 financial crisis, Korea's economic growth rate was halved from 8 percent to 4 percent. Slow growth resulted from low birth rates and an aging population, and the five-day workweek reduced labor input, discouraged investment and weakened Korea's economic supply capacity. Similarly, plant and equipment investment that grew 9.5 percent annually in the mid-1980s dropped to 4.6 percent annual growth from 2002 to 2006. The Bank of Korea attributed the main cause of declining growth potential to the reduction in private sector investment.

Worse, Korea has been thwarted in its search for new growth engines, despite the fact that growth was relatively rapid through government-led development strategies before the 1997 financial crisis. Another factor slowing down Korea's growth was its service sector, one weak in comparison to the manufacturing sector. Korea's service sector is characterized by low productivity and lack of competition from abroad.

A Bank of Korea index measuring South Korea's growth potential fell from an annual average of 6.1 percent during 1991–2000 to 4.8 percent during 2001–2004, mainly due to weak domestic investment. The index, which does not measure actual output but forecasts the economy's potential for sustainable, non-inflationary growth, could drop even further, to an annual average of 4.6 percent during 2005–2014, but could rebound to 5.2 percent in the same period if appropriate efforts were made to boost the economy.

To promote growth potential, Korea needs to expand its factors of production and increase the aggregate demand of domestic consumption and investment. Labor, one of the factors of production, is unlikely to improve due to low fertility rates.

To boost growth potential, the Lee administration has come up with the so-called 747 Plan (increase growth potential to seven percent, achieve $40,000 income, and become the seventh largest economy). The plan includes fostering high-tech industries like financial and medical services and further opening up Korea to international competition. The plan is a supply-oriented policy in which the government would abolish excessive regulations and improve the business environment in order to promote facility investment.

## Hopeless Economic Prospects in North Korea

It is widely believed that the North Korean economy is so poor that it cannot resume a normal growth path without external help. The prevalence of absolute poverty leaves little room for saving, which in turn generates large investment shortages. Unless there is a substantial external infusion of capital, North Korea cannot escape the vicious circle of poverty.

The necessary external economic assistance will not be available until the nuclear issue is completely solved—something that is still only a remote possibility. The decades-long cycle of dialogue, negotiation, and confrontation with North Korea over nuclear weapon development is proof that nothing is done until everything is done.

The gloomy future of the North Korean economy is in a sense a relief for South Korea, in that despite its eroding growth potential it still does not run the risk of being overtaken by the North.

A failed economy makes North Korea more vulnerable to the effects of natural disasters, climate change, diseases, and other non-traditional threats to national security—all of these stand a chance of threatening North Korea's socio-political stability and national security since it lacks the economic resources needed for managing such disasters effectively.

## China's Catching-Up

Korea can find many opportunities in the rapidly growing Chinese economy. Most importantly, China has been Korea's production base with its cheap labor, on top of providing Korea with a vast export market. The volume of bilateral trade increased from $2.6 billion in 1992, when the two normalized relations, to $91.4 billion in 2008, a 34-fold increase in just 16 years.

Nonetheless, China is becoming a potential threat to Korea as well. With the Chinese government providing enormous support for its industries, China's technological competitiveness is catching up with Korea's, thereby threatening the status of Korean companies in all sectors. Improved technology from China is pushing Korean products out of their own domestic markets, and China's advanced products compete directly with Korean goods in global markets. More Korean companies now invest in China instead of Korea; as a result, many jobs leave Korea for China, causing deindustrialization.

Negative signs are becoming clearer. Korea's exports of steel and petrochemical products, two of the major Korean exports to China, are expected to fall sharply with the Chinese government announcing the expansion of production capacity in these industries. Meanwhile, Korean electronic products are facing tougher competition from Chinese products in the global market.

Furthermore, the focus of Chinese industrial policies lies in restructuring existing industries. The competitiveness of Chinese companies is expected to improve dramatically, if China can solve structural problems in its economy through a restructuring plan and recent stimulus package for ten key industry sectors.

Thus, all in all, it depends on Korea's own efforts whether it takes advantage of the prospering Chinese economy or becomes the loser in competition with China. The global economic crisis triggered by the U.S sub-prime mortgage crisis has spread to China, and its economic growth slowed down to 9 percent in 2008, a sharp decline from the previous year's double-digit number. Its growth again plunged to 6.8 percent in the fourth quarter of 2008.

However, one must examine the fundamentals of the Chinese economy in detail with a long-term perspective. The slowdown of China's economic growth may be inevitable due to the deepening global economic crisis, but a hard landing is not quite plausible. Those who warn of such a possibility have some points, but they overstate the negatives, overlook the uniqueness of Chinese society, and miss the effects of the government's policy measures.

The Chinese government has been successful in leading its economy and responding appropriately to risk factors for a long time. As export growth slowed down sharply, the government announced a 4 trillion RMB stimulus package aimed mainly at boosting spending on infrastructure and domestic consumption. It is a shift from an export-oriented development model to a domestic market oriented one.

Although the effects of these measures may be slowed by the global downturn, the Chinese economy is expected to recover gradually in the second half of 2009.

In the meantime, Korea can find some positive signs and opportunities as well because China will remain the fastest growing market.

With China adopting a domestic demand-oriented model over an export-oriented one, Korean companies also need to change their strategies to access Chinese markets. Views of China as the world's factory or as a base for processing trade with cheap labor are outmoded. Korean companies should see China as the world's largest market and focus on penetrating that market. In order to compete with global companies in China, Korean companies need to make an accurate analysis of the Chinese market and take a long-term view, concentrating on brand recognition and technology competition rather than price competition.

### Income Distribution

During the cold war, disparities in the standard of living among different income classes took central stage in the debate between West and East. The socialist camp persistently attacked the free capitalist camp by alleging that the working class was being exploited and mired in poverty. The Korean Peninsula was no exception. Distributive justice occupied the front line of heated propaganda campaigns and the debate on which system was superior. The collapse of the Soviet bloc and China's adoption of the open-door policy uprooted the foundation of this debate, both ideologically and practically. More importantly, the virtual collapse of the North Korean economy since the early 1990s has put an end to the long-standing debate on the comparative systemic approach to income distribution.

Recently, the issue of income inequality has resurfaced in developed and emerging countries. One of the combined and mutually reinforcing consequences of globalization and technological innovation is a widening gap in income and wealth. In Korea, the Gini index shows upward movement since the 1997 financial crisis.

The middle class is shrinking. In a capitalist society, the middle class is the safety valve securing socio-political stability. With a shrinking middle class and rising income inequality, it is fortunate that the ideological debate on income distribution that once raged between capitalist and socialist nations has now abated; otherwise, this would be an opportunity for socialist countries to demonstrate their superiority. Although North Korea is just across the DMZ, there is no active debate on income distribution: South Koreans know that relative poverty in the South is far better than universal absolute poverty in the North.

But the situation could change. Continued aggravation of income equality will result in social and political disruption, which will in turn affect social cohesion, one of the key components of national security.

## South-North Korean Economic Cooperation

The Sunshine Policy during the Kim Dae-jung (Kim Tae-jung) and Roh Moo-hyun (No Mu-hyŏn) administrations (1998–2008) aimed to establish peace in the Korean Peninsula by providing economic assistance to the North and promoting inter-Korean economic cooperation. As South Korea engaged North Korea more deeply, it was hoped, the North would increasingly acknowledge the economic gains from the engagement. This would give it incentives to expand trade and investments to reap more benefits, as well as to open and reform its economy, and to reduce tensions that might present obstacles to closer economic ties.

The Sunshine Policy has been instrumental in expanding economic transactions between North and South Korea. Under it, trade volume increased remarkably, from about $300 million in 1998 to $1.797 million in 2007. Even in the chilled atmosphere of 2008, inter-Korean trade does not seem to have been negatively affected: up until September 2008 exports and imports amounted to $1.392 billion.

However, there have been significant setbacks in this economic cooperation. About 200,000 South Korean tourists visited North Korea's Mount Kumgang over a ten-year period, with total entry payments to North Korea amounting to around $486 million. This tourist program came to an abrupt stop after a North Korean soldier shot and killed a South Korean tourist in July 2008.

In the Kaesong Industrial Region north of Seoul, more than 80 South

Korean factories are now in operation, employing about 33,000 North Korean workers at the region's industrial complex. But its large-scale expansion plan was halted in the midst of turbulent North-South Korean relations. From January to September of 2008, South Korean visitors to North Korea (mainly for business and tourism) totaled more than 140,000. However, the prospect for continued economic cooperation is clouded as the current South Korean government sticks to the reorientation of the Sunshine Policy.

The inter-Korean summit held in October 2007 agreed on multiple ambitious projects, such as building shipyards and extracting mineral ore, but these programs are now all at a stalemate.

The real effects of the Sunshine Policy on easing tension is open to debate. Ostensibly, the infiltration of armed guerrillas, harsh propaganda campaigns, and verbal threats have been replaced by flows of goods and people across the border. North Korea's nuclear and ballistic tests, however, are considerable threats to South Korean security. If the current stalemate lasts longer and economic exchanges scale down, the seemingly peaceful relations between the two Koreas will be in danger.

### Regional Economic Cooperation

North Korea is a country in political, social and economic isolation. In a globalized world, isolated countries are marginalized and face challenges for survival. North Korea has two options: abandon isolation and open up, or move towards further introversion. It is choosing the latter.

The idea of economic integration in Northeast or East Asia has been floating among scholars and policy makers for quite some time. Language emphasizing economic integration has appeared in the joint statements of the annual summit meetings of Asian leaders. China, Japan, and Korea have been studying jointly among their public research institutes the feasibility of arranging trilateral free trade agreements. ASEAN +3 meetings occasionally discuss forming free trade area in the region, but the consensus is still far away.

The current global economic crisis is giving impetus to the desirability and necessity of deepening economic integration in the region. Asian emerging countries have been plagued much worse than was expected by a crisis (with its origin in advanced countries) because of their close global integration via financial flows and trade of manufacturing goods. Unlike their Western counterparts, Asian consumers are not obsessed with excessive spending based on borrowing, and Asian banks are far less exposed to blind investments on opaque financial derivatives.

It is natural for Asian countries to ponder measures to reduce the vulnerability of their economies to outside shocks. Closer economic integration within the region promotes intra-regional trade and investments, thereby giving more cushioning to absorb negative external impacts.

When countries around North Korea are tied more closely through deeper economic integration, North Korea will be isolated more. (Imagine if Switzerland were to shut its doors to nearby countries). Greater isolation leads to greater economic difficulties. If there were greater economic integration among Northeast Asian countries, North Korea would feel enormous pressure to revise its isolationist policy.

It might continue to pursue an isolationist policy and rely on brinksmanship diplomacy using nuclear threats as leverage. However, it will sooner or later discover that this is not sustainable, neither politically nor economically. China, Japan, South Korea must cooperate more systematically in dealing with North Korea. They are well advised to use a stick and carrot jointly by sending implicit pressure for revision of the North's isolationist policy and by proposing an explicit scheme of massive developmental assistance.

## Conclusion

A well-known South Korean political scientist delivered a lecture just before the 1988 Seoul Olympics in which he predicted that if the Seoul Olympics were to end successfully, the race of comparative systems between South and North Korea would reach the finish line in a one-sided victory for the South, and the North would surrender. His prediction has been proven totally wrong.

Likewise, when I think back to the birth of my first son in 1977, I recall believing that my son would not have to be drafted into the military when he grew up. I was also completely wrong—both my sons served two years as ROK infantrymen. My conclusion is that all we Koreans pretend to know about North Korea amounts to nothing more than wishful thinking or subjective beliefs.

For the past ten years, there were no major military clashes between the two Koreas. The sentiments of lasting peace and complacency have been infused into the minds of South Koreans. Few of them seriously believe that the North has either the will or the capacity to start another inter-Korean war, and most believe a full-fledged war against South Korea would lead the North into self-destruction. South Koreans' self-pride and self-confidence stem from the reality that economic power of the South is overwhelmingly superior compared to that of the North.

I wonder whether this sentiment might be another case of wishful thinking. Unlike the case with economic power, neither the North nor the South can boast overwhelmingly superior military power over the other. The North has enough military power to strike the South and inflict enormous damage to its economic security. Thus, the South Korean government needs to declare publicly its firm resolution and capacity to retaliate decisively, in the case of an attack.

The nuclear development scheme propelled by North Korea threatens South Korea's security. It could reverse the economic superiority of the South into a military supremacy of the North. But many South Koreans again fall into the danger of wishful thinking in believing that the North's nuclear weapons do not point to the South, but are only for the purpose of increasing leverage for negotiation with the United States.

The economic superiority held by the South provides a strong foundation for easing military tension but does not fully guarantee peace. Military modernization, a solid determination for defense and a seamless South Korean-U.S. alliance are all vital for national security.

South Korea faces challenges in maintaining and expanding its economic excellence over the North. Its growth potential has been weakening since the 1997 financial crisis. President Lee's ambitious campaign promise to raise the growth potential to seven percent per annum is undermined by the financial tsunami that is sweeping the entire world.

But the South Korean government is exerting its utmost efforts to turn the crisis into opportunity by boldly pushing for reforms through deregulation, privatization and industrial transformation. Korean industries should embody more technology, knowledge and "green" ingredients to successfully overcome the risk of being sandwiched between China and Japan.

The widening gap between the haves and the have-nots within South Korea needs to be addressed as well. Of course, the implications of social inequality in the context of national security are different now compared to the cold-war era. The ideological war between socialism and capitalism has virtually disappeared, and the North Korean economy has collapsed. I am inclined to dismiss the risks of increasing social inequality and the possible ensuing social unrest and their bearing on national security.

For the past ten years, inter-Korean flows of goods and people rose dramatically. At the same time, military tension has been eased. More recently, economic interchanges have slowed down, and the North is intensifying its threat of military action. It seems that there is a trade-off relationship between South-North economic cooperation and security tension.

Deeper Northeast Asian economic integration will play some role in improving the security situation on the Korean Peninsula. Let us suppose that China, Japan and South Korea agree to form a free trade area. This will result in freer trade and investment that would in turn ensure a greater economic prosperity for all three countries. If North Korea insists on maintaining its isolationist policy, its economy will worsen further and it will be degraded to become a "lonely island of misery in the ocean of prosperity." The three neighboring countries need to coordinate their policies toward the North more systematically: these policies should include more sticks against nuclear weapon development and more economic carrots in return for the abolishment of the North's nuclear program.

# ENERGY AND ENVIRONMENTAL CHALLENGES TO SOUTH KOREA'S SECURITY

## *Ji-Chul Ryu*

S outh Korea is a resource-poor country; its indigenous energy resources include only small deposits of anthracite coal and hydropower, thus in order to meet its increasing energy demand it must import most energy sources from overseas, including oil, bituminous coal, nuclear fuel, and natural gas. As shown in Table 8.1, South Korea's energy supply import dependence ratio has steadily increased from 73.5 percent in 1980 to 96.6 percent in 2007 (including nuclear energy).

**Table 8.1 Major Energy Economic Indicators in South Korea**

|  | 1980 | 1990 | 2000 | 2007 |
|---|---|---|---|---|
| Total primary energy demand (million toe) | 43.9 | 93.2 | 192.9 | 242.9 |
| Energy import dependence (%) | 73.5 | 87.9 | 97.2 | 96.6 |
| GDP (2000 trillion won) | 138.9 | 320.7 | 578.7 | 798.1 |
| Per capita demand (toe) | 1.15 | 2.17 | 4.10 | 5.01 |

*Source: Yearbook of Energy Statistics*, 2008, Korea Energy Economics Institute, Ministry of Knowledge Economy.

## Energy Demand Growth and its Drivers

South Korea is the tenth largest energy-consuming country in the world. With its rapid economic and industrial growth, total primary energy demand in South Korea has increased from 43.9 million toe (tonne of oil equivalent) in 1980 to 242.9 million toe in 2007. Per capita energy consumption has increased from 1.15 toe in 1980 to 5.01 toe in 2007, which is a level similar to that of Japan and most European countries (such as Germany and France).

South Korea's high increase in energy demand was due mainly to the expansion of energy-intensive industries during the industrialization period as well as to the effect of income growth (see Table 8.2). South Korea notably expanded the production capacity of energy-intensive industries, such as cement, steelmaking and petrochemicals, for industrial security reasons, and their production has gone up sharply. For instance, the production of ethylene has increased more than twelve times since 1985 and reached 6.8 million tons in 2007. This is one of the major factors to shape out the energy-intensive nature of the South Korean economy, compared with the other economies of a similar income level. Also, as a result of increasing incomes, vehicle ownership has also greatly increased. In particular, the number of passenger cars has increased from 249,000 in 1980 to 12.1 million in 2007.

**Table 8.2 Changes in Major Economic Activities in South Korea**

|  | 1980 | 1990 | 2000 | 2007 |
|---|---|---|---|---|
| Production (million tons) | | | | |
| Cement | 15.6 | 33.9 | 51.4 | 57.1 |
| Pig iron | 5.6 | 15.3 | 24.9 | 29.7 |
| Ethylene | 0.37 | 1.05 | 5.4 | 6.8 |
| Motor vehicle ownership (millions) | | | | |
| Total number | .528 | 3.395 | 12.059 | 16.428 |
| Passenger cars | .249 | 1.916 | 8.084 | 12.100 |

*Source: Yearbook of Energy Statistics*, 2008; Korea Energy Economics Institute; Ministry of Knowledge Economy.

The industrial sector is the largest energy consumer in South Korea, accounting for 57.5 percent of total final energy demand in 2007, while the residential/commercial sector accounted for 19.8 percent, and the transportation sector 20.4 percent (see Table 8.3).

**Table 8.3 Energy Demand by Sector (million toe)**

|  | 1980 | 1990 | 2000 | 2007 |
|---|---|---|---|---|
| Industry | 16.571 | 36.150 | 83.912 | 104.327 |
| Transport | 4.905 | 14.173 | 30.945 | 37.068 |
| Residential/Commercial | 14.034 | 21.971 | 32.370 | 35.916 |
| Public/Others | 2.087 | 2.812 | 2.625 | 4.143 |
| Total Demand | 37.597 | 75.106 | 149.852 | 181.455 |

*Source: Yearbook of Energy Statistics*, 2008; Korea Energy Economics Institute; Ministry of Knowledge Economy.

## Energy Supply Mix

South Korea has experienced a significant structural change in energy mix over the last decade. This is due mainly to the active implementation of a government fuel diversification policy, aimed at enchancing energy security by reducing the vulnerability of the economy to oil price hikes and supply shortages (after two oil shocks occurred in the 1970s–80s). Thus, the share of oil in the total primary energy supply declined from 61.1 percent in 1980 to 43.4 percent in 2007, while those of natural gas and nuclear increased significantly to 14.3 percent and 14.7 percent in 2007, respectively (see Table 8.4).[1]

Table 8.4 Energy Mix by Fuel (thousand toe [%])

|  | 1980 | 1990 | 2000 | 2007 |
|---|---|---|---|---|
| Oil | 26,830 | 50,175 | 100,279 | 105,418 |
|  | (61.1) | (53.8) | (52.0) | (43.4) |
| LNG | — | 3,023 | 18,924 | 34,663 |
|  | — | (3.2) | (9.8) | (14.3) |
| Coal | 13,199 | 24,385 | 42,911 | 60,937 |
|  | (30.1) | (26.2) | (22.2) | (25.1) |
| Hydro | 496 | 1,590 | 1,402 | 1,261 |
|  | (1.1) | (1.7) | (0.7) | (0.5) |
| Nuclear | 869 | 13,222 | 27,241 | 35,734 |
|  | (2.0) | (14.2) | (14.1) | (14.7) |
| Others | 2,517 | 797 | 2,130 | 4,856 |
|  | (5.7) | (0.9) | (1.1) | (2.0) |
| Total Energy Supply | 43,911 | 93,192 | 192,887 | 242,869 |
|  | (100.0) | (100.0) | (100.0) | (100.0) |

*Source: Yearbook of Energy Statistics* 2008; Korea Energy Economics Institute; Ministry of Knowledge Economy.

Imported steam coal actively replaced oil in the 1980s, particularly in the cement industry and power generation sectors. Nuclear energy was also introduced in the 1980s with an emphasis on its use as a fuel for baseload power generation. Natural gas was introduced in the form of liquefied natural gas (LNG) into the South Korean energy market beginning 1987, as a fuel for the residential and commercial sectors and also for cogeneration and district heating systems. However, oil still accounts for the largest share in South Korea's total primary energy mix. In recent years, oil demand has increased, particularly in the transportation and industrial sectors, due mainly

to an increase in the number of passenger cars and expansion of the petrochemical industry.

## Security Concerns in Energy Policy Development: Historical Review[2]

Energy security is always taken as a principle objective of national energy
policy, as it plays a critical role and an essential ingredient of every action
and process in economic activities. However, energy security has multidi-
mensional aspects. Energy security does not simply mean maintaining a stable energy supply, but includes all aspects of energy policies, such as energy
pricing and conservation policy, industrial energy policy, energy diplomacy,
and so on. This implies that energy security can be achieved through harmonization of all energy-related policies.

Given the lack of indigenous energy resources, the South Korean government, setting energy security as a high priority in its energy policy objectives,
promoted a wide range of policy efforts towards this end. Specific measures
to enhance energy security include diversifying energy sources from oil to
coal, natural gas and nuclear; expanding energy infrastructures; encouraging overseas energy development projects; creating emergency strategic oil
stockpiles; strengthening market functions; and implementing energy conservation and encouraging renewable energy.

### Fuel and Import Source Diversifications

The most notable policy development for energy security in South Korea is
the active policy efforts for fuel diversification away from oil to more economic and stable energy sources such as coal, natural gas and nuclear. As
mentioned before, after the second oil shock, the government implemented
active diversification of both energy and import sources in the 1980s.

However, the impetus for fuel diversification was not simply "being out
of oil" but included factors such as long-term supply and price stability, economics, public acceptance, technology feasibility, and so on. For example,
coal and nuclear were introduced for power generation because of their supply stability and economics, while natural gas was implemented because of
public acceptance and environment reasons in urban areas. These criteria
were underlying concepts in energy supply-demand planning for the long-
term and in designing implementation plans and policies in South Korea.

The fuel mix in power generation changed markedly between 1980 and
2007. Since South Korea's first reactor was commissioned in 1978, nuclear
power generation has expanded rapidly and the nation is now the fourth
most nuclear-reliant country in the world. South Korea has 20 nuclear power
plants in operation at four sites. In 2007, nuclear constituted 26 percent of its

electricity-generating capacity and generated 35.5 percent of total electricity supply. Coal and LNG were first used in South Korea for power generation in the early to mid-1980s, with the first LNG-fired power plant completed in 1986 and the first bituminous coal-fired power plant completed in 1983. The shares of LNG and coal in total electricity generation reached 19.4 percent and 38.4 percent in 2007, respectively.

South Korea's oil imports are mainly from the Middle East. Its crude oil import dependency on the Middle East was reduced to 74.3 percent in 1990 from 90.7 percent in 1981, due to the diversification policy for oil import sources. However, the policy to reduce the high dependency on the Middle East has not been very successful. In 2007, dependency on the Middle East for oil is 80.7 percent of the total oil import (see Table 8.5).

Table 8.5 Energy Import Dependence of South Korea

|  | Energy Import Dependency | Energy Import/ Total Imports | Middle East Dependency | |
|  |  |  | 2000 | 2007 |
| --- | --- | --- | --- | --- |
| 1981 | 75.0 | 29.7 | 90.7 | — |
| 1990 | 87.9 | 15.6 | 74.3 | — |
| 1995 | 96.8 | 13.8 | 77.9 | — |
| 2000 | 97.2 | 23.4 | 76.8 | 35.0 |
| 2007 | 96.6 | 26.6 | 80.7 | 50.2 |

Source: Yearbook of Energy Statistics 2008; Korea Energy Economics Institute; Ministry of Knowledge Economy.

Natural gas in the 1990s was imported mainly from regions in Asia such as Indonesia, Malaysia and Brunei.[3] However, imports from the Middle East have risen since 2000 when South Korea started to import from Oman and Qatar, and the dependency on Middle Eastern natural gas was about 50.2 percent in 2007. South Korea is the world's second largest importer of coal after Japan. Although its import sources of coal are diversified, the bulk of imported coal has historically come from Australia, and Australian coal imports have remained stable. South Korea has met the growth in coal demand by dramatically increasing imports from China, which replaced imports from Indonesia and South Africa in recent years. However, it is expected that rapidly growing coal demand in China, particularly for power generation, will significantly reduce China's exports of coal in the near future, so that South Korea may need to diversify its coal import sources from China to other areas, including the Russia Federation and North America.

## Energy Infrastructure Expansion

One of the most important tasks in energy security is to construct and expand energy production and supply facilities in a timely manner to meet increased energy demands accompanying economic and income growth. In South Korea's case, the government set this policy objective as the highest priority in the process of economic development in the 1980–2000s. As shown in Table 8.6 below, energy production capacity in South Korea was rapidly expanded: refinery facility was increased from 640,000 barrels per stream day (BPSD) in 1980 to 2.812 million BPSD in 2007, and power generation capacity from 9.4 gigawatts (GW) in 1980 to 68.3 GW in 2007.

**Table 8.6 Energy Production/Supply Facilities in South Korea**

|  | Unit | 1980 | 1990 | 2000 | 2007 |
|---|---|---|---|---|---|
| Oil Refinery | thousand BPSD | 640 | 840 | 2,438 | 2,812 |
| Power Generation Capacity | GW | 9.4 | 21.0 | 48.5 | 68.3 |
| City Gas Customers | thousand | 99.8 | 1,220.0 | 7,926.6 | 12,722.3 |
| District Heating System Customers | thousand | - | 40.2 | 980 | 1,590 |

*Source: Yearbook of Energy Statistics*, 2008, Korea Energy Economics Institute, Ministry of Knowledge Economy.

Inter- and intra-city gas distribution networks were expanded along with the introduction of LNG in 1987, and thus the number of customers of city gas significantly increased from 99.8 thousand in 1980 to 12.722 million in 2007. South Korea introduced the districted heating system to residential complexes in major cities in 1989, and the number of households receiving heat from the system rapidly increased and reached 1.59 million in 2007.

Expansion of energy production and the supply (network) system is an important energy security measure particularly for end-users in the sense that it can guarantee public accessibility to the energy that they need and want to consume. Since the early 1990s, South Korea has invested heavily in establishing energy network infrastructures; gas and oil pipelines, and power transmission and distribution grid systems were mainly invested in and constructed by the state-owned public utility companies, namely the Korea Gas Corporation (KOGAS) and the Korea Electricity Power Corporation (KEPCO), although the oil and city gas industries in the nation are completely privatized. This policy successfully achieved a relatively well-established domestic supply system/network for oil, gas, electricity and district heating: sufficient electricity capability reserves of more than 10 percent, 1,577 km of domestic oil pipeline, 2,714 km of natural gas trunk pipeline and three LNG receiving terminals, and 142 days of oil stockpiling capacity as of 2007.

## Overseas Energy Development

With no domestic energy reserves, South Korea has promoted overseas up-stream resource development to strengthen the foundation of energy supply security. The state-owned Korea National Oil Corporation (KNOC) is responsible for the exploration, development and production of upstream oil and natural gas. Private companies also have participated in overseas up-stream business for oil and gas.

Table 8.7 South Korea's Overseas Resource Development Projects (as of 2006)

| | Oil and Gas | | Minerals | |
|---|---|---|---|---|
| | Countries | Projects | Countries | Projects |
| Active projects | | | | |
| Production | 15 | 26 | 10 | 31 |
| Development | 8 | 9 | 21 | 49 |
| Exploration | 21 | 48 | 21 | 55 |
| Subtotal active projects | 30 | 83 | 33 | 135 |
| Completed projects | 37 | 83 | 25 | 68 |
| Total | 47 | 166 | 43 | 203 |

Source: Long-term Overseas Resource Development Plan, 2007; Ministry of Commerce, Industry and Energy, 2007.

South Korean overseas resource development projects were launched beginning in 1977. Since then, South Korean companies have participated in 166 overseas oil and gas projects in 47 countries, and 203 mineral projects in 43 countries. Currently, a total of 83 overseas oil and gas exploration and production projects are in progress in 37 countries (see Table 8.7).

With these projects, South Korea has acquired 906 million barrels of oil reserves and 134 million tons (LNG equivalent) of natural gas reserves, as of the end of 2006. Current equity shares held by South Korean companies are only around 2.8 percent of domestic consumption for oil, 4.5 percent for natural gas, and 38 percent for coal (see Table 8.8).

The government fund source for overseas resources development projects is the Energy Project Special Account; other sources include the Exim Bank loan and various pension funds. Exploration projects are mainly funded by the government, and development/production projects are financed by other commercial sources.

**Table 8.8 Performance of South Korea's Overseas Resource Development Projects (as of 2006)**

| | Oil (MM bbl) | Natural Gas (LNG thousand ton) | Coal (million M/T) |
|---|---|---|---|
| Proven Reserves | 906 | 133,900 | 1,178 |
| Total Imports | 888 | 24,605 | 75 |
| Production from Korea's Projects | 25 | 1,116 | 28 |
| Share | 2.8% | 4.5% | 38.0% |

*Source:* Long-term Overseas Resource Development Plan 2007; Ministry of Commerce, Industry and Energy, 2007.

## Oil and Gas Strategic Stockpiling

As a short-term measure for emergency preparedness, in 1980 the South Korean government developed its strategic oil stockpiling system. South Korea's emergency reserves consist of both government and industry stocks. KNOC was established to be responsible for maintaining government stocks. Under the Petroleum Business Act, the government set the amount of oil to be stored by oil companies doing business in South Korea. As of January 2008, KNOC was running nine stockpiling sites; total capacity amounts to 138 million barrels (MMB) with 102 MMB of reserves (including international joint stockpiles). The Third Government Petroleum Stockpiling Plan aimed to increase stockpiling facilities to 146 MMB by 2009.

According to the International Energy Agency (IEA) statistics, South Korea met the requirement for stocks equal to 90 days of net imports, and its oil stocks have never fallen below the IEA's 90-day net import requirement since joining the IEA in 2002. Recent data show South Korea's total stock level of around 142 days as of January 2008 (see Table 8.9).

**Table 8.9 IEA-Member Strategic Petroleum Reserve Duration Days**

| United States | Japan | France | Germany | South Korea |
|---|---|---|---|---|
| 116 days | 144 days | 101 days | 120 days | 142 days |

*Note:* Duration days based on IEA standards (by net daily imports).
*Source:* Korea National Oil Corporation, http://www.knoc.co.kr/.

The government also plans to improve natural gas security through additional storage capacity by increasing its total storage capacity rate from 8.8 percent of annual consumption to 12.7 percent by 2017.

## Strengthening Market Functions

In the late 1990s, the government began to recognize the importance of the market (pricing) mechanism in more efficiently and effectively pursuing energy security. Thus, petroleum prices were completely liberalized in 1997. The government encouraged energy industries towards the facilitation of a market element, and supported energy policies that enhanced the ability to flexibly absorb price or quantity shocks. For a country like South Korea where all required energy sources are imported from overseas, an energy crisis is usually believed to originate from external factors. However, factors impeding energy security are not only from external sources, but also can rise internally from the domestic market. For example, the stability of energy production and supply to the market can be constrained if industry does not make the proper capital investments for energy production/distribution facilities and infrastructures. In this respect, achievement of energy security objectives needs to be accomplished through improving the market environment for industry rather than through direct government involvement and control.

## Energy Conservation and Renewable Energy

Changes in international concerns on environment, following the United Nations Framework Convention on Climate Change (UNFCCC) in 1992 and the Kyoto Protocol in 1997, have triggered the need for a new paradigm of energy policy in South Korea as well, one that supports sustainable development with full harmonization of energy use and environment.[4] With sustainable development as their goal, South Korea's energy policies began to focus on an environmentally friendly energy system as a major task. In order to correct distortions of prices in the energy market due to heavy government intervention in the past and to establish an environmentally friendly low-carbon energy consumption system, the government gradually adjusted the relative prices of petroleum products to the international level to prevent excessive atmospheric pollution during the period 2000–2007; it likewise began to actively promote a wide range of energy conservation and efficiency improvement policies, and to implement policy to encourage renewable energy sources.

## Future Challenges for Energy Security in South Korea

The necessity for energy security will increase steadily in conjunction with South Korea's expanding demand for the energy required to sustain its economic growth. However, in this process, South Korea can expect to encounter a number of internal and external challenges: the securing of a stable overseas energy supply; actively responding to global and local pressures for environmental conservation; and improving energy security in the South Korean Peninsula to resolve energy poverty in North Korea.

### Securing a Stable Supply of Energy from Overseas Sources

South Korea's ever-increasing demand for energy means that it will have to continuously import more energy from overseas sources in order to satisfy its growing needs. Therefore, South Korea must strive to secure energy resources on a long-term basis by establishing energy supply bases in conjunction with energy-producing countries.

South Korea's major energy trading partners have mostly involved energy-producing countries in the Middle East and Southeast Asia. There is no doubt that the Middle East will continue to be a critical source of oil and natural gas for the Asia-Pacific region, including South Korea. Consequently, since OPEC's share of the world's crude oil market is expected to increase, South Korea should redouble its efforts to maintain cooperative relations with Middle Eastern suppliers. However, as the competition to secure steady sources of energy will further intensify in the future, the nation needs to diversify its energy partners and sources of energy to include countries in the regions of Northeast Asia, Central Asia, Africa, and Latin America.

Within Northeast Asia, Russia's Far East is especially well known for its vast amounts of oil and natural gas reserves, as well as hydrological resources that can be used to generate electrical power. South Korea's ability to improve its energy security would thus be substantially boosted by importing energy resources from these nearby areas. In particular, in light of steadily increasing demand for natural gas in the future, South Korea shows a strong interest in importing natural gas from Russia through pipeline networks, and recently meaningful progress was made at the September 2008 summit meeting between South Korea and Russia in Moscow. South Korean president Lee Myung-bak and Russian president Dmitry Medvedev agreed to jointly undertake a project to develop gas routes from Siberia to South Korea and to expand Northeast Asian electrical grid networks. The project features a natural gas pipeline running through the divided Korean Peninsula that would allow South Korea to import 10 billion cubic meters (bcm) of gas annually for 30 years as of 2015.[5] South Korea plans to buy nearly 20 percent of its future natural gas from Russia through this pipeline. And an electric power grid network would allow Russia to supply energy during South Korea's high-demand summer season, while South Korea would supply energy during Russia's high-demand winter season.

As for coal imports, China is the third largest coal supplier to South Korea, following Australia and Indonesia, exporting 17.7 million tons of coal in 2007 (21.2 percent of South Korea's total coal imports). Imported coal from China is mainly used for power generation and for industrial purposes. However, there is a rising concern that China will decrease coal exports in the near future, since China's domestic demand for coal will rapidly increase along with its economic growth. According to a Korea Energy Economics Institute (KEEI) 2008 estimate, China's total export of coal is expected to decrease from 63.3 million tons in 2006 to 38 million tons in 2010, while its total coal imports will increase from 38.3 million tons to 68.0 million tons during the period; thus, China will become a net importer of coal. China's net imports of coal in 2010 are estimated be around 30.0 million tons. This clearly implies that the major importers of China's coal, namely South Korea and Japan, will face a coal supply security problem in the near future and need to find alternative import sources.

### Environmental Concerns and Increases in Demand for Low Carbon Energy Use

South Korea is expected to face strong international pressure to join global joint efforts to mitigate the emission of greenhouse gases, including the carbon dioxide emitted from fossil fuel combustion. South Korea is the tenth largest country in carbon dioxide emissions worldwide, although it was not included as a member of the Annex I group under the Kyoto Protocol, who are obliged to commit to the reduction of greenhouse gas emissions. Also, domestically, the public's enhanced awareness of environmental issues and their adoption of an environmentally friendly consciousness have resulted in increased demands for more stringent environmental standards. Thus, more environmentally friendly energy use will tend to be encouraged. This will lead to changes in demand patterns as a result of an expected increase in demand for new and renewable energy, as well as to high pressure for energy conservation and efficiency improvement.

In August 2008, President Lee Myung-bak announced National Energy Vision and Strategy 2030. The basic outline for this energy strategy is a strong policy emphasis on "Low Carbon, Green Growth," which means achieving sustainable development in a low carbon society.

The three pillars of this strategy are "3Es," namely "Energy Security, Economic Efficiency and Environmental Protection." Four major strategies are established:

- achieving steady growth while using less energy;
- minimizing environmental pollution and using low carbon energy sources;
- turning the green energy industry into a national growth engine;
- and creating a green society that stands strong even in the era of climate change.

It can be clearly stated that future energy challenges for environmental protection, whether global or local, will be highly dependent on technology development and application, particularly for clean energy and energy efficiency improvement. Thus, the South Korean government will respond positively to increased global and domestic concerns and accelerate efforts to expand applications for a lower carbon energy economy for the future.

### Energy Poverty in North Korea and Cooperation Issues[6]

North Korea has suffered from a serious energy supply shortage, which in turn has jeopardized its economy over the last several decades. Accordingly, energy security on the Korean Peninsula is expected to emerge as a critical issue for South Korea in the future, if North-South Korean economic cooperation will begin to be further set in motion.

North Korea is also poorly endowed in terms of natural resources for energy, which are in large part limited to anthracite coal and hydropower. Also, given the lack of capital and technologies to rehabilitate its energy system, North Korea is desperately in need of international cooperation, in particular with South Korea, Russia, China, Japan, and the United States, and with the relevant international organizations as well. For the promotion of international energy cooperation, North Korea is required to:

- Accept demands from the international community for transparency in military and security concerns;
- Closely consult with South Korea in reconstructing the energy systems of both Koreas so they can be integrated into a mutually compatible single system in the future;
- Enhance capacity building for introducing a market mechanism in the energy sector by promoting international cooperation in the areas of training and educating energy experts, jointly undertaking energy project feasibility studies, and policymaking capability;
- Participate in international energy cooperation activities in pursuit of membership in the International Monetary Fund (IMF) and other international financing organizations.

Possible projects for energy cooperation between North Korea and other countries may include:

- Humanitarian aid for the supply of energy products for civilian energy uses: anthracite coal, LPG, kerosene, diesel, and heavy fuel oil for power generation and power supply to limited areas (for example, Kaesong [Kaesŏng], Wonsan [Wŏnsan]);
- Renovation/re-construction of existing energy facilities: coal mines, refineries, power generation, transportation/storage systems with technical, financial and expert assistance from foreign countries;
- Revising legal/market rule structures to create a market mechanism environment;
- Power interconnection between South Korea and the Russian Far East;
- Natural gas pipeline projects from Russia, namely the Sakhalin and Irkutsk projects;
- Providing training/education programs for energy planning/ implementation;
- Resuming the construction of two Korean Peninsula Energy Development Organization (KEDO) light water reactors (LWRs).

## Implication for South Korea–U.S. Energy Cooperation

Historically, energy sector relationships between South Korea and the United States have been close, friendly and cooperative, both on governmental and commercial bases. Most energy business and trade between the two countries are under commercial arrangements: in energy trading between the two countries, South Korea imports coal and uranium from the United States, importing 303 thousand tons of coal (0.4 percent of South Korea's total coal imports) and 84 tonnes of uranium (10.3 percent of South Korea's total uranium imports) in 2007, while the United States is the second largest buyer of South Korea's petroleum product exports after China, importing 6.01 million tons of petroleum products and 5.23 thousand tons of liquefied petroleum gas (LPG) from South Korea in 2007. Also, a U.S. oil company, Caltex, operates a downstream oil business with GS-Caltex, a South Korean company. South Korea and the United States also have a close and strong relationship in the nuclear power generation industry. The Korea Electricity Power Corporation (KEPCO) imported technologies for designing and constructing LWRs from U.S. companies such as Westinghouse, General Electric and the ABB Group. And the Korea National Oil Corporation (KNOC) and some South Korean consortiums participate in oil development upstream projects in the United States, namely the Jaguar/Cougar area, Diamond/Emerald/Platinum/Gold, ANKOR offshore field, and the Gulf of Mexico.

At the government level, South Korea and the United States hold a bilateral Energy Consultation Meeting annually. The major agenda for the meeting in recent years has focused on energy–environment and technological cooperation for developing green energy technologies such as clean coal, $CO_2$ capture and storage (CCS), gas hydrate development, enhanced geothermal systems (EGS), and establishing closer cooperation in the planning, evaluation, and management of R&D projects on energy technology.

Given these successful energy cooperation experiences between the two countries, South Korea and the United States are expected to explore further opportunities for energy cooperation, particularly at the regional basis, in Northeast Asia, where the geopolitics are heavily connected to regional energy issues.

Taking Northeast Asia with North America together, there are big energy consumers/importers, namely the United States, China, Japan and South Korea, and also large producers/exporters—Russia, Canada and the United States. These two regions account for 54 percent of world's total energy consumption as of 2007, adding North America's share (24.2 percent) plus Northeast Asia's share of (29.8 percent). It is also clearly expected that energy demand in the region will continue to increase in the future due to China's robust economic growth. This implies that enhancing regional energy security capability in the region will be a great challenge not only for this region but also at the global level.

The development of energy resources in Northeast Asia, particularly in the eastern Russian region, an area blessed with abundant and untapped oil, natural gas and coal, will have a significant impact not only on the regional energy market itself but also on the North American energy market, since Russia aims to diversify its energy export market to the Asia-Pacific region, including the western coast of North America.

The role of the United States in developing energy resources in the region should be of significance in terms of its strategic importance in the world energy market, its abundant capital and technological capabilities, and its accomplishments in energy development. The United States is clearly a large potential capital investor and technology donor for energy projects and also a significant contributor to improving political stability in the region, particularly around the Korean Peninsula. Then large energy-consuming countries in Northeast Asia, South Korea, Japan and China will be much better off as they are able to secure stable energy supply sources in the region with the advantage of geographical proximity.

Environmental conservation should be pursued in parallel with energy cooperation programs. For example, in order to mitigate air pollution problems caused by coal combustion, particularly in China, the combination of the clean coal technology (CCT) developed by the United States, Japan's capital and South Korea's know-how to construct coal power plants will provide a model for regional cooperation in both the energy and environment sectors. As China's air pollution impacts both South Korea and Japan (e.g., in the form of acid rain), there will be ample incentives to jointly work on this cooperation.

## Notes

1 In general, structural change in energy mix by source occurred as a result of a combination of various factors, such as the government's policy effort for fuel diversification, changes in oil prices, and income increases.

2 For more detail see Ji-Chul Ryu , "Korea's Perspective on Energy Security," (paper presented at the EWC/KEEI Conference on "Energy Security in the North Pacific," Honolulu, HI, December 2008).

3 Until 1990, all LNG imports were coming from Indonesia.

4 South Korea joined the UNFCCC in December 1993 and ratified the Kyoto Protocol in November 2002. Although it belongs to non-Annex I countries classification of the UNFCCC, in which greenhouse gas (GHG) abatement duty has been deferred, it is actively participating in the COP as a member of the UNFCCC and has established national policies to reduce GHGs in 1997.

5 KOGAS and Russia's Gazprom reaffirmed this agreement in early 2011 but implementation is on hold as North Korea has yet to allow the pipeline to run through its territory.

6 For more detail, see Ji-Chul Ryu (Ryu Chi-ch'ŏl), *Nam-, Puk-Han enŏji hyŏmnnyŏk ch'ujin pangan yŏn'gu* [Energy Cooperation Between the Two Koreas] (South Korea: Korea Energy Economics Institute and Ministry of Commerce, Industry and Energy, 2005).

## References

Doh, Hyun-Jae. "Energy Cooperation in Northeast Asia: Prospects and Challenges," *East Asian Review* 15, no.3 (2003): 85–110.

Government of the Republic of Korea. *The National Energy Vision and Strategy 2030.* 2008

Jung, Gi-Chul. "Merits and Demerits of the Kovykta and Sakhalin Pipeline Options." In *Energy Aid for North Korea: Fossil Fuel Options and Denuclearization,* ed. Selig S. Harrison and Ji-Chul Ryu. Woodrow Wilson International Center for Scholars and Korea Energy Economics Institute, 2007.

Korea Energy Economics Institute and Ministry of Knowledge Economy. *Yearbook of Energy Statistics.* 2008.

Lee, Sung-Kyu. "The Trans-Siberian Crude Oil Pipeline: The Impact on the DPRK and the ROK." In *Energy Aid for North Korea: Fossil Fuel Options and Denuclearization*, ed. Selig S. Harrison and Ji-Chul Ryu. Woodrow Wilson International Center for Scholars and Korea Energy Economics Institute, 2007.

Ministry of Commerce, Industry and Energy. "Che-2-ch'a haeoe chawŏn kaebal kibon kyehoek" [The Long-term Overseas Resource Development Plan]. Seoul: Ministry of Commerce, Industry and Energy, 2006.

Pak, Ch'ang-wŏn and Ji-Chul Ryu (Ryu Chi-ch'ŏl). "Tongbuk-A enŏji hyŏmnyŏk ŭl wihan chung-janggi pijŏn mit chŏllyak surip yŏn'gu" [Energy Cooperation in Northeast Asia: Long-term Visions and Strategy]. Seoul: Korea Energy Economics Institute Policy Research Report (March 2005).

Ryu, Ji-Chul. *Energy Cooperation between Two Koreas* [in Korean]. South Korea: Korea Energy Economics Institute and Ministry of Commerce, Industry and Energy, 2005.

Ryu, Ji-Chul. "Korea's Perspective on Energy Security." Paper presented at the EWC/KEEI Conference on "Energy Security in the North Pacific," Honolulu, HI, December 2008.

Ryu, Ji-chul. "Korea's Policy Measures for Energy Security." *Korea Focus* 13, no.5 (Sept-Oct 2005): 81–90.

Ryu, Ji-Chul. "Regional Perspective on Russian Oil and Gas Supplies: A Korean Perspective." Paper presented at the National Bureau of Asian Research's fourth annual energy security conference, "Opportunities and Constraints: Prospects for Russian Oil and Gas Supply to Asia," Washington DC, April 2008.

Ryu, Ji-Chul (Ryu Chi-ch'ŏl). "Tongbuk-A tajagan enŏji hyŏmnyŏk ŭi chedojŏk kiban chosŏng yŏn'gu" Towards the Establishment of an Institutionalized Framework for Multilateral Energy Cooperation in Northeast Asia]. Seoul: Korea Energy Economics Institute Policy Research Report (August 2003).

Ryu, Ji-Chul (Ryu Chi-ch'ŏl) et al. "21-segi enŏji pumun ŭi yŏgŏn pyŏnhwa mit chung-janggi enŏji chŏngch'aek yŏn'gu" [Long-term Energy Outlook and Strategy Development for Korea in the 21st Century]. Seoul: Korea Energy Economics Institute and Ministry of Commerce, Industry and Energy Policy Research Report (March 2001).

To, Hyŏn-jae. "21-segi enŏji anbo ŭi chaejomyŏng mit kanghwa pangan" [On Strategies for Strengthening Energy Security in the 21st Century]. Seoul: Korea Energy Economics Institute Report 03-07 (December 2003).

Yi, Tal-sŏk. "Sahallin enŏji chawŏn wanggu kaebal ch'amyŏ chŏllyak yŏn'gu 2" [Energy Resource Development in the Sakhalin Islands 2]. Seoul: Korea Energy Economics Institute, 2006.

# DEMOGRAPHIC CHALLENGES
# TO SOUTH KOREA'S SECURITY:
# AGING AND DECREASING POPULATION

## Seongho Sheen

South Korea has one of the fastest decreasing and aging populations in the world. For the past decade, its average birth rate was 1.2, the second lowest after Hong Kong; at this rate, those 65 years and older will make up 20 percent of the population in South Korea, and the nation will eventually become a super-aged society within 20 years. The rapid demographic change has raised concern among government officials and social experts. As anticipated, South Korea has already encountered social problems created by the change, and one of the major issues is a labor shortage. The decrease in the labor supply will lead to economic slowdown and reduce tax revenues. Another critical issue South Korea faces is the upgrading of its social welfare program. As the nation transforms into a super-aged society, the demand for social welfare is increasing. As the government is pressured to expand spending on elderly care and retirement pensions, the implications for other government spending—including national security—are dire. South Korea's continued deterrence of North Korean military provocation and efforts to balance military power in the region require defense expenditures that endanger the nation's effort to fund its ambitious project of building a self-reliant defense capability. But with the government trying to catch up with its fellow Organisation for Economic Co-operation and Development (OECD) countries in social welfare spending, the pressure to limit, if not cut, other spending will increase, and defense spending will be the most controversial of these limits/cuts. This chapter examines the impact of the low birth rate and rapid aging on South Korea's national security policy. First, I briefly discuss South Korea's security situation, and then review its latest military reforms; next, I introduce the latest changes in South Korean demographics and their social and economic implications; I will discuss South Korea's new focus on social welfare, with particular attention to its fiscal collision with military spending; and finally, I examine several policy options for South Korea's national security planning under this demographic pressure.

## Security Challenges Facing South Korea

Despite significant changes in the security environment of the Korean Peninsula since the end of the Cold War, South Korea today still has serious national security concerns. It is true that it has established diplomatic relations with China and Russia, and there is deepening economic integration in Northeast Asia between Korea, Japan and China. However, when it comes to national security, South Korea has good reason to build a secure border with neighboring countries and to pursue a strong defense capability.

### The North Korean Threat

Military confrontation with North Korea has been the main security concern for South Korea since the Korean War began in 1950. North and South Korea agreed to an armistice but never signed a formal peace treaty to end the 1950–1953 Korean conflict. Notwithstanding the weakening of the North Korean regime since the end of the Cold War in the early 1990s, South Korea's ten years of sunshine engagement under the two progressive governments of Kim Dae-jung (Kim Tae-jung) and Roh Moo-hyun (No Mu-hyŏn), inter-Korean reconciliations and economic exchanges, the North Korean military threat remains the foremost national security concern for South Korea today. In a 2002 naval skirmish, the North Korean navy, despite obsolete weapons, inflicted serious damage and killed six South Korean sailors. Many military experts have predicted that the North Korean military could destroy a wide range of Seoul with heavy artillery fire alone if war broke out across the Korean Demilitarized Zone (DMZ). North Korea's 180,000-strong commando force poses another lethal threat to South Korean military; it also possesses 600 Scud missiles and 200 Rodong missiles, both capable of reaching any target in South Korea.[1]

A more fundamental and serious North Korean threat comes from its nuclear and non-nuclear weapon of mass destruction (WMD) programs. Many experts see North Korea's conventional military force as losing in competition with South Korea's increasingly powerful and modernizing weapon systems. Since the early 1990s South Korea's defense spending increases have widened the gap with North Korea. As of 2007, South Korea annually spent about $27 billion on defense, while North Korea's spending was below $10 billion.[2] North Korean weapons—tanks, artillery, fighter jets, and warships—date mostly from 1960s, and suffer from chronic shortage of parts and lack of adequate maintenance; in contrast, South Korea continues to improve its major weapons platforms with upgraded versions of fighter jets, state-of-the-art Aegis-equipped battleships and new tanks.[3] North Korea's nuclear development is seen as a rational choice to counter South Korean superiority in conventional and advanced weapons. Since the first nuclear crisis in the early 1990s, North Korea has continued to develop its nuclear capability. North Korea's first nuclear test was conducted in October 2006 after the firing of a long-range missile in July of that year. Despite international efforts to negotiate dismantlement of its nuclear weapon program, Pyongyang conducted a second nuclear test in May 2009, one bigger than the first one and indicative of Pyongyang's progress in becoming a full nuclear power. After the adoption of United Nations Security Council Resolution (UNSCR) 1874 sanctioning North Korea's nuclear programs, North Korea's foreign ministry declared that it would start another nuclear program using uranium enrichment technology.[4] In addition to nuclear weapons, North Korea has developed biological and chemical WMD capabilities.[5] With or without nuclear weapons, North Korea's WMD capabilities and its ballistic missile stocks represent a real and present danger to South Korea.

In fact, inter-Korean relations have deteriorated substantially since the conservative Lee Myung-bak (Yi Myŏng-bak) government took office in 2008. Criticizing the previous government's policy, President Lee has withheld much of the economic aid that was offered to Pyongyang by his two liberal predecessors, saying North Korea must dismantle its nuclear program in exchange for aid. Pyongyang reacted angrily, criticizing the Lee government and calling South Korea a traitor to the reunification of the two nations. In 2009, North Korea issued a grave warning of possible full military confrontation against the Lee government. A message delivered by a North Korean military general announced, "As the South has opted for the road to confrontation with the help of outside powers, ignoring the call for conciliation and cooperation among the Korean people, our revolutionary armed forces have no choice but to take an all-out confrontational posture to trample on it."[6] In 2010 a South Korean warship was torpedoed by a North Korean submarine, losing its forty-six sailors; and four South Koreans, including two civilians, were killed by a North Korean artillery attack on Yeongpyeong Island in the following months. As such, almost two decades after the Cold War and despite ten years of sunshine policy by the South, the North Korean military threat remains real and potent.

*Feeling Pressure from Neighbors*

If North Korea's military threat and nuclear development represent a more immediate security challenge facing South Korea today, growing rivalry for power among China, Japan, and Korea will present a more long term challenge. Prominent realist scholars like John Mearsheimer posit that power shifts among great powers tend to cause a great war. And China's fast rise, according to Mearsheimer, will inevitably lead to a great tension as well as conflict with other major powers in the region,[7] with many seeing the region as "ripe for rivalry."[8] Of course, others caution against such a pessimistic view on the future of Northeast Asia. They say the region is ripe instead for cooperation with growing economic interdependence, a web of new multilateral institutions, socio-cultural exchange, and expanding democracy.[9] Others argue that unique East Asian traditions and cultures will tame China's hegemonic ambition while letting others accept the power shift in a more peaceful manner.[10] Yet, these optimistic views do not directly challenge the realists' pessimistic core assumption, leaving many questions for Northeast Asia's future unanswered. Despite the acceleration of international economic integration and deepening intraregional trade, the readiness of Northeast Asian countries to strengthen their defensive capabilities may lead to a security dilemma. Long-standing political tensions over the Taiwan Straits and the Korean Peninsula present a potential source of major military conflicts in the region. Growing nationalism, fueled by ongoing disputes over history and unsolved territorial issues, only adds to the strong possibility of a great power war in Northeast Asia.[11]

Indeed, rapidly rising military spending and a race for deadly armaments among countries in Northeast Asia have often been cited as convincing proof of growing geo-political rivalry and security tensions. The absolute amount of defense spending in the region has substantially increased over the past decade. In particular, China's escalating defense spending is causing serious concern among major powers in the region. According to a U.S. government report, China's defense budget grew on average 11.8 percent over the past decade compared with an average annual gross domestic product (GDP) growth of 9.2 percent. In 2007 the budget increase was 19.5 percent by Beijing's own count,[12] with a total defense budget of $66 billion, 2.5 times bigger than that of South Korea at $26 billion. As a result, China has increased its military spending by 202 percent between 1998 and 2007 as opposed to a 45 percent increase for the whole East Asian region.[13] Japan is a notable exception with an unchanging 1 percent of GDP spent on defense. Yet, thanks to a large economy, the Japanese defense budget is big enough to put it in the number five spot in world defense spending at $43.6 billion, twice the size of South Korea's.[14] In short, Northeast Asian countries are making serious efforts to modernize their military capabilities and expand regional influence.[15]

## The Koreanization of Korean Defense

Forged by blood during the Korean War and officially created by the Mutual Defense Treaty of 1953, the ROK-U.S. alliance has been the main pillar of South Korea's national security policy. The alliance provided protection from North Korean military aggression, at the same time playing an increasing role as a safety against growing rivalry in Northeast Asia between China and Japan. Meanwhile, there has been a continuing effort by South Korea to build a self-reliant defense capability. Between 1974 and 1996, Korea spent a total of $246 billion on domestic and foreign procurement in order to improve and upgrade its national defense capabilities.[16]

A self-reliant defense has become a South Korean national goal for two reasons. The first comes from fear of abandonment. Despite repeated stating its commitment to South Korea's defense, the United States has tried to reduce its military burden from the Korean Peninsula. South Korea faced a serious security setback when Presidents Nixon and Carter announced substantial troop withdrawals from South Korea. Although the planned reduction did not go through as originally scheduled, there has been a steady reduction of the size and numbers of U.S. troops in South Korea, and the U.S. government has continued to gradually withdraw its troops since the end of the Cold War. Based on its new Asia security initiative,[17] the first Bush administration withdrew 7,800 U.S. troops in just one year between 1991 and 1992. In comparison, the Carter administration's controversial troop reduction plan only achieved a withdrawal of 3,000 troops over the two years between 1977 and 1979. Figure 9.1 illustrates the gradual downward trend of U.S. troop level in the Korean Peninsula since the end of the Korean War.[18]

The second driver for South Korea's self-reliant defense has been its increasing confidence and nationalist sentiment. Over past decades, South Korea has intently pursued the goal of building a military strong enough to deter or fend off military aggression by neighboring countries. Yet, the South Korean military remained very much dependent on U.S. war planning and military protection a decade after the end of the Cold War. If war were to occur on the Korean Peninsula, the South Korean military would be under the commander of United States Forces Korea (USFK), who exercises wartime operational control (WOC) authority as the commander of the Combined Forces Command (CFC) as well as the United Nations Command (Korea) (UNC). In the early 1990s, South Korean president Kim Young-sam (Kim Yŏng-sam) sought to regain WOC. Peacetime operational control was returned to South Korea in 1994. But with the developing nuclear crisis with North Korea in the mid-1990s, discussion of WOC transfer was postponed indefinitely.

**Figure 9.1 United States Forces Korea Troop Levels (1945–2008)**

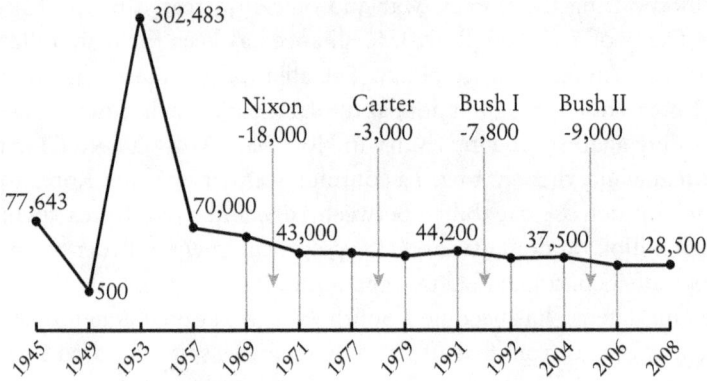

*Source* : ROK Ministry of National Defense.

The discussion about transferring WOC to South Korea from the U.S. army was reopened by the Roh administration in 2002. President Roh expressed a strong interest in building a self-defense capability from the beginning of his presidency. In March 2005, at the Korean Air Force Academy, Roh declared: "We have sufficient power to defend ourselves. We have nurtured mighty national armed forces that absolutely no one can challenge…. [Within a decade,] we should be able to develop our military into one with full command of operations."[19] Roh's strong desire for building a self-defense capability led to a most controversial debate on WOC issue in 2006. In an interview, he argued that the old agreement giving the Americans wartime control of South Korean troops was anachronistic, and a source of shame for today's South Koreans. Roh asserted "saying that we South Koreans are not capable of defending ourselves from North Korea is to talk nonsense. It's shameful. I hope we kick the habit of feeling insecure unless we have layers of guarantee that the Americans will intervene automatically in case of war."[20] In a meeting between the U.S.-ROK militaries in 2005, the two governments agreed to discuss concrete measures to return WOC to the Korean side. If South Korea assumes WOC, it will be gaining more of a voice in its military operations, and the ROK military can take on the heavy responsibility of developing its own capability and strategy to combat a possible invasion. The gradual reduction of U.S. troops in Korea and the transfer of WOC to the ROK military will thus signify the Koreanization of Korean defenses.

## Self-Reliant Military: "Defense Reform 2020"

As its economy grew rapidly, South Korea has increased defense spending to upgrade its military capability throughout the 1980s and 1990s. Even though the defense expenditure as a proportion of GNP fell from 6.0 percent to 3.3 percent between 1980 and 1995, the actual amount spent on defense showed a substantial rise to $15.7 billion in 1996. And between 1974 and 1996, the Korean government spent a total of $246 billion on domestic and foreign procurement in order to improve and upgrade its national defense capabilities. As a result, the 1997 defense budget was 165 times higher than that of 1971.[21]

In fall 2005 the Ministry of National Defense (MND) in South Korea announced a Defense Reform Plan (DRP) with the goal of achieving a self-defense posture by 2020. As announced, the defense budget will be increased by 11 percent each year over a ten-year period. Anticipating an inevitable shortage of manpower for military service due to the low birth rate, the plan called for reducing troop levels from 680,000 to 500,000 by 2020. To make up for the reduced manpower, South Korea sought to field a military with more advanced weapon systems such as advanced mechanized division, next generation fighters, Aegis-class destroyers, submarines, airborne early warning systems and so on.[22] Along with building defense capability, the Roh administration agreed to take over the military missions that had been assigned to the USFK. The two governments agreed to complete transferring ten military missions from the U.S. to ROK army by 2008.[23] Accordingly, as a military expert has observed, "for all its talk of 'cooperative' self-reliant defense, Seoul is also becoming much more independently minded and self-assertive in both security policy and its alliance arrangements with the United States."[24] To achieve this goal, Seoul projected a 621 trillion won increase in defense spending over the next fifteen years.

## National Security Challenges from Within

### Low Birth Rate and an Aging Population

South Korea is experiencing one of the most dramatic demographic changes in the modern world. According to the Korean National Statistics Office, South Korea's birth rate has declined rapidly over the past decades, thanks to an active government birth control policy from the 1960s, one so successful it has become a problem. Today South Korea has one of the lowest birth rates in the world. For last ten years, South Korea's average birth rate has been around 1.2, far below the 2.1 necessary to maintain its current population and the second lowest (after Hong Kong) in the world. As a result, after peaking in 2018 with fewer than 50 million, South Korea's population is expected to decrease. Figures 9.2 and 9.3 show South Korea's birth rate trend and expected population change.[25] Some even predict that South Korea's already low birth rate could drop still further, to below 1.0 in the future. A continued drop in the birth rate could ultimately create a national disaster for South Korea, with a steep decrease in its labor population and economic growth rate. A population expert has warned that if South Korea fails to raise its birth rate, two-thirds of the current population will disappear by 2100, and by 2200 Korea will be left with a population of only 1.4 million.[26]

**Figure 9.2 South Korea's Birth Rate Trend**

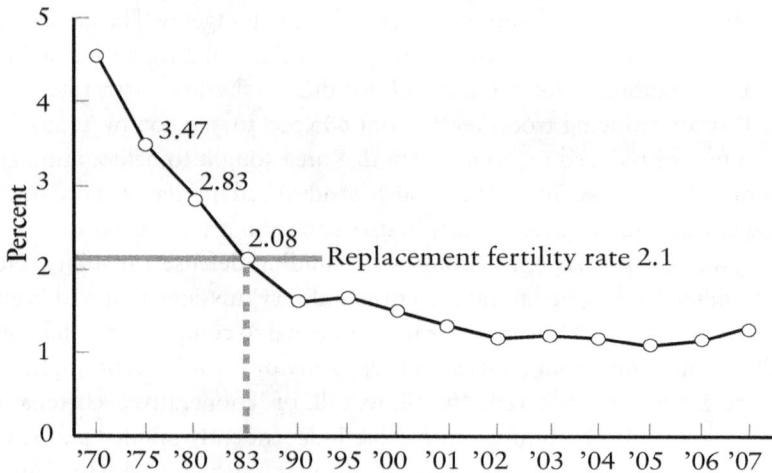

*Source:* Korean National Statistics Office (2009).

The decreasing population has a direct impact on South Korea's long-term economic outlook. According to Figure 9.4, South Korea's economically active population—those between the ages of 15 and 64—will reach its height in 2016 and then begin to decline. In fact, the most important labor population, people between the age of 30 and 49, has already hit its record high in 2006 and has since begun to decline.[27] These declines will have two consequences for the national economy. The first is a labor shortage, something Korea is already experiencing, particularly in it simple manual labor force. The so-called 3D—difficult, dirty, and dangerous—jobs in Korea are largely filled by imported labor from countries like China, Southeast Asia, Africa, and South Asia. Today, there are an estimated one million foreign workers in Korea,[28] a number that would have to increase if the population decline continues. Second, the low birth rate will cause a contraction of the South Korean economy; the domestic market will shrink as demand for education, housing, and labor gradually declines. As Korea's baby boom generation reaches 60 years of age and begins retiring in five to ten years, this will further slow South Korea's future economic growth.[29]

**Figure 9.3 South Korea's Population Trend**

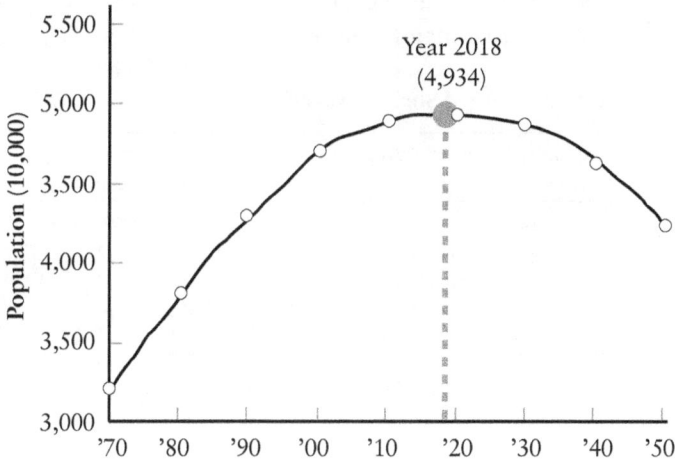

*Source:* Korean National Statistics Office (2009).

**Figure 9.4 South Korea's Labor Population Trends**

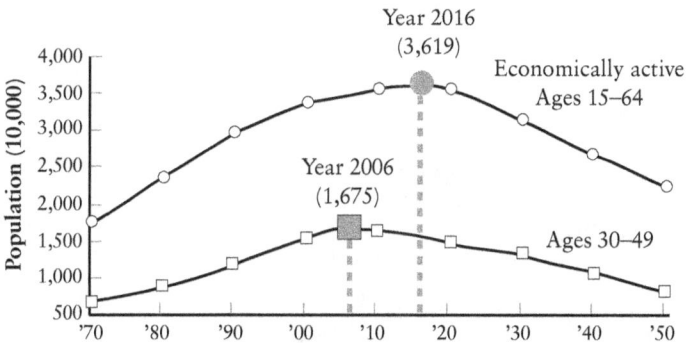

*Source:* Korean National Statistics Office (2009).

This is because, in addition to its record low birth rate, South Korea is also experiencing a record aging of its population. As of 2000, South Korea has become an "aging society" with 7 percent of its population older than 65. By 2018, it is expected to turn into an "aged society" with 14 percent of its population older than 65. This 18-year transition is the fastest ever; yet, the next transition will be even faster, as South Korea is expected to become a "super-aged society," with 20 percent of its population becoming 65 years or older by 2026, just 8 years from the "aged society" stage. South Korea will have made a transition from an "aging society" to a "super-aged society" in just 26 years, breaking the previous Japanese record of 36 years to make the same transition by 2006.[30] Table 9.1 shows how rapidly South Korea's population is aging compared to other major countries.

Table 9.1 Time to Reach Super-Aged Society (years)

| Country | Aging (7%) → Aged (14%) | Aged (14%) → Super-aged (20%) | Aging (7%) → Super-aged (20%) |
|---|---|---|---|
| South Korea | 18 | 8 | 26 (2026) |
| Germany | 40 | 37 | 77 (2009) |
| France | 115 | 39 | 154 (2018) |
| United States | 73 | 21 | 94 (2036) |
| Japan | 24 | 12 | 36 (2006) |

Note: Numbers in parentheses represent the destination years of super-aged societies.
Source: Korean National Statistics Office (2009).

South Korea's rapidly aging society coupled with a low birth rate implies a drastic change in the ratio between young and old population. As Figure 9.5 below shows, the population of those over 65 will be greater than those under age 14 beginning in 2016.

Figure 9.5 Population Transition

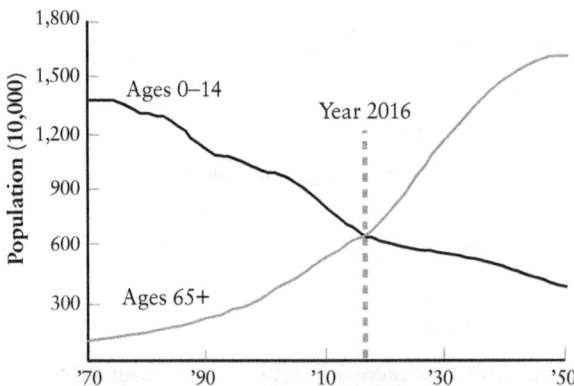

Source: Korean National Statistics Office (2009).

The rise of an aged population will shrink the domestic market as a result of its lower consumption level. The average consumption level of those 60 and older is 65 percent and 70 percent of those in their 40s and 50s, respectively. At the same time, South Korea will have difficult in supplying a high quality labor force as its young population shrinks. If the participation rate remains at the current level, the labor force will decline by 23 percent by mid-century.[31] This translates to an increasing social burden to support an old population. In 2008, for every person older than 65, there were eight economically productive Koreans between the ages of 15 and 64; by 2018 there will only be five, by 2027 just three, and by 2036 there will only be two economically productive Koreans for every person over 65.[32]

### Increasing Demand for Social Welfare: "Vision 2030"

While South Korea's low birth rate will reduce the economic productivity of its labor force, it is increasing the demand for social welfare spending. According to a study, South Korea has two critical economic weaknesses to improve: it has the lowest birth rate and the lowest public social spending among OECD member countries. Figure 9.6 shows that South Korea's fertility rate has dropped below Japan's since 2001,[33] and Figure 9.7 shows that South Korea's 5 percent GDP social welfare spending is far short of OECD average of 20 percent in 2002.[34]

**Figure 9.6 Fertility Rate in Korea, Children per Woman**

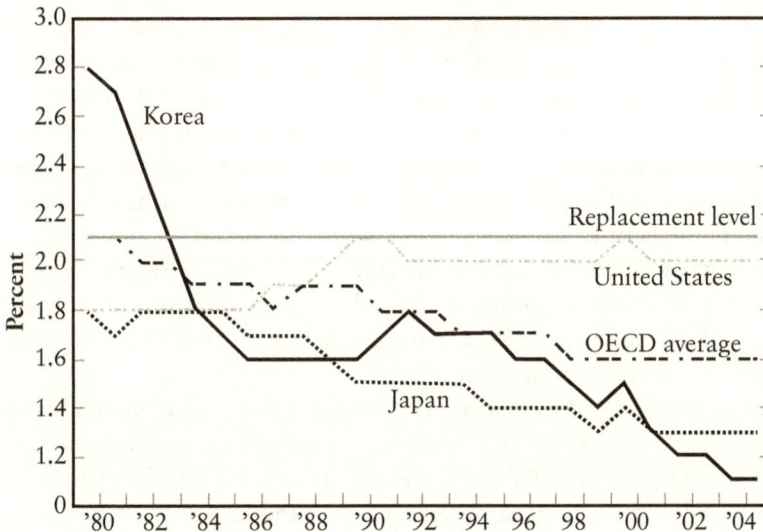

*Source:* OECD (2007).

**Figure 9.7 Korean Gross Public Social Spending (as percentage of GDP)**

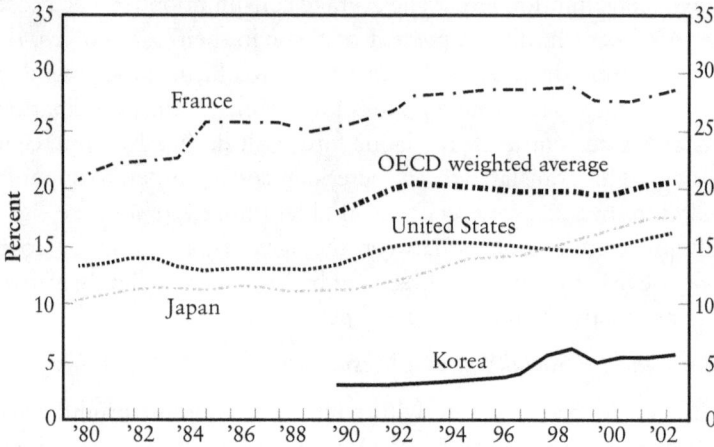

*Note:* The OECD average does not include Hungary and the Slovak Republic due to insufficient data. The national data is converted to US dollars using 2003 PPP exchange rates.

*Source:* OECD, Social Expenditure Database, 1980–2003.

To address the increasing demand and necessity for social welfare spending, the Roh administration announced a major initiative in 2006. In a joint statement issued by the ministries of Finance and Economy, Health and Welfare, and Planning and Budget, the administration defined the low fertility rate, aging population and socioeconomic divide as new challenges facing Korean society. In the statement, it was argued that despite high economic growth, Korea's quality of life was at the lowest level among OECD member countries, with welfare spending a mere one-third of that spent by industrialized countries; pursuing a strategy of both growth and welfare was necessary because, it was argued, one cannot exist without the other. The plan, the first comprehensive long-term national strategy, called for new measures for reforming the national pension system; expanding elderly care; improving health care; educational reform and job training; and closing the social divide. Welfare spending would rise from 6 percent to around the then-current OECD average of 21 percent by 2030. As shown in Figure 9.8, welfare spending was estimated to increase an average of 9.8 percent annually during the period FY 2006–2030, rising to, as a percentage of GDP, the 2001 U.S. level of 15 percent in FY 2019, the 2001 Japanese level of 17 percent in FY 2024, and ultimately to 21 percent, close to the 2001 OECD average of 21.2 percent.[35]

If successful, the "Vision 2030" plan would enable two-thirds of seniors over 60 to receive national pension benefits, as opposed to the current 17 percent. In addition, the national health insurance coverage rate will go up from 65 percent to 85 percent. The rate of public rental housing units will also be increased from 5.1 percent to 16 percent. Discrimination against non-regular workers will be eliminated. Schools will be enhanced with smaller class sizes, after-school activities, and improved child safety. Moreover, those with disabilities and low-income families such as farmer and fishermen will also receive benefits from new social welfare system.[36]

**Figure 9.8 Projected Social Welfare Spending**

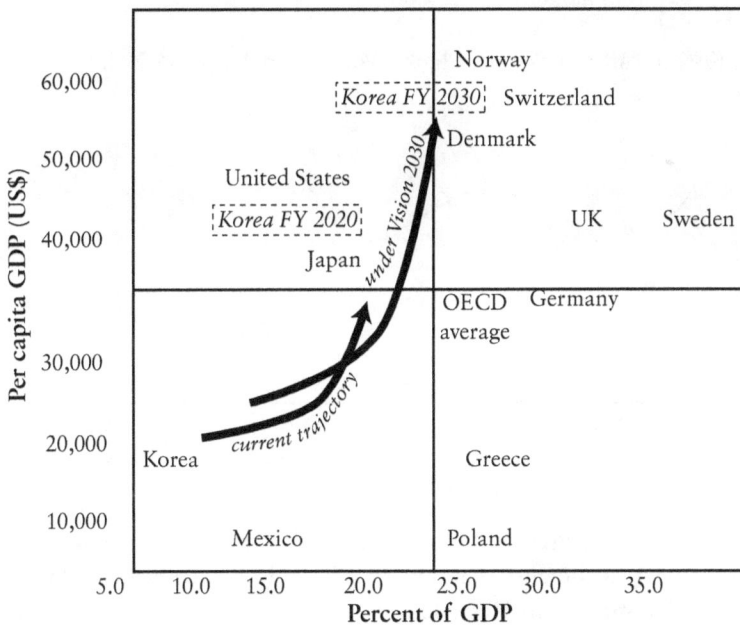

*Sources:* IMF, *World Economic Outlook* (April, 2006); Public social expenditures as of 2001; OECD *Social Indicators* (2005); Vision 2030.

Some, however, advised caution in boosting social spending, as other nations with significant increases in expenditures have seen sharp hikes in tax burdens, with negative consequences for economic growth. Instead of setting an overall spending as a target, it was recommended to focus on developing effective programs in each area of social spending included in the Vision 2030 plan. But there was no question that public social spending would have to rise during the coming decades given the fact of rapid population aging; the proportion of elderly in Korea's population, currently the second lowest among OECD member countries, is projected to be the fourth highest by 2050.[37]

## Implications for National Security Policy: Defense Reform 2020 versus Vision 2030

South Korea's low birth rate and aging population have significant implications for defense planning. First, there will be fewer young men eligible for military service. As shown in Figure 9.9 below, the number of young men eligible for military service at the age of 18 will rapidly decrease beginning 2012, and from 2015 the government will face a recruiting shortage in attempting to maintain current troop levels.[38]

**Figure 9.9 Korean Military Service-Eligible Population Trend (18 Years)**

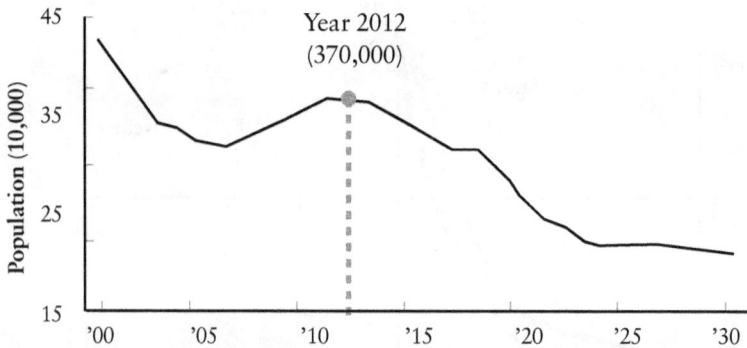

Source: Korea National Statistics Office (2009).

Second, as South Korea's economic growth slows down, it will be increasingly difficult for defense planners to ask for large increases in the defense budget. To implement Defense Reform 2020, South Korea projected spending 621 trillion won on defense, a substantial increase in the defense budget. The plan is problematic. According to Rand Corporation senior defense analyst Bruce Bennett, the "Ministry of National Defense has not been able to achieve its planned budget levels in any year since 2005" and was facing "even more serious reductions in the defense budget" in the coming years.[39] The original reform package of 621 trillion won ($445 billion) was based on the assumption that the country's GDP and government expenditures would grow in parallel at roughly 7.1 percent per year from 2006 to 2020. Defense budget growth was anticipated to be 9.9 percent a year from 2006 through 2010, then about 8.8 percent per year from 2011 through 2015, and then, on average 1 percent per year from 2016 through 2020. South Korea's GDP, however, grew an average of only 4 percent between 2006 and 2008 (see Figure 9.10). The defense budget grew an average 8.1 percent as opposed to 9.9 percent growth under the DRP 2020.[40] Some defense analysts say the planned 621 trillion won defense budget will be eventually reduced by one of 110 trillion won.[41]

**Figure 9.10 South Korea's GDP Growth**

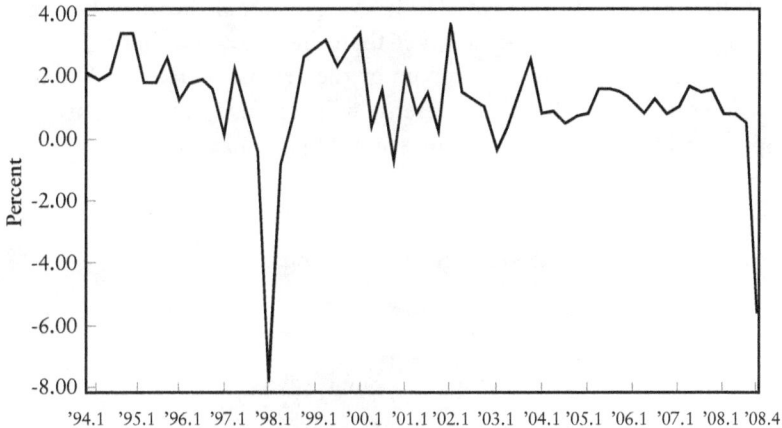

Source: Bank of Korea (2009).

The situation could get even worse due to the recent world economic crisis. For the first time since the 1998 Asian financial crisis, negative growth is expected in 2009.[42] For its 2009 defense budget, South Korea allocated 28.5 trillion won, a 7.1 percent increase from the previous year's budget of 26.6 trillion won.[43] The 2009 budget was based on an expected 4 percent growth in 2008 GDP. However, as Figure 9.10 shows, South Korea was in a serious economic downturn—in particular, the fourth quarter of 2008 had negative 5.6 percent growth.[44] The 2009 GDP did grow at a diminished rate of 0.2 percent, and the defense budget increase was cut down to 3.6 percent.

The third implication of the drastic changes in South Korean demographics is the serious strain put on defense budget increases, brought about by a rapid increase in social welfare spending. Indeed, as the security system and social environment have changed, the ratios of defense expenditures to GDP and to the government budget have followed those changes. Until the early 1980s, the ratios of defense expenditure to GDP and government budget stood at 5 percent to the GDP and 30 percent to the government budget respectively, as the MND had steadily promoted projects such as the "Yulgok project" since the 1970s to build up military strength for self-reliant defense. From the late 1980s, the defense budget has trended downwards until the early 2000s because of the increasing demand for social welfare. Conversely, government spending on social welfare showed the largest increase of all sectors in the 2009 budget (see Figure 9.11). It grew by 7 trillion won, a 10.4 percent increase from the previous year, reaching 74.7 trillion won. As a percentage of the total 2009 budget, social welfare spending (26.3 percent) far exceeded the defense spending (10 percent). The 7 trillion won increase in social welfare spending represented fully 25.6 percent of the overall budget's 27.3 trillion won increase, much larger than the corresponding 7.3 percent portion of the overall increase taken up by the defense increase.[45] The trend of focusing on social welfare over defense will continue as South Korea will attempts to address the increasing pressure of a low birth rate and an aging population.

Figure 9.11 South Korea's 2009 Budget (trillion won)

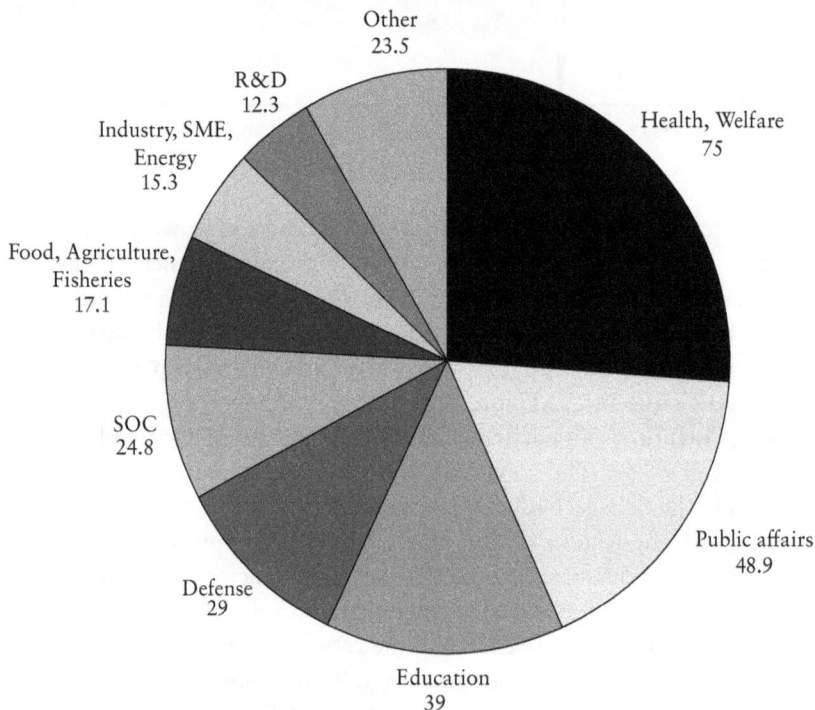

Source: Korea National Statistics Office (2009).

It is unlikely that South Korea will soon reverse these long-term demographic changes but it should make an effort to promote higher birth rates among its younger generation to achieve sustainable economic productivity and a healthy society. The government is now implementing policies to this end, such as tax incentives for newborns, special mortgage benefits for multi-children families, increased subsidies for childbirth, and extra child support. The government is also trying to provide better childcare and job security, and birth holidays for working parents. Despite all this, it will not be easy to reverse the perceptions of and social trends toward smaller families; South Korea is increasingly becoming a post-industrial and more individualistic society. South Koreans now want to enjoy more individual freedom without the heavy economic and psychological burdens of raising many children. The intrinsically linked factors of an aging society, increasing demand for social welfare spending and a slowdown in economic growth mean defense spending will be limited, and South Korea will have to think beyond large military forces and large increases in defense spending as a strategy to build a self-reliant military capability.

## Social Challenges to the National Security Definition

The decreasing population of South Korea poses another fundamental question for the definition and goal of South Korea's national security policy. According to David Baldwin, the most fundamental aspects of a country's national security objective are defined by that nation's social values. The role of national security is, in turn, to reduce the probability of damage to those values.[46] National security planning, then, starts with a society's most important value—in the example of the United States, freedom. The U.S. global war on terror is defined in terms of defending and protecting the freedom of American society. For South Koreans, that national value tends to be defined in terms of the sovereignty and territorial integrity of the South Korean nation. In particular, South Koreans emphasize their thousands of years of national history as one homogeneous and independent nation—which is why Koreans still struggle with the memory of Japanese colonialism in the early twentieth century. National security has been defined mainly as the function of defending the Korean nation as an ideological concept of one nation, one culture, and one history.

South Korea's low birth rate poses a national security problem: simply put, should it continue at the current level, there would be no Korean nation left to defend. The topic South Korea must urgently focus on is how to harmonize traditional Korean national security values and the reality that the Korean population has been ethnically diversified. Although South Korea has been singularly proud of its homogeneous Korean ethnicity, there are now in the nation millions of foreign workers who are filling gaps in the labor force, a mass influx of foreign labor that is changing the composition of Korean society. More than one out of ten newlywed couples are marriages between Korean and foreign nationals; the percentage of interracial marriages rises up to more than 40 percent in rural areas.[47] The central and local governments are now facing the reality of the emerging so-called multicultural family in Korea.[48] Multicultural marriages could create their own set of social issues, including how to provide marriage counseling for foreign brides; protect abused foreign wives; promote the school enrollment of children of multicultural families and prevent social discrimination against foreign workers. With more than ten percent of babies being born in multicultural households, South Korea's ethnic composition will become more and more diversified. This, obviously, will make it difficult to continue defining a homogenous Korean nationhood as the most important value in Korean society. It will be difficult, if not impossible, to teach a new Korean generation with a diversity of national backgrounds to defend the value of one culture, one history. Likewise, when these multicultural children are conscripted into mandatory military service, it will be difficult to ask them to sacrifice their lives for a homogenously defined Korean nation and people. Thus a fundamental question is raised for South Korean society: how to define a national value in light of Korea's new multicultural population. One alternative that could unite these different ethnic groups is a more universal value such as democracy and freedom. It was argued by an expert at a ROK Army seminar that the Korean military would inevitably become increasingly multicultural with the number of foreigners in Korea already more than 2 percent of the whole population. As children from multicultural families reach the age of conscription, the Korean military will face the challenge of incorporating this new population into its forces.[49]

## Policy Options for South Korea

South Korea has several possible policy options to deal with the security challenges caused by its demographic predicament. These options can be roughly divided into two broad approaches: policies that satisfy South Korea's security needs from the supply side and ones that consider the demand side. The former approach would imply additional and improved security measures to deal with national security challenges, including building a more self-reliant, conventional defense capability, developing its own nuclear capability, and strengthening alliances with the United States. Policy options

taking the latter approach would try to lessen South Korea's security demands by reducing the threat from neighbors, including reducing the North
Korean threat by building peace on the Korean Peninsula and lessening the
security dilemma in Northeast Asia by building regional peace mechanisms.

### Strengthening the Alliance with the United States

One approach for South Korea to gain security without spending its own
money would be a return to the "good old days." Throughout the Cold
War, South Korea largely depended on the United States for security against
threats from North Korea and other communist countries. After the Cold
War, the United States continued its military commitment; in particular, it
was the assurance of the U.S. nuclear umbrella that allowed South Korea
to have more confidence in dealing with North Korea, even as at times the
United States expressed unhappiness about Seoul's engagement in the face
of North Korea's defiance. As of 2008, after all the talk of self-reliant defense reform and the Koreanization of Korean defense, there are still 26,500
U.S. troops on the Korean Peninsula, making it the third largest U.S. military
force deployed overseas except in Iraq and Afghanistan (see Figure 9.12).[50]

Figure 9.12 U.S. Global Deployment (March 2008)

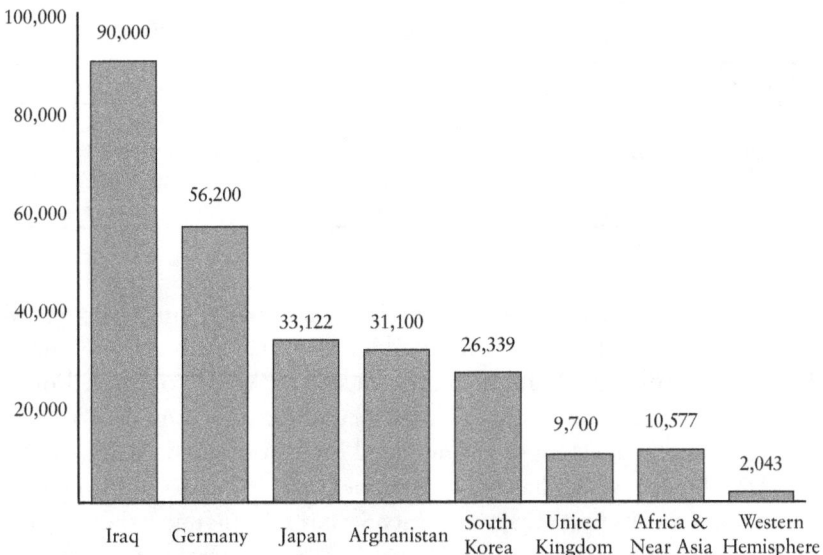

Source: U.S. Department of Defense.

Even in Afghanistan, where it is engaged in a major war against Al Qaeda terrorist groups, the United States has deployed only about 31,000 troops; in the whole African continent including Near Asia and South Asia combined, only about 10,000; and in the entire Western Hemisphere, only about 2,000 troops.[51] The significance of this military commitment of 26,500 U.S. troops to South Korea, from Washington's perspective, cannot be overstated.

This commitment is the reason South Korea's defense expenditures are relatively low comparable to other countries in similar security situations. According to a report from the ROK Defense Ministry (see Table 9.2 below), South Korea's defense budget, 2.4 percent of GDP, is much smaller than "highly insecure" nations like Israel, Saudi Arabia and Kuwait, each who have defense budgets at more than 7 percent of GDP.[52] South Korea's defense spending is even smaller than that of countries with "medium insecurity" like France and Russia, or even China. According to SIPRI, world military expenditures in 2007 corresponded to 2.5 percent of world GDP and $202 per capita.[53] South Korea thus ranks as slightly higher than the world average; even though South Korea is viewed as a nation with a high security threat level, the allocation of national resources for defense "remains lower than other countries facing disputes and confrontations."[54]

**Table 9.2 Security Status and Defense Spending 2004 (% of GDP)**

| Highly Insecure | Medium Insecurity | Highly Secure |
|---|---|---|
| Israel (8.3) | Russia (4.4) | Sweden (1.6) |
| Saudi Arabia (8.2) | United States (3.9) | New Zealand (1.2) |
| Kuwait (7.8) | China (3.7) | Canada (1.2) |
| Syria (7.4) | France (2.6) | Switzerland (1.1) |

*Source: Military Balance 2005–2006 (London: IISS, October 2005).*

With this in mind, it was not surprising that many South Korean experts were concerned about the Roh administration's drive for building a self-reliant defense capability and the transfer of WOC to South Korea. The main critique of the Roh initiative focused on concerns that transfer of WOC would in effect end the Combined Forces Command (CFC) of the U.S.-ROK alliance, which has the commitment of U.S. forces in the defense of South Korea as its first mission priority. Some argue that now that mission has changed to other regional priorities with the introduction of the concept of strategic flexibility of U.S. forces in Korea. Many, especially the conservatives, welcomed the Lee administration's new plan to focus on the U.S.-ROK alliance as the main objective of South Korea's security policy. While it was a desirable move to restore traditional U.S. military commitment to the defense of Korea, it is doubtful whether Washington will reverse its policy of reducing its military burden from the traditional form of a defense alliance in favor of continuing the global war on terrorism.

### Going Nuclear

Increasing budget pressures brought by the weakening of U.S. military commitment to the defense of Korea may lead South Korea to consider a nuclear option. After all, North Korea's nuclear weapons program started with the same dilemma: a shrinking military budget from a weakening national economy and the loss of protective alliances with the demise of the Communist Bloc in the 1990s. Nuclear deterrence on the surface is the surest and most cost-efficient way of providing security for poor nations as well as rich. North Korea itself survived two nuclear confrontations with the United States in the early 1990s and the early 2000s while in the midst of severe economic depression. With a reduction in U.S. military commitment, South Korea is threatened by North Korea's nuclear capability, and many feel the nation needs to consider developing independent power against that capability. After North Korea's nuclear test in October 2006, 65 percent of South Koreans polled responded that the government should push forward the development of an indigenous nuclear capability, even with the U.S.-ROK alliance and nuclear umbrella.[55]

However, the nuclear option presents great risk and huge political costs for South Korea, the greatest being the possible upheaval and unfriendly ending of its bilateral alliance with the United States. The move would create an even more hostile security environment in the region; China and Japan would join the United States in condemning South Korea's decision; and North Korea would surely react angrily with threat of nuclear preemption. Even if an endeavor to develop nuclear weapons succeeded without immediate military confrontation, South Korea might well find itself engaged in a nuclear arms race with North Korea, Japan, and China. For all its possible advantages, going nuclear may cause more harm than benefit for South Korea's long-term security interests.

### Reducing the North Korean Threat

Faced with the economic and demographic difficulties in improving its security posture by increasing arms and troops, South Korea could instead opt to reduce the threat to its national security; since that threat mainly comes from North Korea, building peace will be the first step to take. Kim Dae-jung's sunshine policy was precisely such an effort to promote inter-Korean reconciliation and peaceful coexistence. South Korea's efforts to build peace with North Korea go even further back, when in December 1992 the two Koreas exchanged a "Basic Agreement on Reconciliation, Cooperation, and Peace."

Unless North Korea gives up its nuclear program, the prospect of peace on the Korean Peninsula remains elusive. In that case, the ultimate way to resolve the North Korean threat will involve unifying North and South Korea. It is true that many South Koreans today prefer peaceful coexistence rather than absorbing an impoverished North Korea. According to a recent survey, more than eight out of ten South Koreans think unification should be an important national agenda. However, almost the same percentage is against immediate unification. As for shouldering the cost of unification, opinion was split with 55 percent saying they are willing and 44 percent not.[56]

However, recent news of the unstable health of Chairman Kim Jong Il (Kim Chŏng-il), North Korea's absolute leader, raises the speculation about the country's long-term future. Some see possible regime collapse amidst an uncertain succession scenario after Kim's demise.[57] During her first visit to South Korea in February 2009, U.S. Secretary of State Hillary Clinton echoed this concern about North Korea, saying, "the whole leadership situation is somewhat unclear" with "the uncertainties that come from questions about potential succession."[58] Many questions and doubts remain. Even if there were a sudden regime collapse, it is not clear whether the South Korean people and government are ready and willing to take the opportunity to unify Korea.

### The Northeast Asian Peace Mechanism

If South Korea were successful in reducing the threat on the Korean Peninsula by peaceful coexistence or by unification with North Korea, other threats come from bigger neighbors in the region. Historically, Koreans have often become a victim of great power rivalries. Throughout its long history, Korea fought numerous wars with during various Chinese dynasties. Before its twentieth century colonization by Japan, Korea suffered two sixteenth-century invasions by Japan. Koreans often describe themselves "a shrimp between whales," a popular mantra that defines Korea's geopolitical fate in among great power rivalries. Notwithstanding deepening economic interdependence and social exchanges, Northeast Asian security remains weakened by rising nationalism, unsolved territorial issues and historical animosities. Resolving security dilemmas with bigger neighbors can require shrewd diplomacy. South Korea tried to develop friendly relationships with China, Japan and Russia; in particular, with the end of the Cold War, South Korea established in 1992 diplomatic relations with former enemies China and Russia, and since that time has been actively engaged in regional diplomacy with them. Most recently, the Lee administration launched its ambitious "Global Network Diplomacy" program with China, Japan, Russia and the United States. In a visit to each of their capitals, Lee established a new partnership aimed at upgrading each bilateral relationship, defined variously as "strategic ally" (United States), "strategic cooperative partnership" (China and Russia), and "future oriented matured partnership" (Japan). Lee claimed this diplomacy effort upgraded South Korea's bilateral relations with each partner, promoting peace and stability on the Korean Peninsula, and that these "upgrades" did not work against each other.[59]

There had already been talks of developing a new security mechanism in the region before Lee came to power. Roh emphasized the importance of creating "a regional community of peace and prosperity" in Northeast Asia.[60] And the September 2005 Joint Statement issued by the Six-Party Talks mentioned establishing a Northeast Asia Peace and Security Mechanism (NEAPSM).[61] A working group on NEAPSM was established by the February 2007 Initial Actions Agreement. During the latest Six-Party Talks held in December 2008, Russia, chairing the working group, distributed the draft of "Guiding Principles on Peace and Security in Northeast Asia," receiving positive reactions from all parties.[62]

The Lee administration has also underlined the importance of multilateral security mechanisms. In visits to Washington, Tokyo, Beijing and Moscow, Lee advocated that South Korea and its partner countries should promote a multilateral mechanism to deal with security and other issues. South Korea's emphasis on multilateralism not only calls for more active participation in existing mechanisms such as ASEAN +3, the ASEAN Regional Forum (ARF), the East Asia Summit, and Asia-Pacific Economic Cooperation (APEC), but also eventually calls for the creation of a Northeast Asian mechanism in which all the major parties, Japan and Russia as well as the United States and China, share a common security interest with Korea of building a peace—in other words, a venue in which South Korea and other countries in the region can take advantage of positive-sum dynamics. Implementing such a multilateral initiative would obviously require support by the United States and China. The Obama administration has expressed interest in "forging a more effective framework in Asia that goes beyond bilateral agreements, occasional summits, and ad hoc arrangements, such as the Six-Party Talks on North Korea."[63] Yet, as always, the devil is in the details. No country, including South Korea, has come up yet with a concrete plan on where, when, and how to start building the mechanism.

## Conclusion

South Korea has rapidly expanded its military spending over several decades of economic growth and rising national confidence. Today the nation stands as the 11th largest spender on military expenditure in the world.[64] The continuing threat posed by North Korea's conventional and nuclear arms calls for a continued investment in military readiness, while a weakening of U.S. military commitment and long-term rivalries with China and Japan present an argument for massive military upgrades. Yet, South Korea is also facing increasing demands for increased social welfare spending driven by fundamental shift in demography—a population at once rapidly decreasing and aging. By 2025, South Korea's median age will become 44, older than Europe's 38 today.[65] An increasing number of aged people will increase the government's social welfare spending burden on the government, a burden compounded as South Korea's economic productivity slows down with a decreasing supply of labor caused by the world's lowest birth rate. The demands for increased social welfare spending will strain the government's ability to spend on defense—and there have already been some signs of this. South Korea's ambitious military buildup plan to spend $621 billion over the next fifteen years had to be scaled down from its year of inception as the government announced an equally ambitious plan for doubling its welfare budget within just five years.[66] The worldwide economic recession will only create more demand for the South Korean government to address a deepening social divide and to provide a social safety net.

These demographic changes will force South Korea to find alternative ways of eliminating its security concerns. The nation will find it increasingly difficult to depend on the ROK-US alliance as Washington tries to reduce its military burden and assign more military responsibility to Seoul. Ultimately, developing its own nuclear weapons would cause more harm than benefit, bringing about the possibility of ending the alliance with the United States and the specter of a nuclear arms race around the Korean Peninsula. Working on ameliorating the source of threat would provide South Korea with long-term solution to this dilemma. Making peace with North Korea is the most obvious route to reducing South Korea's defense burden, but with North Korea's ongoing nuclear brinkmanship, the prospect of meaningful inter-Korean reconciliations will remain elusive at best. Another solution would be to create a zone of peace, instead of rivalry, in Northeast Asia. Even though the prospects of establishing a multilateral peace mechanism remains uncertain, there is increasing interests among the parties concerned. There may be common trends that will drive Northeast Asian countries to cooperate in security matters. To be sure, many expect that Northeast Asian countries will continue to increase defense spending and catch up with their American and European counterparts,[67] and given past records and the growing economy, the prediction seems plausible. But it overlooks other important trends in the region. As their economies grow and societies become more affluent, Northeast Asian countries will also face a rising demand for social welfare spending. In fact, China and Japan are also facing the problems of rapidly aging populations and low birth rates. They too will feel a severe strain on defense spending as the demand for social welfare spending continues to rise. South Korea may provide a venue to discuss how to approach these issues in more peaceful and productive way, possibly leading to a "demographic peace" in the region.

## Notes

1 ROK Ministry of National Defense, *Defense White Paper 2008* (Seoul: Ministry of National Defense, 2009), 20–31.

2 Global Security, "World Wide Military Expenditures—2011," accessed February 27, 2011 at http://www.globalsecurity.org/military/world/spending.htm.

3 Jonathan D. Pollack, "The Strategic Futures and Military Capabilities of the Two Koreas," in *Strategic Asia 2005–06: Military Modernization in an Era of Uncertainty,* ed. Ashley J. Tellis and Michael Wills (Seattle: The National Bureau of Asian Research, 2005), 137–174.

4 *Chosun Ilbo,* "N. Korea to Resume Uranium Enrichment," June 15, 2009, http://english.chosun.com/site/data/html_dir/2009/06/15/2009061500279.html.

5 North Korea poses 2,500–5,000 tons of chemical weapons and is capable of producing bio weapons such as anthrax. ROK MND, *Defense White Paper 2008*, 30–31.

6 *Chosun Ilbo,* "North hints at Military Confrontation, putting South on Alert," January 19, 2009.

7 John Mearsheimer, The Tragedy of Great Power Politics (New York: University of Chicago, 2001), 360-402.

8 See Aaron L. Friedberg, "Ripe for Rivalry: Prospects for Peace in a Multipolar Asia," *International Security* 18, no. 3 (Winter 1993/94): 5–33; Richard K. Betts, "Wealth, Power, and Instability: East Asia and the United States after the Cold War," *International Security* 18, no. 3 (Winter 1993/94): 34–77; Barry Buzan and Gerald Segal, "Rethinking East Asian Security," *Survival* 36, no. 2 (Summer 1994): 3–21.

9 See T. J. Pempel, *Remapping East Asia* (Ithaca: Cornell University Press, 2005); Joshua Kurlantzick, "Pax Asia-Pacifica? East Asian Integration and Its Implications for the United States," *The Washington Quarterly* (Summer 2007): 67–77.

10 See David C. Kang, "Getting Asia Wrong: The Need for New Analytical Frameworks," *International Security* 27, no. 4 (Spring 2003): 57–85; see also "Hierarchy, Balancing, and Empirical Puzzles in Asian International Relations," *International Security* 28, no. 3 (Winter 2004): 165–180.

11 See Thomas J. Christensen, "China, the U.S.-Japan Alliance, and the Security Dilemma in East Asia," *International Security* 23, no. 4 (Spring 1999): 49–80; Eugene A.

Matthews, "Japan's New Nationalism," *Foreign Affairs* 82, no. 6 (November/December 2003): 74–90.

12 Office of the Secretary of Defense, *Annual Report to Congress. Military Power of the People's Republic of China 2008*, 31–39.

13 Stockholm International Peace Research Institute, *SIPRI Yearbook 2008: Armaments, Disarmament and International Security* (Oxford: Oxford University Press, 2008), 175-178.

14 *SIPRI Yearbook 2008*, 178.

15 ROK MND, *Defense White Paper 2008*, 12–19.

16 "South Korea's Defense Budget," *GlobalSecurity.org*, accessed February 26, 2009, http://www.globalsecurity.org/military/world/rok/budget.htm.

17 U.S. Department of Defense, *A Strategic Framework for the Asian Pacific Rim: Looking toward the 21st Century* (Washington, DC: U.S. Government Printing Office, 1990).

18 ROK Ministry of National Defense, *ROK-US Military Relationship* (Seoul: MND IMHC, 2003), 672-713; ROK Ministry of National Defense, "USFK Reduction Negotiation Results," news release, October 6, 2004.

19 *Ohmynews*, "No taet'ongnyŏg, kongsa che-53-ki chorŏp mit imgwansik yŏnsŏlmun," March 8, 2005, accessed June 15, 2008, http://www.ohmynews.com/nws_web/view/at_pg.aspx?CNTN_CD=A0000241437

20 Choe Sang-Hun, "Seoul seeks wartime control over its army from U.S.," *International Herald Tribune*, August 10, 2006, accessed December 27, 2006, http://www.iht.com/articles/2006/08/10/news/korea.php.

21 "South Korea's Defense Budget," *GlobalSecurity.org*.

22 ROK Ministry of National Defense, "National Defense Reform 2020," news release, September 13, 2005.

23 See Kathleen T. Rhem, "U.S. to Transfer 10 Missions to South Korean Military," *American Forces Press Service*, November 19, 2003. The missions include the Joint Security Area, counter-artillery operations, and weather forecasting.

24 Richard Bitzinger, *Transforming the US Military: Implications for the Asia-Pacific* (Australia: Australian Strategic Policy Institute, December 2006), 27–30.

25 Korean National Statistics Office, "Hyanghu 10-nyŏn'gan sahoe pyŏnhwa yoin punsŏk mit sasajŏm" [Analysis and implications of social change factors in the next 10 years] accessed January 29, 2009, http://www.nso.go.kr/.

26 Kim Kyŏnghwa, "Ch'ulsanyul 1.0 syok'ŭ Taehan min'guk 'myŏljong wigi'"*Chosun Ilbo*, February 23, 2009, http://news.chosun.com/site/data/html_dir/2009/02/22/2009022200943.html.

27 Korean National Statistics Office, 2009.

28 Including unofficial and illegal workers, the total number could go up to one and a half million. See Yi Yŏng-ch'ang, "Oegugin nodongja 150-man sidae," *Hankook Ilbo*, April 21, 2008.

29 Korea has two baby boom generations: one now between the ages of 45–53 was born between 1955–1963; the other is between the ages of 34–40 and was born between 1968–1974. Together they account for 34 percent of the population with 16.5 million. Korean National Statistics Office, 2009.

30 Ibid.

31 "Economic Survey of Korea 2007: Public social spending in the context of rapid

population aging," OECD, accessed February 28, 2009, http://www.oecd.org/document/ 50/0,3343,en_2649_33733_38794482_1_1_1_1,00.html..

32 Korean National Statistics Office, 2009.

33 "Economic Survey of Korea 2007."

34 Ibid.

35 During the same period, Korea's per capita GDP was projected to jump to $37,000 in FY 2020 and $49,000 in FY 2030, both at 2005 constant price, equaling the 2005 level of Switzerland by 2030. See ROK Ministry of Finance and Economy, "Vision 2030-Korea: A Hopeful Nation in Harmony," August 30, 2006, accessed February 28, 2009,www.korea.net/image/news/Vision2030(060830).doc.

36 Ibid.

37 "Economic Survey of Korea 2007."

38 e-Nara chip'yo (e-National Index), "Pyŏngyuk chawŏn hyŏnhwang" [Military manpower resource index], accessed February 28, 2009, http://www.index.go.kr/egams/ default.jsp.

39 Jung Sung-ki, "Right Course on Defense Reform," The Korea Times, December 22, 2008, accessed February 25, 2009, http://www.koreatimes.co.kr/www/news/nation/ 2008/12/116_36578.html.

40 ROK Ministry of National Defense, "Yesan hyŏnhwang" [Budget report], accessed February 26, 2009, http://www.mnd.go.kr/.

41 Jung Sung-Ki, "S. Korea to Overhaul Modernization Plan," Defense News, December 15, 2008, accessed February 25, 2009, http://www.defensenews.com/story. php?i=3863636.

42 Korea National Statistics Office, "GDP and GNI Growth Trends," accessed February 25, 2009, http://www.index.go.kr/egams/default.jsp.

43 ROK Ministry of National Defense, "Podo charyo," news release, December 13, 2008, accessed February 26, 2009, http://www.mnd.go.kr/.

44 Bank of Korea, "South Korea's GDP Growth Chart," accessed February 28, 2009, http://ecos.bok.or.kr/.

45 ROK Ministry of Strategy and Finance, "2009 Nara sallim" [National Budget 2009], accessed February 27, 2009, http://www.mosf.go.kr/issue/20081001budget/ pdf/2009budget05.pdf.

46 David Baldwin, "The Concept of Security," Review of International Studies 23, no. 1 (January 1997), 5–26.

47 Some studies argue that 20 percent of Korean population will be foreign ethnic groups by 2050. See Sisa Journal, February 26, 2009; Hankook Ilbo, February 21, 2009; and Seoul Sinmun, January 21, 2009.

48 A multicultural family refers to a marriage between two different ethnicities, and their children.

49 Pak Yŏngmin, "Tamunhwa kŭndae pyŏngsa p'ŭrogŭraem kaebal haeya," Kookbang Ilbo, June 24, 2009.

50 U.S. Department of Defense, "Active Duty Military Personnel Strengths by Regional Area and By Country," March 31, 2008, accessed February 15, 2009, http:// siadapp.dmdc.osd.mil/personnel/MILITARY/history/hst0803.pdf.

51 The Obama administration will send 17,000 additional troops to Afghanistan, making troop levels there 48,000, while it will transfer 8,000 marines from Okinawa, Japan to Guam, reducing the total troops in Japan to a level 25,000 lower than the troop

level in South Korea.

52 ROK Ministry of Defense, *Kukpang kaehyŏk 2020-kwa kukpangbi* [Military reform 2020 and defense spending (Seoul: ROK MND, October 2006), 6.

53 SIPRI, SIPRI Yearbook 2008: Armaments, Disarmament, and International Security (Stockholm: SIPRI, 2008)

54 "South Korea's Defense Budget," *GlobalSecurity.org*.

55 Sin Ch'ang-un, "Haetpyŏt chŏngch'aek pakkuŏya 78%, Namhan haek poyu tongŭi 65%," *Joongang Ilbo*, October 11, 2006.

56 The National Unification Advisory Council, "2008-nyŏndo kungmin t'ongil ŭisik yŏron chosa" [2008 Public Opinion on Unification], November 2008.

57 Paul B. Stares and Joel S. Wit, *Preparing for Sudden Change in North Korea*, Council Special Report no. 42 (New York: Council on Foreign Relations, January 2009).

58 Hillary Rodham Clinton, "Putting the Elements of Smart Power into Practice," briefing en route to Seoul, South Korea, February 19, 2009, accessed February 24, 2009, http://www.state.gov/secretary/rm/2009a/02/119411.htm.

59 South Korean Ministry of Foreign Affairs and Trade, *Yi Myŏnng-bak chŏngbu chubyŏn 4-kuk oegyo sŏnggwa* [Lee government's diplomatic achievement with four neighboring countries], December 2008.

60 Roh Moo-hyun, "On History, Nationalism and a Northeast Asian Community," *Global Asia* 2, no. 1 (April 2007): 10–13.

61 According to Article 4 of the Joint Statement, the parties "committed to joint efforts for lasting peace and stability in Northeast Asia" and also "agreed to explore ways and means for promoting security cooperation in Northeast Asia." See U.S. Department of State, "Joint Statement of the Fourth Round of the Six-Party Talks," Beijing, September 19, 2005, http://www.state.gov/r/pa/prs/ps/2005/53490.htm.

62 "Chairman's Statement of the Six-Party Talks," *China View*, December 11, 2008, http://news.xinhuanet.com/english/2008-12/11/content_10491337.htm.

63 Barack Obama, "Renewing American Leadership," *Foreign Affairs* 86, no. 4 (July/August 2007): 12.

64 In 2007 South Korea spend $22.6 billion. See *SIPRI Yearbook 2008*, 178.

65 Nicholas Eberstadt, "Power and Population in Asia," *Policy Review*, no. 123 (February 2004): 1–21.

66 It was under the same Roh Moo-hyun administration that Defense Reform 2020 (2005) and Vision 2030 (2006) were announced.

67 See Ashley J. and Michael Wills, *Strategic Asia 2005-06, Military Modernization in an Era of Uncertainty* (Seattle: The National Bureau of Asian Research, 2005); see also Richard A. Bitzinger, "The Asia-Pacific Arms Market: Emerging Capabilities, Emerging Concerns," *Asia-Pacific Security Studies* 3, no. 2 (March 2004).

# PROSPECTS

# GLOBAL TRENDS 2025:
# IMPLICATIONS FOR SOUTH KOREA
# AND THE U.S.-ROK ALLIANCE

## *Thomas Fingar*

Koreans and Americans, like everyone else, view the world through lenses shaped by their own experience, concerns, and geographic circumstances. This phenomenon has been expressed in many ways—from "what you see depends on where you stand," and "what you see depends on where you look"—but my favorite is Saul Steinberg's often-imitated 1976 *New Yorker* magazine cover, which illustrates how denizens of Manhattan see the rest of the United States and nations across the Pacific.[1] The image is humorous because it is exaggerated, but remains justly famous because it reflects a fundamental truth about people everywhere. What we perceive, what we fear, what we desire, and how we pursue our goals reflect our circumstances, priorities, and perceptions of what is (and is not) possible.

Although it is sometimes tempting to disparage the views of others as myopic or parochial, they cannot be dismissed. Political leaders disregard their constituencies' concerns, and indeed those of rival nations, at their peril. Recognizing and attempting to appreciate how others see the world, and why they perceive it as they do is vital for success in international affairs. As the chapters in this volume illustrate, it is difficult to understand and explain our own idiosyncrasies, more difficult to accommodate the perceptions and priorities of two players, and even more difficult to factor in the concerns and objectives of additional countries.

Political leaders in all nations, especially democratic ones, must be sensitive to the perceptions and priorities of their own citizens. This limits their freedom of action. Perceptions and priorities are not immutable, but they cannot be changed quickly or by fiat. All political leaders find it challenging to strike the right balance between steps to accommodate and steps to change perceptions in order to achieve national security objectives. The magnitude of the challenge depends, in part, on the stability and competence of government institutions. Competing claims on limited resources (e.g., money, time, and political capital) compound the problem. The process and effects of globalization complicate matters further, and it is increasingly the case that developments anywhere can constrain—or create—possibilities everywhere.

Strategic thinkers and political leaders in the United States and the Republic of Korea (ROK, or South Korea) have long and deep experience in dealing with the consequences of the fact that the United States is a global player with interests and responsibilities "everywhere," whereas the ROK focuses more narrowly on the Korean Peninsula and the immediate region. Working through the resultant perceptual and practical differences is not easy, but we know how to do it. Indeed, our experience, success, and inventory of proven solutions to recurring problems enhance our confidence that we can successfully meet future security challenges. On balance, this is a good thing, but it also presents a potential impediment to continued success. Tweaking familiar formulas and slightly modifying what has worked in the past may no longer be adequate or appropriate to meet current and coming challenges.

One reason why old approaches may not—and probably will not—be viable in the future is that definitions of national security now subsume a wider and more varied array of interests and essential elements. The ability to detect, deter, and defeat military aggression has been joined, and in some cases superseded by imperatives to ensure access to energy supplies and other key resources, preserve economic competitiveness, and protect populations from infectious disease and certain consequences of global climate change. These and other dimensions of security are being debated in countries around the world and the outcome of these debates will shape national budgets, diplomatic strategies, and military deployments.

The trend summarized above implies that the requisites and modalities of U.S.-ROK security cooperation will increasingly be shaped and constrained by developments beyond Northeast Asia, and that both countries will have to revise their worldviews to include more places, problems, and political dynamics than ever before. At a minimum, this means that decision-makers in Washington and Seoul must be aware of, and sensitive to the security concerns and strategic priorities of governments in every region, as well as an increasing number of countries. In other words, we must develop more complex and comprehensive perceptual maps of the world to replace the *New Yorker* cover-like frameworks of the past. Toward that end, the next section of this chapter outlines some of the issues that will likely command policymaker attention during the next fifteen years.

## Global Trends and Drivers

The discussion that follows draws upon and extrapolates from the findings of the 2008 National Intelligence Council (NIC) study titled *Global Trends 2025: A Transformed World*.[2] The goal of the study, which the NIC conducts every four years, is to stimulate strategic thinking. It neither predicts what will happen nor prescribes what should be done to prevent, manage, or take advantage of specific developments. Rather, it seeks to identify key trends and where they appear headed, as well as the key factors that may drive or inhibit their evolution. The issues discussed here are a subset of the longer list developed by the NIC after consultations with hundreds of academics, government officials, and other members of the foreign policy elite in dozens of countries on six continents. The list's accuracy, completeness, and assessment of the way trends and drivers interact may be less important than the fact that influential people have begun to think about and prepare for them. In other words, decision-makers already view the trends described below as important, incipient shapers of political debate, policy decisions, and public discourse. They, in turn, will define the perceptions and priorities that affect the future of the U.S.-ROK alliance.

### *Globalization Continues*

Despite the extent and severity of the global financial crisis that began in 2007, *Global Trends 2025* anticipates recovery long before 2025 and expects that trends subsumed under the rubric of "globalization" will resume, though possibly more slowly than before the financial meltdown. The pace and pattern of the recovery will have differential impact on specific industries, countries, and regions, but over time, and probably rather quickly, economic activity and international trade will grow and the world will become more integrated and interdependent. Both integration and interdependence are likely to result more from decisions and developments made by firms and other nongovernmental actors than by governments or multilateral institutions.

As globalization resumes and encompasses even more places, peoples, and realms of activity, it will continue to facilitate unprecedented levels of prosperity. More people, in more places, will be more prosperous than ever before. However, globalization will likewise continue to exacerbate inequalities, both within and among nations. In other words, more people will become rich, the rich will become richer, and the poor will become somewhat better off but relatively poorer in comparison to others in their communities, countries, or other frames of reference. Living conditions will improve, expectations will rise, and, primarily as a result of the communications revolution that is part of globalization, people everywhere will become more cognizant of how their own situations compare to different reference groups (e.g., citizens of neighboring countries, other adherents of their religion, or urban dwellers in their own state or region). Both those with greater wealth and those in relatively greater poverty will have incentives and avenues to press their own governments for specific—and very different—benefits.

All governments, even the most authoritarian, will find it increasingly necessary to appear responsive to such demands. Doing so will stress the administrative capacity and the budgets of governments at all levels, from local jurisdictions to nation states. It is not too much of an overstatement to characterize their dilemma as one in which failure to appear—and actually be—responsive to growing citizen demands will erode legitimacy and endanger stability. On the other hand, seriously attempting to meet escalating demands will overtax the capacity—fiscal and otherwise—of government agencies and programs, increasing the risk of system breakdown. I describe the other factors contributing to the severity of this challenge—including demographic change and the effects of global climate change—in the ensuing sections.

The net effect of globalization will be positive—greater prosperity, better jobs, more education, better health, and more opportunities for more people—but the process will often be disruptive. Traditional ways of doing things will no longer suffice; replacing institutions, societal norms, and other established underpinnings of societies, economies, and polities will be difficult and contentious. For example, a seemingly inevitable consequence of the trends subsumed under the heading of "globalization" is that governments at all levels, in every country, will find it increasingly difficult to control or cope with developments within their own purview because critical drivers and other influences operate across administrative boundaries and beyond the reach of communities and governmental authorities affected by them. Local authorities will appeal to upper echelons of their own system for help and resources, thereby increasing the stress on higher level governmental capacity. Even national governments will find it increasingly difficult to manage the resultant challenges. Moreover, other dimensions of globalization will limit their options. If, for example, a government attempts to extract more money or other benefits from a corporate investor, the globalized world gives that investor many alternatives. It might pull out or decide not to expand activity in that jurisdiction. Alternatively, if a government attempts to deal with discontent and demands by taking repressive measures, news of its actions will be communicated instantly to higher-level authorities in its own country and to the world, with predictable and unpredictable consequences.

## Rise and Relative Decline

One concomitant of globalization is the unprecedented transfer of wealth from West to East, the "rise" of many nations, most notably the so-called BRICs (Brazil, Russia, India, and China), and the relative decline of the United States. Each of these developments has captured the attention of pundits and politicians but, in my view, many of their views are simplistic or exaggerated. This is not the place for a detailed critique of what others have written, but the developments are extremely important and germane to South Korea's security challenges and the U.S. role in helping to meet those challenges. I discuss how and why in the sections that follow.

The transfer of wealth from West to East is unprecedented in scale and may have unpredictable consequences, both because much of it is going to new destinations (primarily China) and because globalization has expanded the range of possible ways in which to use accumulated wealth. Nevertheless, what we are witnessing now and can expect to see in the years ahead is essentially the continuation of developments and trends that began in the 1970s. The two most important strands or interrelated streams of this development are the rise of "Asian tigers"—first Japan, then the ROK and Taiwan, and then others, the most impressive being China—as the world's primary producers of consumer items (and later, producer goods) and windfall profits from escalating demand for commodities, especially oil and natural gas.

Though an oversimplification, the traditional pattern had been as follows. Commodity (oil and gas) earnings flowed mainly to the Middle East and the Soviet Union/Russia, and manufacturing revenues flowed increasingly to Asia. Significant but declining portions of this revenue then flowed to the Middle East for energy resources to fuel the increasingly prosperous countries of Asia. Countries in the Middle East invested their newfound wealth in the West, primarily the United States and Western Europe, and Asian countries did the same, at least initially. But Asian countries also used their earnings for domestic investment in infrastructure, education, and health care. In the case of Japan and South Korea, they modernized their military forces and covered some of the costs of U.S. forces stationed in those countries. This process engendered new issues and frictions in the U.S. relationships with Japan and the ROK, but we worked our way through them and the outcome was continued stability, enhanced security, and greater prosperity for all.

The so-called rise of China continues the familiar pattern with one very important difference: China's size and potential impact. Again oversimplifying, the international system absorbed, accommodated, and benefited from the rise of Japan and the "little tigers" of Asia. However, China's size—its vast population, foreign exchange reserves, and demand for energy and other commodities—raises questions, concerns, and fears about the ability of the existing international order to accommodate its greater role and influence. Precisely how this plays out will be a function not just of China's aspirations, but also of what many nations do. That said, two points are worth noting, in keeping with the focus of this book. First, China, like the Asian states that preceded it on the road to greater wealth and influence, benefits enormously from the existing international order and has many incentives to preserve the status quo. Second, China's rise will be a factor in public discourse, political debate, and policy deliberations in Washington, Seoul, Tokyo, Moscow, Pyongyang, and most other national capitals for years to come. Precisely how this phenomenon will shape national security decisions affecting South Korea and the U.S.-ROK alliance is impossible to predict with confidence. That the impact will be significant is virtually certain.

From a U.S. perspective, the rise of China and the other BRICs—and the prospective rise of Indonesia, Turkey, and others in the "next wave"—is a positive development in many ways analogous to the earlier rise of Japan and the little tigers. Like the earlier recovery and renewal of Western Europe, the rise of Japan and the little tigers decreased the relative power and prosperity of the United States (particularly in comparison to its allies) but actually added to American wealth and military capabilities. The BRICs' cases are different because none is a U.S. ally and two (China and Russia) are still seen by many as competitors and potential adversaries.

The rise of the BRICs could ultimately be detrimental to U.S. power and prosperity, but such an outcome is by no means inevitable. That said, it must be acknowledged that U.S. preeminence has been in decline for a long time and almost certainly will continue to abate. But this diminution does not mean that the United States is in decline. The United States has continued to prosper even as—and perhaps because—other nations have become wealthier, stronger, and more engaged in international affairs. What it does mean is that the United States' ability to exercise unchallenged leadership of the international community as it once did in the "free world" is a depleted asset unlikely to be replenished. This has many implications, including the need to work out new "burden sharing" arrangements to preserve peace and stability in specific regions and the international system as a whole. Such agreements will, in turn, affect U.S. security relationships with and expectations for its allies and partners.

Before concluding this summary examination of what Fareed Zakaria has called, correctly in my view, the "rise of the rest" and the putative decline of the United States—and by implication, of Japan and the ROK—I offer two observations important to the discussion below.[3] The first is to note the connection between the declining ability of governments to control or manage effects within their purview that are triggered or exacerbated by developments beyond their own jurisdiction, and the diminution of Washington's ability to prescribe solutions to problems in the international system. The success of the institutions that were put in place after World War II, with strong U.S. leadership, facilitated the unprecedented increase in global prosperity and the "rise of the rest." Those institutions, and U.S. global leadership, in large measure define the status quo international system that has proven so beneficial to so many. Second, while some delight in the relative decline of U.S. influence, few appear eager to share the "system maintenance" costs or responsibilities that the United States has borne to date.

### Aging Institutions

Despite—or perhaps because of—the efficacy and longevity of the post-World War II institutional order (such as the World Bank, the International Monetary Fund, the General Agreement on Tariffs and Trade/World Trade Organization, the United Nations (UN) and its specialized agencies, and numerous bilateral security treaties between the United States and allies such as Japan and the ROK), many existing multilateral organizations appear increasingly ill-suited to the needs of the twenty-first century. Exhibit A in this regard is the impotence and irrelevance of existing institutions during the 2007 global financial crisis. Exhibit B is the composition of the UN Security Council. These institutions have performed well, but they were created to deal with problems and players of a bygone age and are increasingly unable to provide timely, effective solutions to today's problems.

The need to revitalize, reengineer, or reinvent critical components of the international system is increasingly apparent, but several factors make doing so very difficult. Perhaps the biggest impediment is reluctance to fiddle with or abandon mechanisms that have served so well for so many years, especially when there is no obvious alternative. A second impediment is the erosion of deference to the United States. In the 1940s and for a long time thereafter, others in the "free world" accepted or acquiesced to American leadership. The United States remains the most powerful nation, but its preeminence has diminished, U.S. pronouncements on what is best for the international system are no longer taken at face value, and there is no consensus on how the international order should be reformed or which countries should be entrusted to make the critical decisions. There is no obvious answer to the question, "What is the alternative to U.S. leadership of any effort to remake the international system?" Without an answer to that question—one that is acceptable both to the United States and to "all" the major powers (a group that has yet to be defined and cannot gain consensus—we are doomed to live with institutions that we know have diminished and declining relevance to the world of today and tomorrow. The situation may have to become much worse before it can be made significantly better.

What is true of international financial and political institutions is also true, mutatis mutandis, of international control regimes such as the Nuclear Non-Proliferation Treaty (NPT), and the U.S.-led system of bilateral and multilateral alliances. The North Atlantic Treaty Organization (NATO) is often described as the most successful alliance in history—it preserved the peace and witnessed the demise, without war, of the adversary it was designed to counter—but what does it do for an encore? Indeed, why does it still exist? To say the NATO allies hold different views on these questions is an understatement, but all are reluctant to abandon or significantly change a demonstrably successful instrument just because its raison d'être has vanished. The U.S. alliances with the ROK and Japan are not so obviously outmoded as is NATO, but it is appropriate to ask whether hub-and-spoke bilateral security arrangements can still work for Northeast Asia and whether any and all alliance structures should have out-of-area responsibilities.

### Aging…and Exploding Populations

Global population will increase by 1.2 billion between 2009 and 2025. Less than 3 percent of the increase will occur in the West (defined here to include Japan, but the percentage would be the same if we also include South Korea). India will grow by 240 million and surpass China (which will add 100 million) to become the world's most populous nation. Sub-Saharan Africa will add 340 million and there will be 100 million more people in South and Central America. Much of the developing world will face the challenges of large and growing youthful populations that require education and jobs, but often distrust authority. Other nations—Japan, South Korea, Russia, and most of Europe—face very different challenges because their populations will be older, aging, and stagnant if not actually declining in number. Fewer young workers will be available to support growing numbers of senior citizens, or to serve in the military.

Plotting demographic projections on a map of the world reveals a number of interesting patterns. For example, the "rising" states of India and China will have to provide for the basic needs—education, health care, and jobs—for huge numbers of youth, in addition to the young people already in the pipeline. To do so will require sustained growth rates of 8 percent or more to maintain current levels of prosperity that, for most people, are still very low. Already struggling governments in Sub-Saharan Africa will have to cope with youth bulges that will severely tax and may even overwhelm their capabilities. Impatient youth in countries with ineffective governments, many of them authoritarian or flawed democracies, will challenge the legitimacy of existing regimes unless they vastly improve government performance on issues that matter to young people (notably, education suitable to securing rewarding, twenty-first century jobs). Countries in the "arc of instability" running across Northern Africa, the Middle East, and Central and South Asia will experience declining rates of population growth and have more breathing space to address issues that have alienated young people and thereby provided recruits to insurgencies and extremist groups.

The list of demographic challenges could easily be extended and refined but the point I make here is that governments almost everywhere will have to devote time, energy, and resources to issues triggered, exacerbated, or transformed by changes in the size and age composition of their populations. Countries with low or negative population growth will have to consider immigration as a partial solution, with all the attendant problems of absorption, especially in more homogeneous societies such as those of Japan, Korea, and much of Europe. Those with burgeoning, ambitious, and alienated youth bulges face the prospect of "brain drain" to more prosperous or promising countries and must decide whether repression can forestall likely challenges to regime legitimacy.

### Effects of Global Climate Change

Climate scientists tell us that the effects of global climate change will begin to affect everyday life during the next twenty years and that nothing can be done to prevent those changes from occurring.[4] The best that can be accomplished in the short run is to mitigate their consequences for populations at risk. Current projections anticipate that the impact of climate change on agriculture, the availability of water, the frequency and severity of storms, changes in sea level, and storm surges will be more pronounced in other regions than in Northeast Asia. These projections should provide little comfort, however, because Northeast Asia will be affected by climate change beginning in the decade after 2025. The region will also attract even greater international opprobrium than it has to date. Appeals for resources to ameliorate adverse effects elsewhere will inevitably escalate, as nations and nongovernmental organizations debate new climate change agreements.

The increased political salience of climate change effects will engender stepped-up efforts to "prevent," or at least minimize, further damage by taking "immediate" steps that will begin to have an impact a decade or more in the future. As major producers of greenhouse gases, the United States, China, and India will be blamed for what is already happening and pressed to "do more" to reduce harmful emissions. China argues that current problems were caused by other, richer, more developed nations, as well as the developing world, (of which China is a part despite its status as a BRIC), and that it should not be expected to slow its own drive for prosperity to compensate for the sins of those who modernized first. That argument, though understandable, sounds increasingly hollow given the size of China's foreign exchange reserves.

The United States appears prepared to do more than it was during the administration of George W. Bush. However, its budgetary problems—underscored by the huge increases in debt incurred to address the global financial crisis—will constrain its ability to underwrite mitigation efforts by third parties and put increased pressure on other expenditures, including those for security arrangements with other nations. South Korea and Japan are already taking steps to reduce their carbon footprints, but as wealthy nations in comparison to most of the world, they will be expected to do even more to underwrite the costs of prevention and amelioration, both within the region (China) and beyond.

Many other climate change-related developments will affect future decisions. My key point here is that the Northeast Asian nations will be compelled, by circumstances and international politics, to devote more time, attention, and resources to climate change. In the end, doing so will engender or exacerbate friction among those countries, and the frictions and competing demands for money, attention, and other scarce resources will affect not only South Korea's security challenges but also the potential for addressing them.

## The Geopolitics of Energy

The global financial crisis and economic downturn that began in 2007 reduced competition for—and the price of—energy resources, but growth will resume and energy will again move toward the top of national agendas. Developed and developing countries alike need ever-larger supplies of energy to fuel their economies and facilitate the lifestyles their people desire. Relative scarcity and competition drive up prices. Wealthy countries can, albeit reluctantly, pay prices that poorer countries cannot. The importance of assured supplies is more than a matter of cost, however. Exploitable oil and natural gas reserves are already concentrated in relatively few countries; even if there are new discoveries and/or new technologies, the number will decrease further by 2025. Concentration creates the potential for political influence and, at least in some quarters, has rekindled interest in mercantilist alternatives to reliance on markets to assure access. Assured access, at affordable cost, does not eliminate other potential threats to energy security. Transport routes—by sea, rail, road, or pipeline—must be protected because they are inviting targets for pirates, political insurgents, and the desperately poor. Simply stated, assured energy supplies are a critical component of national security.

High prices for hydrocarbons and pressure to reduce greenhouse gases combine to increase the appeal of, and desire for nuclear power plants. This will be a worldwide phenomenon with many positive consequences, but it will entail solving—or at least seriously addressing—a host of difficult security and political issues. Aspirations for greater energy independence will spark interest in and/or reinforce arguments for indigenous fuel cycle capabilities. Expense and technical requirements make this impractical for most nations, but not for all. Iran already argues that it is "entitled" to possess all elements of a complete fuel cycle because it adheres to the NPT. It appears to be only a matter of time until North Korea makes a similar argument. Given their perceived security requirements, these countries will argue strongly that they cannot rely on the goodwill of other nations to provide the fuel required to operate power plants essential to meeting economic and social needs. This creates both an imperative and an opportunity to establish an international fuel cycle regime of some kind, but that will take time, be difficult to achieve at the global level, and likely progress on a much different timeline than is desirable to alleviate security concerns on the Korean Peninsula.

There are other, obvious dimensions of the quest for greater energy security that will influence what happens in Northeast Asia and how that, in turn, will affect South Korea's security requirements and the future of the U.S.-ROK alliance. These considerations include China's effort to expand its naval reach and capabilities to defend strategic lines of communication (for oil, but also for many other commodities), and opportunities and impediments to naval cooperation among the United States, Japan, the ROK, China, and Russia. Their global interests and status as permanent members of the United Nations Security Council will require the United States, Russia, and China to address nuclear power and nuclear control regimes at the global level, even if or as they continue to work on denuclearization of the Korean Peninsula through the Six-Party Talks or other regional forums. In theory, arrangements devised to address regional challenges in Northeast

Asia could serve as prototypes for more inclusive global arrangements, but it now appears likely that pressures to develop global solutions—mainly to address Iran's nuclear ambitions—will cause the United States, Russia, and China to seek global solutions long before denuclearization of the Korean Peninsula has been achieved.

## Competing Demands and Complicating Factors

This chapter only skims the surface of the range, complexity, and interrelationships among issues now capturing the attention of attentive publics and political leaders. Many other topics—terrorism, infectious disease, state fragility, a shift toward asymmetric military approaches to deterring and defeating much stronger conventional forces—must also be factored into any equation to address South Korea's security challenges. The net result of the interaction between the trends and considerations discussed above is a situation and decision matrix far more complex than at any previous period in the history of the U.S.-ROK alliance. This does not mean that the situation now is more—or less—dangerous than in the past. It probably does mean, however, that old approaches to updating and reinvigorating the alliance will almost certainly be inadequate. Any new approach must consider at least all of the following dimensions and parameters:

- The ranking and relative priorities of the different elements of national security (e.g., economic security, energy security, old age security, and military security) are changing; security from aggression no longer automatically trumps all others. Defining a nation's security challenges and requirements is no longer solely the provenance of military officers, defense ministry civilians, and arms manufacturers. A much wider and more varied array of political actors and organizational interests participate in the process, shape national security policies, and influence budget decisions.

- Globalization has made the world smaller and more integrated. What happens far from a nation's borders can be as or more important to its security, broadly defined, than events and capabilities in its immediate neighborhood. The ROK is more dependent on—and impacted by—what happens beyond the peninsula and Northeast Asia than in the past. The United States has long been a global player, but the number and scope of places and problems judged important to U.S. security are greater than ever. By contrast, the resources available to address the global security agenda are both smaller than they have ever been, and continue to diminish.

Developments and drivers of the kinds described in this chapter raise questions about the continued suitability and utility of many long-standing assumptions and approaches. For example, is it still the case that security in Northeast Asia is best served by bilateral alliances centered on the United States? Is it time to consider broader and more inclusive arrangements? Given changes in the nature of military conflict and U.S. global responsibilities, and the stake that others have in continuing what has been called "Pax Americana," should the U.S.-ROK and U.S.-Japan alliances be redesigned to include more sharply defined divisions of labor with complementary capabilities that might be employed beyond Northeast Asia? How should the dimensions of South Korea's security challenge that require military preparedness be addressed in the context of budget deficits and competing priorities?

The list of questions could easily be extended for many pages. This and other chapters in this volume suggest an equally long list of opportunities and possibilities to enhance security by thinking outside of traditional frameworks. Many new approaches to meet our security challenges are possible; none will be easy to achieve. But we must explore alternatives to the status quo. The only thing that is certain is that doing what we have always done will not be adequate to meet the challenges we face.

## Notes

1 See the famous cover illustration for the March 29, 1976 issue of *The New Yorker*, www.saulsteinbergfoundation.org/gallery_24_viewofworld.html.

2 National Intelligence Council, *Global Trends 2025: A Transformed World*, November 2009, www.dni.gov/nic/PDF_2025/2025_Global_Trends_Final_Report.pdf.

3 Fareed Zakaria, *The Post-American World* (New York: W. W. Norton, 2008).

4 See *National Intelligence Assessment on the National Security Implications of Global Climate Change to 2030*. House Permanent Select Committee on Intelligence and House Select Committee on Energy Independence and Global Warming, June 25, 2008, www.dni.gov/testimonies/20080625_testimony.pdf.

# ABOUT THE CONTRIBUTORS

**Jae Ho Chung** is a professor of international relations at Seoul National University. Professor Chung is the author or editor of eleven books, including *Central Control and Local Discretion in China* (Oxford University Press, 2000), *Charting China's Future* (Rowman & Littlefield, 2006), *Between Ally and Partner: Korea-China Relations and the United States* (Columbia University Press, 2007), and *China's Crisis Management* (Routledge, 2011). He serves on the editorial committees of *The China Quarterly*, *Pacific Affairs*, *East Asia*, *Politics*, *Asian Perspective* and *China Perspectives*, and is the founding coordinator of the Asian Network for the Study of Local China (ANSLoC, http://www.ansloc.net) and project manager of the MacArthur Foundation's Asia Security Initiative grant on "Managing Sino-Korean Conflicts and Identifying the Role of the United States" for 2009–12 (http://masi.snu.ac.kr).

**Thomas Fingar** is the Oksenberg/Rohlen Distinguished Fellow in the Freeman Spogli Institute for International Studies at Stanford University, where in 2009 he was the Payne Distinguished Lecturer. From May 2005 through December 2008 he served as the United States' first Deputy Director of National Intelligence for Analysis and, concurrently, as Chairman of the National Intelligence Council. Dr. Fingar served previously as Assistant Secretary of the State Department's Bureau of Intelligence and Research, Principal Deputy Assistant Secretary (2001–2003), Deputy Assistant Secretary for Analysis (1994–2000), Director of the Office of Analysis for East Asia and the Pacific (1989–1994), and Chief of the China Division (1986–1989). Between 1975 and 1986 he held a number of positions at Stanford University, including senior research associate in the Center for International Security and Arms Control. Dr. Fingar is a graduate of Cornell University (AB in government and history, 1968), and Stanford University (MA, 1969, and PhD, 1977, both in political science).

**Donald W. Keyser** was the 2008–09 Pantech Fellow at Stanford University's Shorenstein Asia-Pacific Research Center. He retired from the U.S. Department of State in 2004 after 32 years. His career focus was on U.S. policy toward China, Taiwan, Hong Kong, Japan and the Korean Peninsula. He also served as ambassador/special negotiator for regional conflicts in the former USSR; as the principal deputy assistant secretary for intelligence & research; as a senior inspector of overseas diplomatic missions; and as the director for global counter-narcotics and international law enforcement cooperation (excepting in Latin America).

**General (Retired) Byung Kwan Kim** served as the Deputy Commander of ROK-U.S. Combined Forces Command and the Commander of Ground Component Command (2006–2008). Prior to that, he served as Commanding General of the 1st Field Army (2005–2006); the 7th Mechanized Corps (2003–2005); and the 2nd Infantry Division (1999–2001). General Kim has also served in various strategic positions, including as Director General of Force Planning for the Joint Chiefs of Staff of the Republic of Korea (2001–2003). More recently, he was the inaugural Koret Fellow at Stanford University's Shorenstein Asia-Pacific Research Center during 2008–09.

**Jongseok Lee** is a senior fellow at the Sejong Institute in Korea. A significant portion of his research is concerned with North Korea, inter-Korean relations, North Korea-China relations, and Northeast Asia. He received his PhD in political science from Sungkyunkwan University in 1993, and was a research fellow at the Sejong Institute from 1994 to 2003. He authored the following publications: *A Study on the Workers' Party of Korea* (1995) (in Korean), *The Study of Unification in a Divided Period* (1998) (in Korean), *Understanding of Contemporary North Korea* (2000) (in Korean), *North Korea-China Relations: 1945~2000* (2000) (in Korean) (it was published in 2005 in Chinese). He was the Minister of Unification and chairman of the Standing Committee of the National Security Council in 2006. In addition, he was the deputy secretary-general in the ROK National Security Council from 2003 to 2006.

**Kyung-Tae Lee** is currently president of the Institute for International Trade at the Korea International Trade Association. Dr. Lee is also a Distinguished Professor at the Graduate School of International Studies, Korea University. He has served as the president of the Korea Institute for International Economic Policy (KIEP), and was dispatched as ambassador of Korea's Permanent Delegation to the OECD. Dr. Lee received his PhD in economics from the George Washington University.

**Alexandre Y. Mansourov** is a visiting scholar at the U.S.-Korea Institute at Johns Hopkins University's Paul H. Nitze School of Advanced International Studies and member of the U.S. National Committee on North Korea. He is a specialist in Northeast Asian security, politics, and economics, focusing primarily on the Korean Peninsula. Dr. Mansourov worked as professor of Security Studies at the Asia-Pacific Center for Security Studies from 2001 to 2007. He received his PhD in political science from Columbia University. He has edited three books, including *A Turning Point: Democratic Consolidation in the ROK and Strategic Readjustment in the US-ROK Alliance* (2005), *Bytes and Bullets: Information Technology Revolution and National Security on the Korean Peninsula* (2005), and *The North Korean Nuclear Program: Security, Strategy, and New Perspectives from Russia* (2000), as well as having published numerous book chapters and academic articles on Korean and Northeast Asian affairs.

**Ji-chul Ryu** is a senior fellow at the Korea Energy Economics Institute (KEEI). He is an expert in the areas of strategic development energy research, international energy cooperation, and energy planning and modeling. He joined KEEI in April 1987 and served as vice-president of the Asia Pacific Energy Research Centre (APERC) in Tokyo, Japan, from 1996 to 2000. He also served as a senior counselor to the Minister of Energy and Resources at the Korean Government in 1991-1992. Dr. Ryu holds a PhD in economics from the Australian National University and a B.S. in mathematics and statistics from Seoul National University.

**Benjamin Self** is the inaugural Takahashi Fellow in Japanese Studies at the Walter H. Shorenstein Asia-Pacific Research Center. Prior to joining the center in 2008, Self was a senior associate at the Henry L. Stimson Center working on Japanese security policy, beginning in 1998; while there, he directed projects on Japan-China relations, fostering security cooperation between the U.S.-Japan Alliance and the PRC, Japan's nuclear option, and confidence-building measures. Self has also carried out research and writing in areas such as nuclear non-proliferation and disarmament, ballistic missile defense, Taiwan's security, Northeast Asian security dynamics, the domestic politics of Japanese defense policy, and Japan's global security role. From 2003 until 2008, he lived in Africa—in Malawi and Tanzania—and is now studying the role of Japan in Africa, including in humanitarian relief, economic development, conflict prevention, and resource extraction. Self earned his undergraduate degree in political science at Stanford in 1988, and an MA in Japan studies and international economics from The Johns

Hopkins University's Paul H. Nitze School of Advanced International Studies.

**Seongho Sheen** is an associate professor at the Graduate School of International Studies, Seoul National University. He has been a visiting fellow at the East-West Center in Washington, D.C., a CNAPS fellow at the Brookings Institution, and an assistant research professor at the Asia-Pacific Center for Security Studies (APCSS), Honolulu, Hawaii. His research focuses on international security, U.S. foreign policy, Northeast Asian politics and the Korean Peninsula. His recent publications include "Nuclear Sovereignty vs. Nuclear Security: Renewing the ROK-U.S. Atomic Energy Agreement" in *Korean Journal of Defense Analysis* (June 2011); "North Korea's Nuclear and Long Range Missile Development and its Implication for Northeast Asia" in *Strategic Studies* (March 2010, in Korean); and "To Be or Not To Be: South Korea's East Asia Security Strategy and Dilemma of Unification" in *The International Spectator* (Spring 2009). He received his PhD and MA from the Fletcher School of Law and Diplomacy, Tufts University and his BA from Seoul National University.

**Gi-Wook Shin** is the director of the Walter H. Shorenstein Asia-Pacific Research Center; the Tong Yang, Korea Foundation, and Korea Stanford Alumni Chair of Korean Studies; the founding director of the Korean Studies Program; a senior fellow at FSI; and a professor of sociology at Stanford University. As a historical-comparative and political sociologist, his research has concentrated on areas of social movements, nationalism, development, and international relations. Dr. Shin is the author/editor of numerous books and articles. His latest books include *History Textbooks and the Wars in Asia: Divided Memories* (2011); *South Korean Social Movements: From Democracy to Civil Society* (2011); and *One Alliance, Two Lenses: U.S.-Korea Relations in a New Era* (2010). Due to the wide popularity of his publications, many of them have been translated and distributed to Korean audiences. His articles have appeared in academic journals including the *American Sociological Review*, the *American Journal of Sociology*, *Nations and Nationalism*, *Comparative Studies in Society and History*, *International Sociology*, *Pacific Affairs*, *Asian Survey*, and *Asian Perspectives*. Before coming to Stanford, Dr. Shin taught at the University of Iowa and the University of California, Los Angeles. After receiving his BA from Yonsei University in Korea, he was awarded his MA and PhD from the University of Washington.

**David Straub** has been associate director of the Korean Studies Program (KSP) at the Walter H. Shorenstein Asia-Pacific Research Center at Stanford University since 2008. Previously, he was the 2007–2008 Pantech Fellow at the Center. Straub retired in 2006 from the U.S. Department of State as a Senior Foreign Service Officer after a 30-year career focused on Korean and Japanese affairs. At the Department, he served as director of Korean affairs from 2002 to 2004, and played a key role in the Six-Party Talks in Beijing on ending North Korea's nuclear weapons program. Straub has also taught at The Johns Hopkins University School of Advanced International Studies and Seoul National University's Graduate School of International Studies. He has written a number of essays and book chapters on U.S. policy and Korean and Japanese affairs, and is a frequent commentator on U.S. policy toward Northeast Asia in American, South Korean, Japanese, and other media.

# RECENT PUBLICATIONS OF THE
# WALTER H. SHORENSTEIN
# ASIA-PACIFIC RESEARCH CENTER

**BOOKS** (DISTRIBUTED BY THE BROOKINGS INSTITUTION PRESS)

Jean C. Oi, ed. *Going Private in China: The Politics of Corporate Restructuring and System Reform.* Stanford, CA: Walter H. Shorenstein Asia-Pacific Research Center, 2011.

Karen Eggleston and Shripad Tuljapurkar, eds. *Aging Asia: The Economic and Social Implications of Rapid Demographic Change in China, Japan and South Korea.* Stanford, CA: Walter H. Shorenstein Asia-Pacific Research Center, 2010.

Rafiq Dossani, Daniel C. Sneider, and Vikram Sood, eds. *Does South Asia Exist? Prospects for Regional Integration.* Stanford, CA: Walter H. Shorenstein Asia-Pacific Research Center, 2010.

Jean C. Oi, Scott Rozelle, and Xueguang Zhou. *Growing Pains: Tensions and Opportunity in China's Transition.* Stanford, CA: Walter H. Shorenstein Asia-Pacific Research Center, 2010.

Karen Eggleston, ed. *Prescribing Cultures and Pharmaceutical Policy in the Asia-Pacific.* Stanford, CA: Walter H. Shorenstein Asia-Pacific Research Center, 2009.

Donald A. L. Macintyre, Daniel C. Sneider, and Gi-Wook Shin, eds. *First Drafts of Korea: The U.S. Media and Perceptions of the Last Cold War Frontier.* Stanford, CA: Walter H. Shorenstein Asia-Pacific Research Center, 2009.

Steven Reed, Kenneth Mori McElwain, and Kay Shimizu, eds. *Political Change in Japan: Electoral Behavior, Party Realignment, and the Koizumi Reforms.* Stanford, CA: Walter H. Shorenstein Asia-Pacific Research Center, 2009.

Donald K. Emmerson. *Hard Choices: Security, Democracy, and Regionalism in Southeast Asia.* Stanford, CA: Walter H. Shorenstein Asia-Pacific Research Center, 2008.

Henry S. Rowen, Marguerite Gong Hancock, and William F. Miller, eds. *Greater China's Quest for Innovation.* Stanford, CA: Walter H. Shorenstein Asia-Pacific Research Center, 2008.

Gi-Wook Shin and Daniel C. Sneider, eds. *Cross Currents: Regionalism and Nationalism in Northeast Asia*. Stanford, CA: Walter H. Shorenstein Asia-Pacific Research Center, 2007.

Stella R. Quah, ed. *Crisis Preparedness: Asia and the Global Governance of Epidemics*. Stanford, CA: Walter H. Shorenstein Asia-Pacific Research Center, 2007.

Philip W. Yun and Gi-Wook Shin, eds. *North Korea: 2005 and Beyond*. Stanford, CA: Walter H. Shorenstein Asia-Pacific Research Center, 2006.

Jongryn Mo and Daniel I. Okimoto, eds. *From Crisis to Opportunity: Financial Globalization and East Asian Capitalism*. Stanford, CA: Walter H. Shorenstein Asia-Pacific Research Center, 2006.

Michael H. Armacost and Daniel I. Okimoto, eds. *The Future of America's Alliances in Northeast Asia*. Stanford, CA: Walter H. Shorenstein Asia-Pacific Research Center, 2004.

Henry S. Rowen and Sangmok Suh, eds. *To the Brink of Peace: New Challenges in Inter-Korean Economic Cooperation and Integration*. Stanford, CA: Walter H. Shorenstein Asia-Pacific Research Center, 2001.

**STUDIES OF THE WALTER H. SHORENSTEIN ASIA-PACIFIC RESEARCH CENTER**
(PUBLISHED WITH STANFORD UNIVERSITY PRESS)

Yongshun Cai. *Collective Resistance in China: Why Popular Protests Succeed or Fail*. Stanford, CA: Stanford University Press, 2010.

Gi-Wook Shin. *One Alliance, Two Lenses: U.S.-Korea Relations in a New Era*. Stanford, CA: Stanford University Press, 2010.

Jean Oi and Nara Dillon, eds. *At the Crossroads of Empires: Middlemen, Social Networks, and State-building in Republican Shanghai*. Stanford, CA: Stanford University Press, 2007.

Henry S. Rowen, Marguerite Gong Hancock, and William F. Miller, eds. *Making IT: The Rise of Asia in High Tech*. Stanford, CA: Stanford University Press, 2006.

Gi-Wook Shin. *Ethnic Nationalism in Korea: Genealogy, Politics, and Legacy*. Stanford, CA: Stanford University Press, 2006.

Andrew Walder, Joseph Esherick, and Paul Pickowicz, eds. *The Chinese Cultural Revolution as History*. Stanford, CA: Stanford University Press, 2006.

Rafiq Dossani and Henry S. Rowen, eds. *Prospects for Peace in South Asia*. Stanford, CA: Stanford University Press, 2005.

The authorized representative in the EU for product safety and compliance is:
Mare Nostrum Group
B.V Doelen 72
4831 GR Breda
The Netherlands

www.ingramcontent.com/pod-product-compliance
Lightning Source LLC
Chambersburg PA
CBHW020340270326
41926CB00007B/259